WITHDRAWN

B32976

'The central message of this work should make it a "must-read" for all social workers, managers and those concerned with and about social work. As with all great ideas and concepts, the joy is that at their heart they are simple. What this book does beautifully is unpack the simple idea, exploring the key components of how social workers should place relationship-based social work at the centre of their practice. In a world too driven by technocratic responses, digital solutions and robotics, the one thing we can be sure of is that social workers will not be replaced by robots! This book explains why – you should read it.'

– Dave Hill, CBE, Executive Director, Social Care and Education at Essex County Council and past President of ADCS

Relationship-Based Social Work

of related interest

Relationship-Based Research in Social Work
Understanding Practice Research
Edited by Gillian Ruch and Ilse Julkunen
ISBN 978 1 84905 457 7
eISBN 978 1 78450 112 9

Doing Relationship-Based Social Work
A Practical Guide to Building Relationships and Enabling Change
Edited by Mary McColgan and Cheryl McMullin
ISBN 978 1 78592 014 1
eISBN 978 1 78450 256 0

Inspiring and Creative Ideas for Working with Children
How to Build Relationships and Enable Change
Deborah M. Plummer
ISBN 978 1 84905 651 9
eISBN 978 1 78450 146 4

Innovations in Social Work Research
Using Methods Creatively
Edited by Louise Hardwick, Roger Smith and Aidan Worsley
ISBN 978 1 84905 585 7
eISBN 978 1 78450 145 7

Mastering Communication in Social Work
From Understanding to Doing
Linda Gast and Martin Bailey
ISBN 978 1 84905 444 7
eISBN 978 0 85700 819 0
Part of the Mastering Social Work Skills *series*

Improving Child and Family Assessments
Turning Research into Practice
Danielle Turney, Dendy Platt, Julie Selwyn and Elaine Farmer
ISBN 978 1 84905 256 6
eISBN 978 0 85700 553 3

RELATIONSHIP-BASED
SOCIAL WORK
Second Edition

Getting to the Heart of Practice

Edited by
GILLIAN RUCH, DANIELLE TURNEY and ADRIAN WARD

Foreword by David Howe

Jessica Kingsley *Publishers*
London and Philadelphia

Contains public sector information licensed under the Open Government Licence v3.0.
Figure 14.2 reproduced with kind permission of Tony McCaffrey.

First edition published in 2010
This edition published in 2018
by Jessica Kingsley Publishers
73 Collier Street
London N1 9BE, UK
and
400 Market Street, Suite 400
Philadelphia, PA 19106, USA

www.jkp.com

Copyright © Jessica Kingsley Publishers 2010, 2018
Foreword copyright © David Howe 2018

Front cover image source: iStock.

All rights reserved. No part of this publication may be reproduced in any
material form (including photocopying, storing in any medium by electronic
means or transmitting) without the written permission of the copyright owner
except in accordance with the provisions of the law or under terms of a licence
issued in the UK by the Copyright Licensing Agency Ltd. www.cla.co.uk or in
overseas territories by the relevant reproduction rights organisation, for details
see www.ifrro.org. Applications for the copyright owner's written permission to
reproduce any part of this publication should be addressed to the publisher.

Warning: The doing of an unauthorised act in relation to a copyright work
may result in both a civil claim for damages and criminal prosecution.

Library of Congress Cataloging in Publication Data
Names: Ruch, Gillian, editor. | Turney, Danielle, editor. | Ward, Adrian,
1953- editor.
Title: Relationship-based social work : getting to the heart of practice /
edited by Gillian Ruch, Danielle Turney and Adrian Ward.
Description: Second Edition. | Philadelphia : Jessica Kingsley Publishers,
[2018] | Revised edition of Relationship-based social work, 2010. |
Includes bibliographical references and index.
Identifiers: LCCN 2017038353 | ISBN 9781785922534
Subjects: LCSH: Social service--Case studies. | Interpersonal relations--Case
studies.
Classification: LCC HV40 .R373 2018 | DDC 361.3/2--dc23
LC record available at https://lccn.loc.gov/2017038353

British Library Cataloguing in Publication Data
A CIP catalogue record for this book is available from the British Library

ISBN 978 1 78592 253 4
eISBN 978 1 78450 543 1

Printed and bound in Great Britain

Contents

Section 1. Setting Out the Terrain: Historical Trends, Conceptual Models and Frameworks

Section 2. Working with the Relationship in Practice

Section 3. Sustaining, Supporting and Developing Relationship-Based Practice in a Reflective Context

Foreword

Of course it's never really gone away. It has always been there in social work, one way or another: the practitioner's relationship with her client, the service user. Whatever intentions you have, whichever technique you use, the medium in which matters are conducted is the relationship you have with the other, and the other has with you. The quality and character of these relationships therefore matter, they matter a great deal. Not surprisingly, outcomes have been shown to vary depending on the technique used or intervention chosen. However, more critically, outcomes have also been found to vary depending on the skill and quality of the relationship created by the practitioner as she engages with her client, no matter what technique or method she is using. In a sense then, all social work is relationship-based. There is no choice. In which case, it's vital that we do it well.

It was back in the late 1960s when I began my career as a social worker. I worked in a pre-Seebohm Children's Department. One of the books that helped me make sense of what I was doing, and perhaps also what I could and should do, was Margaret Ferard and Noel Hunnybun's 1962 book *The Caseworker's Use of Relationships* (with a foreword by John Bowlby, no less). Later that same year I came across Isca Salzberger-Wittenberg's 1970 book *Psycho-Analytic Insight and Relationships: A Kleinian Approach*. This gave my enthusiasm for understanding the way we relate to clients a further boost. Even though over the years the idea of relationship-based social work was destined to go in and out of fashion, I never lost faith in its fundamental importance. Like many of my colleagues, the decades saw me flirt with all manner of ideas and theories, fashions and fads, but wherever the ideological winds were blowing me, I tried to ground whatever I was thinking or doing, researching or writing, on the bedrock of the worker–client relationship. I worried that if social work could no longer see that relationship-based practices were its core strength, then it was in danger of losing its humanity and with that its right to exist in any meaningful way.

The relationship between one human being and another is a complicated, tricky place. There is both confusion and delight as my thoughts, feelings and behaviours affect, and are affected by, your thoughts, feelings and behaviours. This is particularly the case when feelings are running high during moments of anxiety, fear, anger, love, shame, sadness. And social work, of course, is a place where feelings, almost by definition, routinely run high.

The idea of relationship-based social work is therefore both simple and complex. Simple in the sense that it is unavoidable. We all know about relationships because that is the everyday world, personally and professionally, in which we live and have our being. But as we've seen, it's also a complex place where there is endless scope for misunderstanding and confusion, connection and collaboration, anger and disappointment, joy and belonging, possibility and hope.

To help us understand and navigate this world, at least in the context of social work, Gillian Ruch, Danielle Turney and Adrian Ward have brought together a number of leading experts to write about relationship-based practice. Packed into these pages are so many good ideas, useful explanations and helpful practices that you will finish the book not only humbler and wiser but also feeling more convinced and determined.

There is a natural logic to the book as each chapter deals with one of the key aspects of doing relationship-based social work. The compilation begins by making the case for relationship-based practices in which there is a need to help the client achieve a balance between their internal and external needs. At times of upset and arousal we seek to regulate our emotions and have them managed and contained. If we can achieve this, then we can begin to think, think about our feelings, our behaviour, our needs and how best to meet them. The theories that help us to understand the relationship and the use of self are outlined, described and discussed.

Social work takes place in a variety of places and over different periods of time. There are excellent chapters on worker–client relationships when encounters are brief, and when they are long term, complex and sustained. There are fascinating chapters on working with strong feelings – fear, anger and aggression; hopelessness, despair and depression; love and attraction. And when the work is done, or the relationship, for whatever reasons, has to stop, we learn a lot from the essay that discusses endings, completions and letting go.

So although we may feel that simply living life teaches us how to do relationships, it becomes clear that there is much to understand, learn and improve if we are to do them well. The book's final chapters therefore talk about how students can be helped to develop a relationship-based practice, the importance of supervision, and the value of having emotionally intelligent professional leadership. How we learn, how we are supervised, and how we are managed should be consistent with the principles of relationship-based social work. Recognising the importance of practices that are both reflective and reflexive runs as a golden thread throughout the book. *Relationship-Based Social Work: Getting to the Heart of Practice* celebrates the power of the human relationship to hold and to heal. Read this splendid book and warm *your* heart and sharpen *your* mind.

David Howe
Emeritus Professor of Social Work
University of East Anglia, Norwich

Preface to the Second Edition

This second edition of *Relationship-Based Social Work: Getting to the Heart of Practice* is being published eight years after the first one. Since the appearance of the first edition, macro-level political changes have influenced – largely negatively in our view – the ways in which individuals, families and groups facing difficulties are perceived, configured and responded to. In the context of these changes we feel that this book is more important than ever for social work practitioners who are working in a politically hostile landscape.

In the substantive chapters we have retained the book's overarching focus on psychodynamic and systemic understandings of human behaviour and on professional interventions, but have profiled more explicitly a commitment to anti-oppressive practice and diversity issues. Two new chapters have been included: a chapter on working with service users and carers replaces the first edition's service user perspective chapter and an additional chapter focuses on professional leadership in contemporary social work practice, acknowledging the central importance of relationship-based leadership for effective everyday practice.

It is our aim that this second edition will help to equip social workers with relationship-based knowledge, skills and values that resist the adverse effects of the prevailing political agenda, offering hope and new possibilities to people experiencing vulnerability and distress.

Gillian Ruch, Danielle Turney and Adrian Ward
September 2017

Introduction

ADRIAN WARD, GILLIAN RUCH AND DANIELLE TURNEY

This book aims to address a familiar theme in a new way. It is perhaps a truism that 'the relationship' is central to good practice in social work – this has always been recognised to some degree, whatever one's theoretical stance. What is new is that we now want to examine and explore what this means in contemporary practice, with its complex bureaucratic and interdisciplinary requirements and its frequent realignments in terms of ideology and professional identity. In this shifting context, what does it actually mean to place 'the relationship' at the heart of practice? What does it look like (and feel like) in practice, and how does this approach sit within current social work preoccupations? These are some of the questions we have begun to address in this book.

The book grew out of the work of an informal grouping of social work teachers and researchers with an interest in psychosocial, psychodynamic and systemic approaches. As we shared ideas and experiences, both about practice and about teaching and research, what emerged was a realisation that despite all the continuing upheavals in policy and procedure, social work would always begin and end with a human encounter between two or more people – even if this was sometimes a brief or fraught encounter. What the social worker will always have to do is make the most of this encounter, understand the multilayered complexity of the relationship which develops, and use his or her skill to ensure that (at the very least) the relationship works in support of the social work task and not counter to it. At its best, what social work can offer to people in need of help is a supportive and understanding relationship which will enable them to resolve their difficulties and to feel enhanced rather than undermined in the process.

What we rediscovered in editing the book is that, although it may sound a relatively simple proposition to place the relationship at the heart of practice, it is not a straightforward matter at all. In particular, we needed to think about the contested nature of contemporary practice, in which (for example) all 'professionalism' may be questioned in terms of its assumptions about power and the locus of expertise. We needed to think about the origins of the social work project and how some of its early and well-intentioned assumptions had to be rethought in the light of some challenging critiques from a range of perspectives. We also needed to address the enormous expansion of models of welfare: social workers now practise in a huge and diverse range of settings, sometimes as a lone practitioner in a complicated multiprofessional network and sometimes as a powerful force within a local government agency driven by compelling national agendas.

At the same time, we felt that there is not always sufficient understanding within this range of agencies of the subtleties and dilemmas of the social worker/service user relationship. After all, if this relationship was always as straightforward as some would wish to imagine, then why is the work so challenging and sometimes so stressful? Why do things go wrong, such as risks not being fully understood or people's true intentions or motives not being recognised? Why do service users sometimes feel unheard, undervalued or misunderstood, and, likewise, why do social workers sometimes feel that the true nature of their work is not appreciated or understood more widely?

We realised that the common ground in all of these situations was the relationship between social worker and service user, and that this common ground had certain main features which we could usefully explore in the book and which would actually help us to structure the argument of the book. Thus:

- First, in every case, such a relationship would have a beginning, a middle and an ending, each phase bringing its own characteristic challenges and demands, so we needed to give specific attention to each of these phases of practice.

- Second, in every case, because they are often encountering people in the midst of crisis and uncertainty, there was the potential for the social worker to have to work with some very powerful feelings, so we needed to acknowledge this reality and to address some of these feelings directly.

- Third, we realised that if the common ground is the relationship, then it is the demands which working *in* and *with* this relationship may place on the social worker's self – their human, personal nature – which must be recognised, so we needed to ensure that we included a clear focus on the professional 'use of self'.

- Fourth, it then became clear that, in order to work in this way, social workers require a distinctive kind of support and development, in terms of training, supervision and leadership, and that the organisational and policy contexts in which they have to operate will have a critical effect on their capacity to work effectively, so we needed to address these issues too.

- Finally, if this whole enterprise is going to succeed, it has to be based in sound and coherent theory, rather than just being left to the intuition of the worker, so we needed to address the theoretical grounding for this approach to practice – and that is where we decided to begin.

It is out of these realisations that we have built the structure of this book. We begin with a revisiting of the theoretical foundations of the work in the first two chapters and a discussion of the use of self in the third. The second section of the book focuses directly on practice, following the sequence suggested above, from beginnings through to endings, but also – in the 'sustaining' phase – focusing directly on a number of the powerful feelings which may be encountered, including fear, anger, depression and despair, but also liking and love. For these chapters in particular, we asked contributors either to begin with or to feature prominently some substantial examples from practice which would help to bring the material to life, and there is certainly some powerful case material in this section. In the third section, we move to the issues of training, supervision and the organisational and policy contexts, to explore the challenges that welfare organisations face in trying to facilitate this approach to practice, and also to think about how it can be incorporated in leadership and management. Finally, we conclude with some brief reflections on the journey we have undertaken in compiling this book.

This is only a beginning, and we have inevitably had to restrict our scope to cover only part of the range of possible applications of this theme. But it is also only a beginning in terms of reworking the theory base. There are many possible takes on relationship-based practice, and as editors we have largely focused on an approach rooted in psychodynamic, systemic and attachment theories – which themselves are all contested fields. Not all of our contributors would align themselves under the same banner, however, and we feel the book is actually enhanced by this diversity. It will be noticed that whereas some are strongly identified with either the psychodynamic or attachment models, others draw on quite different models such as liquidity or empowerment. We wish to promote a broad and inclusive approach, although at the same time we accept that this makes it difficult to come up with a definitive account of relationship-based practice.

As acknowledged in the introduction to the first edition, discrete definitions of the concept of 'relationship-based practice' are, and remain, elusive. An observable development since the first edition has been the adoption of the term 'relationship-based practice', particularly in practice contexts, where it is often associated with a specific practice methodology. Despite these narrower, more fixed interpretations of the term, we remain content to hold the book open on an absolute definition of what relationship-based practice might be. In fact, holding this position probably reflects the nature of the relationship-based practice terrain, which is rich and diverse and may always be hard to pin down to a simple formula. The challenge for us all is to engage in a thoughtful, curious and open-minded way with the issues raised by attempting to work *in* and *with* the relationship, and to aim to draw on whatever combination of ideas resonates with our professional experiences. It is in this spirit that the book has been written, and we hope it will enable those who read it to enhance their own relationship-based practice as a result.

SETTING OUT THE TERRAIN

Historical Trends, Conceptual Models and Frameworks

Chapter 1

The Contemporary Context of Relationship-Based Practice

GILLIAN RUCH

Cathy glared across the courtroom to where Aisha stood in the witness box giving evidence against her. 'Killing me with every word, you are', she muttered, not quite under her breath. And louder: 'Not happy with taking every child I've ever had, but now taking the next one too. Taking my future...' She shook her head, banged her foot on the floor and fixed Aisha vividly with her eyes. Cathy's solicitor put a hand on her arm to calm her.

Aisha continued, saying how, with real regret, she had to recommend that Cathy's unborn child should be removed at birth and placed immediately for adoption. The history – which had been detailed in the reports and rehearsed in the court – was awful, indicating serious risk of physical and emotional harm if Cathy was allowed to keep the child. She spoke of her lengthy involvement with Cathy and the times she had had to remove her other children, but she also spoke about how Cathy seemed quite unable to change her behaviour with regard to her chaotic lifestyle, her drug habits, the severe neglect of her children and her repeated choice of dangerous and violent partners. At this, Cathy smiled wistfully and, with what might have been a nervous giggle of acknowledgement, she nodded her head, looked at her solicitor and nodded again, this time whispering, 'She's right, you know, the cow.' But then she suddenly shook her head again and tapped her foot repeatedly on the floor.

The court eventually made its decision. The unborn child was to be removed to a place of safety and placed for adoption. Cathy had known this would happen and seemed both resigned and enraged, bemused and almost amused – in fact, quite lost in the formal processes and confused about this latest twist in her desperately unhappy life. Aisha came slowly across the courtroom to talk with her, half-expecting to be verbally if not physically attacked, and yet somehow also knowing that she would be able to carry on working with her, that Cathy was sufficiently in need of her support, and sufficiently aware of that reality, that the work would continue: in fact, Aisha was determined that it would continue. Sure enough, after a further vicious glare and shake of the head, Cathy said to Aisha with another wistful smile, 'I suppose you're happy now?' but held her arm and led her away from the solicitors and court ushers, saying, 'Buy us a cup of tea, will you?' They walked out of the court buildings arm in arm and found a cafe. Aisha knew now that she would be able to retain her involvement with Cathy, supporting her in sustaining her access visits to her children in long-term foster care.

Understanding relationship-based practice

This real account of care proceedings might at first sight read as overly sensational and soap opera-like, but based as it is on the recall of a case with which one of the editors of this book was involved, it speaks powerfully to the complex, multi-faceted nature of the professional relationships social workers have to navigate on a daily basis.

The final twist to Cathy's story may have a familiar ring to many social workers who have worked closely with service users in the greatest need and difficulty, balancing the requirements for care and control, yet somehow holding on to a working relationship with the very person who in many ways sees them as the problem rather than the solution. So what is going on here, and how has this social worker managed to retain (apparently) the trust and respect of Cathy, despite all that she has had to do?

At one level, we might imagine that Aisha is a particularly empathic listener who has engaged Cathy sufficiently so that she will still feel listened to despite everything, or that she has been especially persuasive in convincing Cathy that it is still in her interest to stay in communication with her social worker. But Cathy is, in most respects, a person whose life is in a state of permanent shipwreck – disaster, danger and loss have been with her for as long as she can remember – and she has fallen out with virtually every professional she has encountered. So how can we explain the persistence of this particular relationship?

It might also be argued, of course, that Cathy has a kind of dependency on the woman who is in reality her oppressor, or who at least has played a key role in removing her children, and that, instead of promoting this dependency, Aisha would have been better employed providing Cathy with better housing, with more support for her children and with stronger action against the string of abusive short-term partners. And yet whatever material improvement Aisha has managed to secure for Cathy seems to have made no difference at all to her capacity to regulate her own life and offer security and consistency for her own children. (If it had made a difference, Aisha might have been able to argue differently in court.)

On the other hand, we might look at what Aisha may think and feel about all this. She probably sees her key responsibility as not only ensuring that Cathy's children are safe but also trying to provide ongoing support and containment to prevent Cathy from doing further damage to herself, perhaps resulting in a seriously self-destructive outcome. Aisha places a high premium on working 'in the relationship', against all the odds, as it sometimes feels. She wants to sustain the relationship, not only as a vehicle to offer support and, as necessary, an element of social control, but also in the hope that the experience of this continuing and unflinching personal commitment will enable Cathy to learn something which she has so far been unable to achieve by any other means: the ability to understand and regulate her own life and its pressures, and eventually to live a more fulfilled life. In other words, the relationship is not only the medium but part of the message: that it is possible to deal with life's crises without panic, pandemonium and despair, and that positive human relationships are what makes this possible. Through the lens of attachment theory, Aisha might be seen as offering a secure base to Cathy, in the hope that over time Cathy will be able to use the experience of being in a continuing, honest and reliable relationship to reframe her own internal working model, which may enable her to live a less difficult life.

It is a complicated relationship: Cathy sees Aisha as a powerful figure but she has also been able to confide in her through some very difficult times and to talk with her about her own childhood experiences which were painful and abusive. Aisha, too, has very mixed feelings: at times over the years Cathy has been inconsistent, hostile and even abusive towards her (such that Aisha has at times had to take precautions for her own safety), but she also retains respect for the dogged determination with which Cathy clings on to the wreckage, as well as a personal liking for her humour and open manner. Aisha has excellent and detailed supervision on her work and has frequently used this to think through the balance of the working relationship with Cathy and to ensure that she remains on task and that she picks her way through the emotional minefield of Cathy's existence without either making matters worse or losing her.

What is being described here is typical of much social work practice: demanding, confusing and paradoxical at times, and requiring of the worker the ability to stay with people in distress or turmoil and continue to provide a mixture of personal support and pragmatic guidance, largely through the medium of a reliable, engaged and constructive relationship. Such relationships are at the heart of good practice – and very often when practice goes wrong, it emerges that either there was not a solid helping relationship in place or that the relationship had become distorted or too tenuous to sustain the work, or sometimes that the social worker was too overloaded by other tasks to engage fully with the relationship.

The nature of the social work task

On a daily basis, social work practitioners are required to engage with difficult interpersonal situations and with distressed individuals such as Cathy. The individuals with whom social workers engage are experiencing social and emotional difficulties for which they need support and assistance. Within this context, the focus of social work practice uniquely straddles the intersection of the psychological and social contexts of people's lives. Whether the service user is an older person, someone with a disability, a young person with an offending history or a vulnerable child, it is usually both the psychological and social factors impinging on their experience that are the focus of social work interventions. While attending carefully to the social context in which people's difficulties are located, practitioners are simultaneously drawing on internal, often unconscious, dynamics to make sense of these professional encounters. It thus becomes clearer that working in relationship-based ways is complex and demanding. It also becomes easier to understand why it can be difficult to sustain the focus on the relationship and apparently easier to conceive of professional involvement in a more straightforward or simplistic way that prioritises, for example, form-filling and computer-based, as opposed to face-to-face, activities. Such professional behaviours may seem to make sense in the face of distressing, potentially anxiety-provoking, situations which are located in all too often resource-deficient welfare contexts.

This risk of minimising the importance of the relationship in professional practice provides a vivid example of one of the key concepts in relationship-based approaches – avoidant defensive strategies – explored below. The challenge social workers face in practice is to 'defend and sustain complexity' (Burke and Cooper 2007, p.193) and, in particular, the complexity of human behaviour, in the face of powerful pressures to oversimplify it. The emotionally charged nature of all social work encounters requires practitioners to reflect on how the work impacts on them and to draw on the understanding which reflection affords, to inform their practice. It is precisely because the bread and butter of social work is emotionally charged, and because resources to address the issues are often insufficient, that the professional relationship is so important as a key resource.

On a political level and in a climate of continuing austerity, this might sound like a cop-out, implying that an emphasis on relationships can be used to mask a shortfall in resources. Equally, it could be construed that if sufficient material resources (e.g. day centres, preventative child care packages, etc.) were available, then the professional relationship would not matter. Clearly neither of these positions is acceptable. The centrality afforded to professional relationships cannot be allowed to excuse inadequate resourcing of welfare provision, nor should material resources in isolation be considered capable of resolving all of the social and psychological difficulties which people may face. Certainly if resources were more abundant, some of the pressures on service users would be lifted, and this political dimension should not be disregarded. Featherstone et al.'s (2014) book *Re-imagining Child Protection* makes an important contribution to reasserting the significant part played by structural inequalities in the lives of families engaged with Children's Services. That said, adopting a binary, either–or, individual–structural response to Cathy's circumstances is not the answer. In Cathy's case, gaining understanding of her own experiences, and their impact on how she behaves and utilises resources made available to her, is integral to any effective and sustained changes, and that is a longer-term task.

Bower (2005, p.11), referring to the potential benefits of the relationship in practice, comments that, 'a thoughtful and emotionally receptive stance to clients can have therapeutic value without anything fancy being done'. Within this statement there is something of a paradox because, on one level, working 'in the relationship' is a straightforward and obvious way of practising. In reality, however, this requires practitioners to be appropriately equipped to understand the potentially complex dimensions of such relationships. If relationship-based approaches are to be taken seriously, they cannot be done on the cheap. To be a relational resource, practitioners need time and thinking space to develop appropriate professional understanding, and ongoing support to use it effectively, as we shall see throughout this book. Thoughtful and emotionally receptive responses do not, as Bower suggests, need to be 'fancy', but this should not imply they are undemanding for the practitioner concerned, as emotional receptivity and responsiveness require understanding of the intra- and interpersonal dynamics at work. Later chapters in Section 3 explore wider implications of relationship-based approaches, including how they can be embedded from the outset in social work education and training (Chapter 11) and be an integral part of the ongoing support provided for practitioners through supervision (Chapter 13).

One of the fundamental tensions that practitioners face is to balance the internal and external needs of service users – and to respond to both, or at least with both in mind. In essence, it is as simple and as difficult as that. Given the increasingly restrictive budgetary context of welfare provision, Bower's claim for the impact of effective professional relationships deserves careful attention. In a paper that conceptualises the relationship between structural and individual factors shaping an individual or family's life, Hingley-Jones and Ruch (2016) refer to the dynamics of relational austerity, an unintended outcome of financial austerity, and one which aligns itself closely with Bower's position. If the creation of a meaningful professional relationship is as important as the provision of material resources, then it could be argued that, on grounds of effective practice and economic expediency, relational resources need mobilising as a matter of urgency. This is not to suggest they should replace other resource provision, but that they should be understood as an integral component of effective interventions.

In this book we will look at many aspects of professional relationships within social work: how they may start; the range of strong feelings which they may involve, including love, fear, sadness and despair; and eventually how they finish. Although the relationship between Cathy and Aisha is a long-term ongoing one, some social work relationships are very different in time, focus or content and may sometimes be only fleeting or fluid, even though they will still be important. Although all social work includes some element of relationships, our focus here will be on an approach known as 'relationship-based practice', in which much attention is paid to the detail and significance of the relationship: its dynamics or components, the factors which make it challenging or at times paradoxical. This approach also involves looking below the surface to make sense of the less rational or tangible aspects of the social work relationship: the unconscious elements which may have a critical effect on the work, such as the ways in which unspoken anxieties about powerful feelings, including fear or despair, may cloud the judgement of the worker or impede the progress of the work.

The main message of the book is that to be effective in relationship-based work the social worker needs knowledge and skill in the handling of the complex dynamics of helping relationships. In particular, the demanding nature of practice means that it is potentially fraught with anxiety: the dilemmas and difficulties which service users face may evoke considerable uncertainty and anxiety. Such anxiety – if not fully understood and addressed – may distort judgement and communication and seriously affect the outcomes of the work. How else do we explain the social worker who allows a young child to remain in a family home which she and other professionals are too scared to enter, or who misses the crucial signs that a mentally ill adult has suddenly become a much greater risk to himself and others?

What, then, does a contemporary relationship-based model of practice look like, and what prevents or inhibits social workers' capacity to develop relationship-based practice?

A relationship-based model of social work practice

Relationship-based practice is not a new phenomenon and the model we are proposing draws partly upon the psychoanalytic influences informing child care and mental health social work from the 1940s onwards and the psychosocial model associated with Hollis (1964). Key features of these earlier models include:

- recognition that past experiences affect current attitudes and behaviour

- understanding that we do not always consciously realise how our experiences affect our behaviour

- realisation that professional relationships and the feelings they evoke can be associated with other, often unconnected and not always conscious, earlier experiences (Stevenson 2005, p.xi).

We consider that these ideas still have resonance and see them as important features of the model, but in developing a more inclusive theoretical approach, psychoanalytic perspectives are complemented by ideas rooted in systems theory and attachment theory. This theoretical framework concurs with McCluskey and Hooper's (2000, p.9) definition of psychodynamic thinking as:

> an approach informed by attachment theory, psychoanalysis and systems theory, which together offer ways of understanding the complexity and variability of the ways in which individuals develop and relate to one another within particular social contexts, via a focus on their past and present relationships.

In adopting an inclusive theoretical stance, the model reflects the opening up and 'cross fertilisation of ideas, research findings and the testing out of ways to apply this growing understanding [of psychodynamic thought] to practice across the range of caring professions' (Brearley 2007, p.87). Burke and Cooper (2007, p.194) similarly underline the importance of social work approaches embracing diverse perspectives and specifically highlight the creative potential of systemic and psychoanalytic ideas:

> Social work is the ideal terrain on which to create a dialogue between systemic and psychoanalytic approaches. It has always been a pioneering profession in attempting to bridge the gap in the theorising of the connection between the personal and the social. It is in social work practice that ideas are applied of how the wider societal context shapes subjectivity and personal relationships. If neither psychoanalytic nor systemic ideas are disqualified in the

process of attempting to create a dialogue, nor banal similarities drawn, our thinking should be enriched.

Alongside this shift to a more theoretically inclusive approach, the model has sought to respond to a key criticism levied at earlier models of relationship-based practice: that they had a tendency to pathologise service users, to individualise problems and to position the professional as 'expert'. Some of the more radical or overtly political critiques of a narrowly defined psychodynamic approach focused on the lack of acknowledgement of the broader social/economic/political context within which lives are lived and an underestimation of the impact on individuals of structural problems such as poverty, racism and homophobia.

These criticisms of relationship-based approaches in the 1980s were important to acknowledge, and they changed the terms of some of the discussions about the role and meaning of the professional relationship. However, an undesirable consequence was a significant shift towards predominantly socially orientated practice which paid insufficient attention to the psychological dimensions of people's lives. Such exaggerated swings in professional emphasis are not uncommon in response to external factors, but they are invariably unhelpful because they do not acknowledge the critical balance of psychological and social perspectives that social work endeavours to hold in tension and which distinguishes its activities from other professional groups. The model we are proposing seeks to redress these polarised positions. Developments in relation to anti-oppressive practice, understandings of power in professional relationships and the importance of working in ways that utilise service users' knowledge, and facilitate partnership and collaboration, are recognised as integral components of relationship-based practice and of respectful and empowering relationships.

From this inclusive perspective, the model proposed is characterised by the following key understandings of social work practice:

- Human behaviours and the professional relationship are an integral component of any professional intervention.

- Human behaviour is complex and multi-faceted. People are not simply rational beings but have affective (both conscious and unconscious) dimensions that enrich but simultaneously complicate human relationships.

- The internal and external worlds of individuals are inseparable, so integrated (psychosocial), as opposed to one-dimensional, responses to social problems are crucial for social work practice.

- Each social work encounter is unique, and attention must be paid to the specific circumstances of each individual.

- A collaborative relationship is the means through which interventions are channelled, and this requires a particular emphasis to be placed on the 'use of self'.

- The respect for individuals embedded in relationship-based practice involves practising in inclusive and empowering ways.

The model proposed seeks to offer a joined-up way of thinking about relationships that acknowledges the visible and invisible, conscious and unconscious components that comprise all relationships, and recognises the important connections between the intrapsychic, interpersonal and broader social contexts in which they are embedded. It aims to help practitioners engage in meaningful practice which makes sense of the uniqueness of individuals' experience and behaviours. In so doing, the focus of interactions is not simply on their content but is also on the process and dynamics involved. Importantly, it recognises that both practitioner and service user bring a range of experiences and emotional responses into the encounter and that each participant's understanding of themselves and the 'other' will have a bearing on the relationship and its meaning (Turney 2012). This allows practitioners to keep in touch with both their thoughts and feelings about the relationship and to be alert to not only the cognitive but also the affective responses which inform how the uniqueness, risk and uncertainty that characterise all social work relationships are addressed.

Attention to depth, as opposed to surface understandings is of importance given the widespread recognition that shortcomings in practice have been attributed to practitioners not engaging effectively with service users. This emphasis on the word 'effectively' highlights how it is not simply a question of engagement but the quality of the engagement that matters. Following the death in 2000 of Victoria Climbié, Cooper (2005, p.8) commented on how difficult it is for professionals who encounter unimaginable aspects of human behaviour and their tendency to see, but not see, and to 'turn a blind eye'. Similar dynamics can be identified in relation to the death of Peter Connelly, initially reported in the media as Baby Peter in London, in 2007, who, despite 'being seen' on 60 separate occasions by a range of health and social care professionals at home and in professional settings, was not removed from his abusive carers. Practitioners using relationship-based approaches should be able to develop what Ferguson (2005, p.791) refers to as 'deep' relationships and to move beyond surface understandings and interactions. In placing the relationship at the heart of social work practice, the model focuses on the relationship as the vehicle through which interventions are mediated, as well as potentially being of intrinsic value as an intervention in its own right.

It is not enough, however, to propose a model for relationship-based practice without attending to some of the obstacles to its effective implementation. Paradoxically, it is precisely because of these obstacles that there is the need for such a model to become more widely established in practice. The challenge to relationship-based ways of working arises from the contemporary social and political context in which practice is located, and it is this wider context that has in recent decades inhibited its development.

Marketisation, managerialism and the commodification and bureaucratisation of the individual

Social work occupies an ambivalent social space, and its particular relationship to the individual or the state is defined according to the prevailing dominant political ideologies (Howe 1994; Parton 1994, 2014; Rogowski 2016; Yelloly and Henkel 1995). Since the 1980s the social work profession and practice has been significantly influenced and constrained by its broader social, political and economic contexts and specifically the twin forces of marketisation and managerialism. The welfarist approach to social work which dominated the 1950s, 1960s and 1970s was replaced in the 1980s by a neoliberal political philosophy which emphasised individual rights and responsibilities and the role of economic market principles – in essence the 'marketisation of welfare'. The impact of the market culture on social work practice was evidenced by new terminology permeating practice with notions of 'best value', consumers and purchaser/provider splits becoming increasingly visible (Howe 1994; Munro 2000; Parton 1994). The effects of these governing principles for the social work profession were a reduction in the interventionist role of the state, a greater emphasis placed on the right of the individual to freedom of choice and more scrutiny of the efficiency of social work practice. It has been argued that, as a direct result of these changes in emphasis, there was an increase in the number of marginalised and excluded people requiring help and a simultaneous decrease in resource provision (Parton 1998a), and furthermore that practice became increasingly resource-led rather than needs-led, and system-centred rather than client-centred (Audit Commission 1994; Preston-Shoot 1996; Smith 1996) – trends that have continued under later administrations.

A significant consequence for the practitioner/client relationship was a shift from nurturing and supportive to contractual and service-orientated approaches to practice. Transactional and economically driven approaches replaced the therapeutic and interpersonal stance that historically had been the dominant characteristics of practice (Howe 1996). The centrality for practice of the professional relationship based on trust (Hollis 1964) was replaced, according to Parton (1998b), by the notion of audit. Practitioners became managers, as exemplified in the title 'care manager' introduced for social workers located in adult services, whose primary tasks were to assess, commission and review services. Practice was increasingly seen in terms of technical-rational competencies rather than professional values, knowledge and skills (Adams 1998; Smith and White 1997). Howe (1996, p.92) described how this managerialist approach, derived from a neo-political ideology, 'is antithetical to depth explanations, professional discretion, creative practice and tolerance of complexity and uncertainty'.

Similarly, Parton (1998b, p.6) outlined how under such regimes:

> the essential focus for policy and practice no longer takes the form of a direct face-to-face relationship between the professional and the client but resides in managing and monitoring a range of abstract factors deemed liable to produce risk for children.

These tensions between marketised models of welfare provision and professional practice have long been recognised (Howe 1986; Jones 2015; Jordan and Drakeford 2012) and the continued colonisation of practice by market forces has been a sustained, steady process. One significant consequence of these shifts in understandings of practice has been an increasingly narrow focus which prioritises measurable outcomes that 'prove' economic efficiency and effectiveness. While it is of course important to identify how best to support families and what interventions are most likely to facilitate change, there has been a tendency to construe this in increasingly narrow terms. Trying to define 'what works' – and what counts as evidence – poses challenges in situations where the main resource is the practitioner rather than – or at least in conjunction with – any more formal method or approach that has been adopted.

Under such conditions, any aspect of practice which is not measurable – such as 'mindfulness, the process and nature of relationships, managing the affective component of the work, "the artistry of social work"' (Youll 1996, p.39) – is in danger of being considered less important. Indeed, a perceived 'undue' emphasis on such activities can leave a practitioner open to the kinds of shaming and blaming management practices used to exercise control over staff that have been identified by Gibson (2016). Aymer and Okitikpi (2000, p.69) also recognised how the emergence of managerialist social work practice became characterised by the separation of action from reflection:

> what it achieved was to change the ethos of the professional intervention from one of trust to that of contract culture where everyone involved from providers and purchasers to customers (people) only related to each other through contractual obligations that had been agreed… guidelines, procedures, manuals act as a defence against the anxiety of 'not knowing'.

The emphasis on markets, choice and minimal state intervention, which epitomises the neoliberal stance that continues to pervade and shape social work practice, has had a fundamental impact on how service users are understood and engaged with and how practitioners understand themselves and their professional role. Embedded in the principles of welfare markets are the notions of customers and suppliers, based on commodity transactions. The principles that govern business and economic activities have been translated into the domain of interpersonal relations.

It is not difficult to see the shortcomings of such configurations for social work. Individuals in this model of practice are configured as customers whose choices are based on purely rational principles with no reference to their psychosocial needs or circumstances. Equally, practitioners are expected to adopt the role of service commissioner or provider on a similar basis, with no regard to the complexities of people's lives. The commodification of the individual and welfare practices over the past two decades has undermined the importance attributed to human relationships, and the need for relationship-based practice has tended to be screened out as social work has become increasingly predicated and practised on a rational/business basis.

A corollary of the marketisation of welfare has been the colonisation of professional practice by bureaucratised and managerialist practices (Blaug 1995) which have been another dominant sociopolitical trend for the past 20 years and more. Such practices are compatible with market perspectives as they too configure individuals primarily as rational beings. They also seek, albeit unsuccessfully, to reduce the anxiety aroused by heightened awareness of uncertainty and risk in professional practice by identifying ostensibly 'risk-free' solutions to unsettling realities. In so doing, they aim to minimise the uncertainty embedded in human situations. This reductionist and rationalised approach to social work practice has been further exacerbated by the burgeoning of the digital economy and increasing reliance on computer-based systems as the 'best' way of managing practice (Parton 2008). One visible manifestation of this has been the increasing amount of time social workers spend inputting data into complex computer systems designed to safeguard children. The coincidence of the enquiry into the death of Peter Connelly, who was killed by his carers despite professional involvement, and the publication of research into the Integrated Children's System, introduced following Victoria Climbié's death (Pithouse *et al.* 2009; Shaw *et al.* 2009), have brought home forcibly the challenging nature of social work and the inadequacies of overly bureaucratic responses to complex, interpersonal situations (see also Munro 2011b).

Reconfiguring the service user and practitioner

One way of understanding and conceptualising the shift towards marketised and managerialist practices in the social work profession is as a defence against the anxieties inherent in the nature of the work being undertaken. From this perspective, with its over-reliance on bureaucratic interpretations of practice, the increasingly impersonal nature of the social work relationship protects practitioners and managers from the emotionally demanding and distressing dimensions of individuals' circumstances. The risk of adopting such a stance, however, is considerable as it may impair professional judgements and decision-making by constricting the professional relationship and reducing the amount and type of knowledge that is drawn on to inform critical decisions. Up-to-date computer records do not equate to good practice, yet the fear expressed by social workers (Ferguson 2005), if they fail to comply with the administrative demands of their work, can directly impact on their involvement with service users. Under such pressure, the professional relationship is at serious risk of being compromised.

In his exploration of the nature of contemporary social work practice, Ferguson (2005) highlights how the managerialist culture has impacted on how service users are understood and related to. The 'sanitisation' of social work practice and the fear of acting oppressively have resulted in tendencies within social work to avoid engaging with the distasteful and difficult aspects of practice (Ferguson 2005). Such constrained forms of engagement are inevitably ineffective as they fail to address the core issues under the guise of wanting to sustain a 'professional' relationship and be non-discriminatory. Avoiding addressing, for example, the personal hygiene issues associated with a service user, or challenging an individual's aggressive and threatening behaviours towards professionals, can potentially have the opposite effect and be oppressive on the grounds of failing to engage with the whole person and establish a meaningful and honest relationship. Being anti-oppressive as a practitioner does not mean abandoning professional value positions but requires these positions to be negotiated through the medium of honest and meaningful relationships that address the more challenging aspects of an individual's life. Aisha's engagement with Cathy provides a vivid illustration of such authentic practice. To respond in this way is to embrace fully both relationship-based and anti-oppressive practice.

For relationship-based practice to take hold, there needs to be a significant shift in how individuals are perceived. The realisation that people are not simply commodities within a market system, or objects that can be reduced to a computer record, but are unique individuals with complex intersubjective experiences needs to be reclaimed. Recognition of the inability of computerised systems to capture the complexity of human lives is beginning to be accepted (Pithouse *et al.* 2009; Parton 2008) and there is evidence, at least within academic circles, of a shift from the 'electronic turn' in social work practice (Garrett 2005) to a 'relational turn'. An important feature of this reconfiguring of individuals from rational to relational beings is the acknowledgement that this reconfiguration needs to embrace professionals as well as service users.

The reduction of practitioners to care managers and commissioners denies the emotional dimensions of their professional experiences and relationships and overlooks the necessary resources they need to undertake their work effectively. Reconceptualising the practitioner means acknowledging their emotional responses and the emotional impact of practice on them. The anxieties that arise from the complexity, ambiguity and uncertainty of contemporary practice need containing, not only for service users but also for practitioners.

Offering such containment is not an easy task. The paucity of attention given, until quite recently, to relationship-based practice in social work settings can be understood in part as a result of the dominant market and bureaucratic forces shaping models of practice. It can equally be understood in terms of the operation of defence mechanisms. Relationship-based practice requires practitioners, managers and policymakers to engage with the messy realities of practice. Avoidance and denial are common responses which enable individuals and organisations to defend against troubling and unacceptable aspects of experience. Any attempts to reorientate social work practice to a more relationship-based position risks provoking defensive responses. In advocating a shift in emphasis in practice from managerialist to relational approaches, with less emphasis on procedures and legalistic responses and more on uniqueness and relationships, professionals are forced into less familiar territory and required to confront aspects of practice which up until now they may have avoided. Given this situation, to realise widespread acceptance of relationship-based approaches to practice at all levels within organisations – policymaking, management, practice – requires sensitive handling. The work of Menzies-Lyth (1988) on the social systems that organisations develop to defend against anxiety (see Chapter 2) is very pertinent for social work settings and for understanding the resistance that can arise to embedding relationship-based practice within the organisation.

Dealing with defences

Awareness of these defensive dynamics underlines the importance of identifying and providing the necessary support structures that will enable practitioners and managers to sustain relationship-based approaches (see Chapters 10 and 12). In contrast to current permutations of practice which rely heavily on technical-rational, prescriptive and bureaucratic interventions, relationship-based approaches require practitioners to rely more heavily on their practical/moral knowledge base, grounded in their intersubjective experiences. As a consequence, it is essential that appropriate sources of support are provided that will enable practitioners to make sense of their experience. It is almost impossible to overestimate the demands of relationship-based practice. To engage meaningfully, responsibly and effectively in relationship-based practice requires practitioners to be theoretically informed and equipped with practice skills that can recognise, tolerate and make sense of the complexities and ambiguities of human experience.

Conclusion

Since the inception of social work, the importance attributed to the relational aspects of social work practice has varied in response to sociopolitical forces and theoretical trends. Developments over the past two decades have pushed the relational aspects of practice to the margins, although there are now grounds for optimism. The limitations of practice that fails to embrace sufficiently the role of the professional relationship are beginning to be recognised and responded to. It is never helpful, however, to polarise issues, and building new approaches to relationship-based ways of practising should not preclude the potentially positive contributions that management systems and bureaucratic procedures can make. Crucial to the effectiveness of such integrated relationship-based approaches is the recognition of the human dimension of social work's primary task. There is an urgent need for practitioners, managers and policymakers to be both intellectually and practically equipped with the knowledge, skills and values required to realise this task, and it is to this body of knowledge that this book seeks to contribute.

Chapter 2

Theoretical Frameworks Informing Relationship-Based Practice

GILLIAN RUCH

Introduction

In Chapter 1 a contemporary model of relationship-based practice was outlined, and psychoanalytic, systems and attachment theories were identified as the three key theoretical and conceptual frameworks informing it. This chapter explores in more detail some of the concepts associated with each of the three theoretical traditions and illustrates how, by drawing on these ideas, it is possible to work with service users creatively, constructively and collaboratively through the medium of the professional relationship.

Early relationships, powerful feelings, anxiety and uncertainty

In both the psychoanalytic and attachment traditions, great emphasis is placed on the significance of early experiences for an individual's subsequent development. Associated with these early experiences are powerful or what are sometimes referred to as 'primitive' feelings. To understand the power of such feelings, we only need to observe a distressed infant for a few minutes to experience their full force. Ordinary human responses, such as an overwhelming urge to pick up and cuddle the infant, offer some insight into the powerful communicative potential of such behaviours and, in most cases, our need to offer comfort.

However, the extreme force of such feelings can also lead to much more serious reactions in other circumstances. For adults whose emotional development may have been seriously impaired, and who may also be subject to other intolerable pressures, the experience of an infant expressing her vulnerability and neediness in such immediate and intrusive ways can feel unbearable and may ultimately elicit responses ranging from avoidance to abuse. Perhaps one of the most difficult aspects of human behaviour to comprehend is the capacity of adults to inflict injury upon or, in the most extreme cases, to kill babies and children. The deaths of children in which carers were complicit underline the importance of recognising how babies and children can be experienced by some adults as attacking and persecuting. Very often it is the understanding of the adults' own traumatic childhood experiences and impaired emotional development that can help us to understand such extreme responses. Although these are extreme examples of the worst excesses of uncontained feelings, they serve to emphasise the intensity of our most basic, 'primitive' feelings, the destructive capacity of human nature and the importance of all efforts to minimise the risk of such incidents recurring.

In endeavouring to understand relationships, it is necessary to recognise the part played in psychological development by these powerful feelings and anxieties. Central to relationship-based practice is an understanding of the role played by anxiety in response to distressing and uncertain situations (Brearley 2007; Trowell 1995). The ways in which anxiety is experienced and managed may play a powerful role in influencing how an individual responds to situations and challenges arising in their life, and if people have not developed effective ways of managing their anxiety earlier in life, they may have continuing difficulties later on. Extreme or disproportionate anxieties of this sort may be exhibited in a variety of ways, including aggressive and hostile behaviours, hysteria and mania, as well as acute and chronic depression. All of these behaviours are familiar to social workers and are often most effectively responded to if understood in relation to anxiety. It is from this perspective that seemingly irrational behaviours can take on a more understandable dimension. We shall now look briefly at how such anxiety may be understood by psychoanalytic, attachment and systemic theories respectively.

A psychoanalytic stance understands anxiety to be an individual's natural response to basic fears such as not having their basic needs met – of annihilation. Bion (1962) refers to this fear as 'the nameless dread', the non-existence of a relationship with another. Klein's 'object relations' theory (Trowell 1995) argues that the emotional development of an infant is always in relation to another person; she refers to the other as the 'object' (as distinct from the 'subject' who is experiencing the feelings); therefore this approach to understanding relationships is known as 'object relations'. From a Kleinian perspective, the experience of anxiety is closely associated with ambivalent loving and hateful feelings towards another person. Anxiety arises where these feelings become polarised – between the fears of losing the loved object and of being confronted by the hate object. The developmental task is to be able to integrate these polarised feelings. To achieve this task, infants require parental care which enables them to resolve the conflicting feelings they experience.

Klein referred to this necessary, but conflictual, development stage as the 'paranoid-schizoid position', in which the infant is at risk of being overwhelmed by fear of their feelings and unable to experience good and bad in one object (person). For infants who experience positive parenting, their capacity to tolerate conflicting feelings enables their emotional development to progress to what Klein referred to as the 'depressive position': in this context, 'depressive' has a positive connotation and is representative of a healthy, integrated and balanced emotional stance. The extent to which infants have been able to develop integrated emotional responses influences the extent to which they can later exhibit such responses as adults. Although not irreversible, early experiences and the emotional development that is shaped by them have a powerful effect on experiences in later life (Howe 1995).

The experiences of young people leaving care provide a vivid example of how anxiety may underpin behaviours. The task of the relationship-based social worker is often to recognise the external pressures on the care leaver arising from their new social circumstances and context, while simultaneously trying to understand what internal needs the individual's behaviour might be expressing. It is not uncommon for young people leaving care and embarking on independent living to present themselves to their social workers in the early stages of the transition with numerous crises. Often these difficulties will be highly charged, and frequently they seem to arise on a Friday afternoon, perhaps influenced by their having to make another transition, from the 'known' routine of the week to the unknowns of a weekend. Although the presenting problem might be a shortage of money or food for the weekend, underlying these practical requests there may also be anxiety about coping on their own and adjusting to not having caring adults in immediate proximity.

It is not difficult to see that these vulnerable young people's immediate and concrete experience of being alone may trigger unconscious feelings associated with annihilation and a deeper despair. How such experience is communicated may also offer insight into the inner world of the young person, as hostile, aggressive behaviour is often likely to elicit rejecting responses from professionals, which may well reproduce the young people's earlier experiences of parental relationships. In the case of young care leavers, it is not uncommon for these earlier experiences to have impaired their emotional development, resulting in aggressive and attacking behaviours, associated with unintegrated, paranoid-schizoid reactions which may sometimes lead them to perceive others, including the social worker, as entirely bad and unhelpful. Acknowledging the pressures young care leavers experience in developing their independent lives is a critical task within the professional response, alongside seeking practical solutions to overcome these pressures they are experiencing. Equally important for any response to be effective, however, is the capacity to help the young person understand their actions and gain some insight into their behaviour.

Hussain is 17 and has been living with a foster family for seven years, prior to moving into an independent living scheme for care leavers. In the early stages of this transition, Hussain's social worker, Joe, undertook to visit him regularly once a week. Despite having known Hussain for some time and having developed a positive relationship with him, Joe was surprised by the hostility with which Hussain treated him when he visited. Joe was not deterred, however, and continued to visit on a regular basis. Even when Hussain was not there several times in a row, Joe kept visiting and always left a note letting Hussain know he had visited.

Gradually, as Hussain adjusted to his new circumstances, he was able to talk with Joe about the experience. For Hussain, during the initial stages of the move, it was impossible for him to be able to relate to Joe positively as he experienced him as responsible for the difficult experiences and feelings he was encountering. Despite Joe's expressions of concern and support, for a long time Hussain could not accept them, choosing to see Joe as 'the baddie', the bad object responsible for his distress. Through his persistent and consistent pattern of visits, Joe was able to offer Hussain a reliable model of adult concern and support, and eventually, through this 'containing' experience, Joe enabled Hussain to accept his help and support and in the process to develop the capacity to experience other individuals as sources of both positive and negative feelings.

Within attachment theory it is possible to identify similar dynamics at work, although the roots of the behaviours are understood rather differently. As with object relations theory, attachment theory is premised on the need of infants to be in relationship to others, and, in line with Freudian thinking, it attributes this to the survival instinct and the search for proximity to a care giver – a 'secure base' – through attachment-seeking behaviours – for example, crying (Aldgate 2009). Through their experience of positive secure attachments, infants develop an internal working model, similar to Klein's depressive position, which allows them to thrive within from what Winnicott (1986) referred to as 'good enough' parenting. Infants with secure attachments exhibit sound development across all the developmental domains – physical, social, emotional, cognitive and moral – compared with infants who exhibit insecure attachments, whose development is often impaired in one or more domains. The interconnections between emotional and cognitive development are particularly interesting and can be understood in part in terms of the process referred to as 'containment', discussed below.

Although the focus in psychoanalytic approaches is predominantly on intrapsychic dynamics and how relationships have become internalised and shaped behaviours, from systemic perspectives, individual behaviours are understood in the context of interpersonal relationships in the here and now. The anxiety experienced in family systems can be understood as a response to uncertainty about what is happening or why. Although systemic perspectives do not relate this to annihilation in the way psychoanalytic approaches do, the uncertainty generated can be understood in terms of a threat to an individual's identity and their relationship network. Helping individuals and families to tolerate uncertainty and retain their curiosity about what is taking place within their social systems is central to relationship-based practice.

This understanding of the role that primitive feelings, anxiety and uncertainty have in shaping human behaviours is pivotal to relationship-based practice. With this knowledge and awareness, it is possible to think about how practitioners can engage with service users in ways that respond to both the conscious and unconscious communications being delivered. To understand how a relationship-based model of practice engages with and responds to the less visible, unconscious communications involves an exploration of the dynamics of transference and counter-transference, defence mechanisms and containment.

Making the invisible visible
Transference and counter-transference

If we are to think about the unconscious aspects of communication, it can be helpful to use metaphor, in terms of looking 'below the surface' to experience these less visible but still very powerful underlying currents of feeling. These deeper levels of communication mean thinking about the process as much as the content of interactions, and often involve trying to make sense of the tensions between the surface and the depths, and the intertwining between feelings associated with the past and the present, as well as the ways in which these tensions can influence or distort our behaviour and experience.

Central to the psychodynamic view is the concept of transference – the idea that in our current relationships and interactions we may unconsciously 'transfer' feelings into the here and now which actually belong in our previous relationships. Most commonly, this is taken to mean that we tend to use our most powerful early relationships with our mother and/or father as a template for understanding our current relationships (although we might use other templates too). This might mean, for instance, experiencing authority figures in our lives as if they were our own parent – for better or worse. In most everyday interactions and relationships, such templates may not be of much consequence, but when combined with the kinds of deep anxiety or insecurity described earlier, they may have a more serious consequence.

For example, if all our earliest experience were of unreliable or even hostile parental figures, we may be likely to read such templates on to our current interactions (and perhaps to revert to our earlier ways of trying to cope), which may make it very difficult to sustain positive dependent relationships. Such feelings might also make it difficult for us to accept help from a social worker, if our unconscious expectation is always that those who should be helping us will actually neglect or even attack us. Social workers therefore need to try to take account of such unconscious patterns, both in their assessments of people's experience and behaviour and in making sense of their relationships with service users.

To complicate matters, it is, of course, not just service users whose relationships have an unconscious element, but social workers too. Not only may we as social workers carry around our own transference templates, but we will also be affected by the unconscious ways in which service users may transfer their feelings on to us. Thus we might react to someone seeing us as a punitive parent by unwittingly going into that role and acting precipitously or harshly, or, equally, we might react against such feelings by unconsciously overcompensating, trying to avoid being seen as too harsh and perhaps making too many allowances. Such reactions to the transference are known as the counter-transference. What makes it complicated is that because these patterns develop unconsciously, we are not likely to be aware of them as they are happening, although we may be able to make them more 'visible' through later reflection or supervision – which is one reason why supervision is so important.

One further useful distinction is between the personal and the diagnostic counter-transference. In the personal counter-transference, our own templates may have become inappropriately activated, as in the example above, drawing us into reactive or avoidant patterns. In the diagnostic counter-transference, we can (on reflection) learn to use our understanding of the ways in which we may risk being drawn into an unfamiliar or inappropriate response to help us to make sense of the other person's unconscious communications. The familiar question which we may pose to ourselves in confusing or conflictual situations – 'Is it them or is it me?' – is one way of expressing this distinction.

What is important is how social workers use such thoughts in conjunction with service users. Awareness of being 'caught off guard' or 'acting out of character' can sometimes, if the practitioner is alert to it, be sufficient information in itself to feed back to the service user to explore its significance.

For example, the social worker might say, 'When you said that, I felt…(confused/angry/protective)…towards you – I wonder why that should have been so?' In fact, a significant part of developing an active helping relationship can come through this ability to reflect with the service user on the ways in which both parties seem to be experiencing the relationship.

Contemporary relationship-based models of practice play down the hierarchical 'professional expert' approach. Instead, the emphasis is on engaging collaboratively in partnership with service users, to allow the insight afforded by the professional relationship to inform subsequent interactions. It is such interactions that enable in-depth relationships and process-based interventions to become established. Practitioners therefore need to be especially self-aware and to develop the skills of reflection if they are to be able to recognise and use these transference and counter-transference dynamics. This 'use of self' is an integral dimension of relationship-based practice and is explored more fully in Chapter 3 and elsewhere throughout the book.

Mirroring

Within systemic theoretical frameworks, the process of mirroring has a role similar to transference to play in helping the professional understand the experience of the service user more fully and accurately (Boyd 2007). Mirroring or isomorphism occurs when the dynamics of a situation are replicated in a different but related context.

> In supervision, Marie, the supervisor, became aware that however she approached the issue that Dave, the social worker, was describing in his work with a particular service user, she was met with a defeatist response and a reluctance to consider any intervention as potentially helpful. Marie recognised Dave's response to be out of keeping with his usual positive outlook. On raising this with Dave, the ensuing discussion highlighted how Dave's pessimistic perspective on the situation appeared to be unconsciously mirroring the attitude of the service user being discussed. With this awareness, Dave was able to identify a way of returning to the family concerned to explore with them what made it so difficult to believe the situation could change.

Because phenomena such as mirroring are unconscious, we will not usually be aware of them at the time, although if we are on the alert for them, we may develop the capacity to use the information and insight which such awareness offers. The 'Seminar Method' described in Chapter 10 offers one way of learning to develop sensitivity to this process, and Mattinson (1970) described how the unconscious 'reflection process' in supervision could sometimes help to illuminate and make sense of the work being discussed.

In systemic practice, 'reflecting teams' (Anderson 1987) have been found to offer a useful mechanism for responding to the dynamics observed within a family situation. In this model, one or two practitioners will meet with the family and the remaining practitioners (the number will vary, but usually between two and four) will observe the session behind a one-way screen, if available, or from a discreet distance in the room if there is no screen. The practitioners engaging with the family invite the reflective team, at an appropriate point in the meeting, to hold a conversation about what they have observed in front of the family. Once this is completed the practitioners then re-engage with the family and invite them to discuss which aspects of the reflective team's conversation have interested them. Being 'one removed' from direct engagement with the family affords the members of the reflective team a space to focus on the processes and dynamics operating, with less risk of becoming involved in the content of the session. From this position they can more easily focus on the affective impact of the session and offer their observations of this when conducting the reflective conversation in front of the family. Not only is the team able to be reflective on multiple levels; it is also open to mirroring the unconscious dynamics itself, and this possibility must always be held in mind. It is not uncommon for team members to unconsciously re-enact the dynamics of a family situation, with different practitioners allying themselves with individual family members and mirroring their behaviours and dynamics within the team.

Not all contexts have the resources to operate reflecting teams, but the principles underpinning them can inform all professional relationships, whether the work is undertaken by one practitioner on their own or as part of co-working. Mirroring is also a feature of interprofessional work contexts. Being able to take a step back and acknowledge what might be being played out within the professional context can offer helpful insights into how the professional system can then collaborate in the interests of all members of the family. The challenge for practitioners is being able to have the time, space and insight to take the necessary step back. If it is not taken, however, the risk is that the professional responses will reinforce the existing dysfunctional dynamics.

The importance of communicating understanding of transference issues in a respectful and empowering manner to families applies equally to the awareness gained from the mirroring processes. A feature of reflective teams is their commitment to conveying their views in a tentative and open manner, refraining from adopting a position of expertise. From a social constructionist systemic perspective, all views carry equal weight and no one truth is sought after (Hedges 2005).

Individual and organisational defences
Individual defences

Alongside being able to recognise and work with the dynamics of transference and counter-transference, relationship-based practitioners also need to have an understanding and awareness of the role that defence mechanisms play in human interactions. Both Freud and Klein recognised the importance of defences. When positive experiences of containment or internal working models are absent, individuals may resort to alternative strategies for survival. Fundamental to understanding defences is the realisation that they are normal and healthy responses to threatening situations. The dysfunction arises when they become so embedded in an individual's behaviour that they define all interactions, regardless of the presence of a genuine threat.

To refer to someone as 'acting defensively' or 'being defensive' is part of everyday vocabulary, but underlying these generic phrases are more specific behaviours. Freud identified several defensive responses including denial, repression, avoidance and displacement (Trowell 1995). Denial refers to the unconscious inclination to avoid pain by minimising the acknowledgement of distressing feelings. Often short-lived and in response to a crisis – for example, the sudden death of a close relative – denial may temporarily protect individuals from having to encounter the painful reality associated with loss. As part of the bereavement process, denial can be understood as a normal reaction, provided it is only temporary and does not become entrenched. Repression refers to the burying of feelings, rendering them more difficult to recall. For adults with traumatic childhood experiences, it is sometimes many years after the events took place that they feel safe and contained enough to allow repressed memories to surface. Avoidance, displacement and sublimation are similar in nature and are apparent when energy is invested in other activities to avoid having to face up to emotionally distressing issues. As mentioned elsewhere in this book, the current preoccupation within contemporary social work on paperwork and procedures can sometimes be understood as an avoidant or displacement activity which enables practitioners to divert their attention from the painful situations they are faced with.

Developing Freud's ideas of transference/counter-transference and defence mechanisms, Klein devised the defensive concepts of splitting and projection to explain the capacity for an individual to rid themselves of unwanted, anxiety-provoking aspects of their experience. As a defensive strategy, splitting reinforces the propensity to polarise good and bad feelings. At an everyday 'normal' level, splitting is exhibited in young children who view one parent as embodying all the good aspects of the parental relationship and the other parent all the bad elements.

Such splits are generally not permanent and will be reconfigured as events change. For damaged and traumatised individuals, the capacity for conflicting feelings to become integrated may be more challenging, and part of the social work role is to assist this process. Projection refers to the placing of the unwanted 'split-off' feelings – for example, hatred, anger, resentment, fear, confusion, envy – into another person. In its most potent form, this is known as projective identification, with the recipient of the unwanted feelings being indirectly made to experience them as if they were their own. Similar to the transference dynamic, projective mechanisms can elicit unexpected responses in the recipient.

> Sue had been working with Karen, a 14-year-old girl with a complex abusive history, for several months. Following a difficult and chaotic 'direct work' session with Karen, the session ended with Karen appearing to be quite calm, despite the nature of the session, and departing in an unusually amicable and straightforward way. Immediately after the session, Sue went out to a cash machine to take out some money. In the process of entering her PIN, Sue became aware she simply could not remember it as her brain felt

'scrambled'. On reflection, she recognised that she had been left feeling confused following the session with Karen and realised that, unconsciously, the feelings of confusion that Karen could not tolerate had been projected on to her.

With insights such as Sue's, there is opportunity in subsequent sessions to explore with Karen what feeling so confused is like and to empathise with her about how unsettling it can be. Empathising in this way can be experienced as containing and offers individuals such as Karen the opportunity to tolerate what (until it was acknowledged and understood) had felt overwhelming and anxiety-provoking. In order for Karen to be able to move on from her traumatic experiences, she needs to be able to understand and accept the intolerable feelings which she can currently only deal with by 'evacuating' or projecting them on to others. This example highlights how, unless an individual's emotional experiences are understood, any number of resources – in Karen's case, positive foster placements, creative opportunities for young people and school activities – are unlikely to be effective because of Karen's confused understanding of her circumstances and their implications for her self-image and self-worth. While these remain unresolved, the likelihood is that Karen's behaviours will undermine any potential positive impact such resources might have. In order for a good experience to really mean anything, we need to be able to accept it and take it into ourselves; the risk for Karen was that she could not hold on to any good feelings about herself.

Social workers in adult mental health settings will be familiar with working with service users whose emotional development is at the unintegrated, paranoid-schizoid level. Understanding how threatening relationships can be from this developmental perspective assists workers in responding in effective ways. A common way for service users to express their emotional state is through 'splitting' – that is, attributing good and bad characteristics to different professionals with an inability to recognise that each individual might have elements of both. Social workers are all too familiar with being treated as the 'bad', intrusive and unhelpful professional, whereas health visitors, for example, may be attributed with all the positive and helpful professional qualities. In interprofessional working contexts, such behaviours by service users can have a powerful impact on professional dynamics and relationships between service users and professionals, particularly when some professionals are unaware of the unconscious processes operating. Being perceived as unconditionally positive by a service user, even if it is not an accurate or integrated perception, can be appealing to practitioners. The risk that this generates is one of professional collusion, with positively connoted practitioners exhibiting a reluctance to challenge a service user for fear of jeopardising the ostensibly positive professional relationship they have established (see Chapter 7).

From an attachment perspective, avoidant attachment behaviours can also be construed as defence mechanisms because the behaviours characteristic of this attachment type (insecure self-sufficiency and compulsive self-reliance) allow individuals to bypass the source of anxiety (inadequate, rejecting care givers) and encourage false and premature independence (Howe *et al.* 1999). Understanding the internal working model associated with this attachment type enables social workers and substitute care givers to shape their interactions in ways that acknowledge the behaviours of the individual and offer alternative affirming, care-giving experiences. For younger children who have been forced to take on adult roles, prematurely adjusting to more appropriate adult/child relationships can be challenging and the new roles are not always easily accepted.

Relationship-based practitioners must be attentive to defensive dynamics and, while sensitive to their normality in most contexts, must resist colluding with them in their more dysfunctional forms. Understanding their roots in anxiety and the purpose they serve enables practitioners to shape responses which recognise the unique configuration of experiences that individuals face.

Organisational defences: professionals have anxiety too

Understanding how anxiety-provoking situations might explain the behaviours of service users is only one side of the coin. Considering how anxiety shapes professional responses is equally important for relationship-based practice. As has already been acknowledged, the failure of professionals to see the dangers in family situations such as Baby Peter is explicable by the inhibiting effects of anxiety on individuals' ability to think about what is going on and what is being seen. As Bower (2005, p.4) recognises, the emotional impact of practice on social workers can leave them feeling 'confused, fragmented, inadequate, despairing or enraged'. Bower goes on to say that such feelings can lead practitioners to behave 'in ways which are not typical of them, for example, being punitive or indulgent'. In the case of Victoria Climbié, what Laming referred to as the 'rule of optimism' is a similar example of the inability of the professionals involved (not just the social worker) to see what was really happening. Cooper's 'turning a blind eye' (2005, p.8) is another manifestation of an anxiety-ridden avoidant professional response. In addition to individualised responses, the work of Menzies-Lyth (1988) identified the powerful influence of organisational defences on professional conduct. In her study of a London teaching hospital, Menzies-Lyth identified social systems which had become established as a defence against the emotional pain nurses experienced in caring for sick people. Among the most significant defensive practices were the de-personalisation of the patient, the routinisation of tasks, the abdication of responsibility and delegation of responsibility to senior staff. The parallels with contemporary social work practice are easy to see: the reduction in time spent with service users; the preoccupation with procedures and computerised systems, and the bureaucratisation of decision-making (Whittaker 2011; Lees *et al.*, 2013). Taylor, Beckett and McKeigue (2008) have explored how decision-making in child care social work settings could be understood through the lens of organisational defences. In the context of child care court cases, they identified projective dynamics leading to the denigration of the practice of other colleagues and professionals, the abdication by practitioners of responsibility for decision-making to 'expert witnesses' and the ritual performance of tasks. All were understood to be defences against anxiety. An edited collection by Armstrong and Rustin (2015) comprises a diverse and insightful range of contemporary applications of social systems as defences against anxiety, highlighting its ongoing relevance particularly for public sector professions.

In order to practise in relationship-based ways, social workers have to be alert, therefore, not only to their own personal defensive strategies but also to the prevalence of organisational defences which can distance professionals from those they engage with and diminish the nature of the professional relationship. A more detailed discussion of how these dynamics are played out in contemporary organisational contexts can be found in Chapter 14.

Containment, curiosity and 'not knowing'

So far this chapter has traced the roots of human behaviour in the powerful feelings, and in particular anxiety, associated with early experiences and outlined the defensive responses developed to cope with these experiences. Once these dynamics are understood, what is required are strategies for engaging with them in constructive empowering ways, and this is where the concepts of containment, already referred to in this chapter, and curiosity come into play. Containment and the container/contained relationship are derived from the work of Bion (1962) and the concept of curiosity is associated with Cecchin (1987).

For Bion, containment offered a framework for enabling individuals to be able to think about their affective experiences – their feelings. Building on Klein's ideas of projection and introjection, Bion studied the intimate relationship between mothers and infants and introduced the concept of 'maternal reverie' – the capacity of the mother (care giver) to be attentive and responsive to the infant's needs. When, on the grounds of hunger, discomfort or fear, the infant expresses his primitive feelings, the carer through her actions – holding, feeding, changing the infant – acts as a container of these feelings and returns them to him in a manageable form. Consistent experiences of containing responses gradually enable the infant not to be overwhelmed by his experiences, but to tolerate and make sense of them on a cognitive as well as an affective level. It is this affective-cognitive connection that Bion recognised as so important for the overall development of infants. When the connection cannot be made due to the absence of an effective container, what Bion referred to as 'attacks on linking' arises, and the affective and cognitive development of an individual is impaired – it is especially the ability to make links between emotion and rationality that are undermined here, meaning that powerful irrational feelings may dominate the person's way of thinking and of acting.

> Hussain's relationship with Joe during his transition phase into independent living, outlined earlier in the chapter, highlights how Joe was able to model a containing presence for Hussain through simply maintaining regular contact regardless of Hussain's responses. Joe did not allow Hussain's confused, chaotic and

challenging behaviour, arising from his anxiety about how he would cope on his own, to affect his (Joe's) commitment to visit Hussain weekly. As Joe was able to acknowledge how unsettled Hussain was, Hussain became more able to talk, albeit briefly, about his concerns. Gradually his capacity to understand and tolerate his anxious feelings enabled him to be in his flat when Joe visited each week, and his behaviour became more settled.

In a similar vein, attachment theory recognises the connections between feeling and thinking. Poor internal working models and insecure attachments impede the development of cognitive and social skills, as the additional energy required to manage unsettling emotional experiences detracts from that available for other developmental domains. Secure attachments established through consistent, positive care-giving experiences increase the potential for integrated development.

Social workers in all contexts have the potential to act as the container for distressed individuals, by tolerating and understanding their distress and expressing confidence in their ability to learn to manage their own distress. What this requires is a receptiveness to the distress being experienced (without becoming overwhelmed oneself) and the capacity to provide a space in which unbearable feelings and unthinkable thoughts can be safely confronted and explored. In the context of mental health social work, self-harming or other physically damaging behaviours can be understood as concrete expressions of mental pain or intolerable anxiety. People who have been traumatised and who self-harm often describe these behaviours as a form of emotional relief, with suicidal behaviours representing the most extreme version of this. As a result of the experience of a containing relationship, individuals can be helped to better understand and tolerate their experiences and to generate the capacity to integrate feeling and thinking, emotions and thoughts. Through the creation of affective-cognitive connections, individuals who self-harm can develop the capacity to talk about their feelings as opposed to acting them out. This is one very direct way in which the use of the relationship can be of great value to a distressed service user.

In seeking to embody containment, social workers need to be aware of how they verbally contain individuals through the conversations they have. The capacity to listen attentively, to articulate affective responses and to explore with service users any transferential dynamics or defensive behaviours in a non-threatening manner may enable service users to understand and take more control of their behaviour. Equally important are the non-verbal forms of containment that can speak more powerfully than words – for example, the capacity to sit in silence with a distressed, bereaved elderly person, or the commitment to turning up at a regular time to meet with a young offender, irrespective of whether he turns up. Offering consistent, sensitive attention helps to surface anxiety and allow it to be thought about. Clearly if social workers are to be able to work in this way, they need to 'know themselves' well (see Chapter 3) and they will need similarly understanding support and supervision in their own right (see Chapter 12).

The systemic equivalent to containment is encapsulated in two concepts: 'not knowing' and curiosity. An important quality for systemic practitioners to model for service users is their capacity to tolerate the uncertainty surrounding the dysfunction being experienced. While seeking with the individual(s) concerned to make sense of events and relationships, practitioners need to be able to tolerate 'not knowing' what is going on in order to explore fully the circumstances. In so doing, service users are afforded a space to think about the behaviours being exhibited and how the relationships between the individuals concerned might be shaping them.

Complementing the capacity to tolerate uncertainty and to 'not know' is the concept of curiosity (Cecchin 1987). When working with individuals and families, systemic practitioners invite all members of the system to express what it is they are curious about in a situation, in order to explore fully the difficulties being encountered and potentially to unearth aspects of the situation that had not been considered. Multiple perspectives and an inclusive 'both/and', as opposed to a polarised 'either/or', stance are embraced. In the same way that containment creates a safe space to explore the issues being faced, a curious stance allows for inclusive, non-threatening thinking that is respectful of each individual perspective and does not seek to attribute blame but to gain a fuller understanding of the problem. With a fuller understanding of the issues being faced, the likelihood of reaching meaningful and effective ways to move forward is increased.

Conclusion

Drawing on these diverse but complementary theoretical and conceptual ideas, social workers can equip themselves with a sound knowledge and skills base for developing relationship-based practice. Given that an integral feature of relationship-based practice is the acknowledgement that each person and their circumstances are individual and unique, it might seem contradictory to suggest, as this chapter does, that there are frameworks that offer collective explanations for individual behaviours. However, the two positions need not be mutually exclusive, as the skilled practitioner is one who is familiar with the theoretical and conceptual frameworks explored in this chapter, and who can draw on this knowledge in ways that respect and make sense of the individual with whom they are engaged. To be able to achieve this, one of the key capabilities such a practitioner must possess is a sound understanding of their 'use of self' in the professional context, and it is to this dimension of practice we now turn.

Chapter 3

The Use of Self in Relationship-Based Practice

ADRIAN WARD

Introduction

New recruits to social work often struggle with questions about how they should relate with service-users, such as 'Am I supposed to be their friend?', 'How much should I reveal about myself?' and 'Should I get "involved" with them?' These are all very significant questions which are not to be dealt with lightly, as they remain important throughout practice, and especially to service-users themselves – who, of course, may not have thought about such matters in the abstract but will certainly bring their own hopes, fears and expectations to any encounter with a social worker, including sometimes the wish for a friend or at least an ally – or the fear of finding an enemy – in what may well be a time of great uncertainty or anxiety. Social work has always struggled with the tensions between on the one hand the organisational requirements to deliver an efficient and focused service and on the other hand the need to do so in a personal, friendly and supportive way – even where there is an element of compulsion or control. It is through learning how to handle this sort of tension that new social workers start to learn about the use of self.

Social workers do indeed have to be 'friendly' towards those they are employed to help, but being friendly is not the same as becoming someone's friend, as new recruits to the profession soon discover. Being friendly may mean showing interest and receptivity, even though the relationship cannot and should not be the truly reciprocal one which real friendship involves. A social worker may offer warmth and understanding but will not necessarily expect it in return. Likewise a social worker will invite and even at times demand self-disclosure on the part of the service-user but will not necessarily offer it in response – unless she decides this would be helpful and appropriate. A social worker may invest hope and expectation in a service-user's potential for change and development, and may be disappointed or frustrated if this never quite materialises, but will not usually express this disappointment directly to the service-user, unless she judges this an appropriate and constructive thing to do.

What emerges from this discussion, then, is that social workers do need to relate with their service-users, but that they will do so from within a set of judgements and decisions about what is likely to be helpful and in keeping with their professional task. These judgements are made at several levels. For example, the worker will be operating within organisationally determined procedures that will allow certain types of response but not others. She will also be working within her professional code of ethics, which sets out certain moral and ethical guidelines to which she should conform. These externally determined guidelines are both necessary and helpful for the practitioner, and they set the broad parameters within which all practice must be conducted, although they do not tell the whole story. There is also inevitably a more immediate and contingent set of decisions to be made in every situation, and these have to be operated at a much more personal level, which is why our opening questions remain always pertinent: how do I 'relate' interpersonally with this service-user and how should I 'manage' this relationship, for example, how much of myself should I disclose or actively draw upon – and how much control do I really have over self-disclosure anyway?

It is questions such as these which open the way into thinking about the use of self in practice, because they draw our attention to the inevitability that social work practice will always make demands on the self of the worker, and will therefore require the worker to think about how to handle their *use* of self. Novices soon discover that too much self-disclosure may weaken their perceived authority, although too little 'give' on their part may mean that they are perceived as remote and uninterested, and may therefore mean that they are less likely to establish a working rapport. However, it is much more complicated than this: beyond the questions of conscious decisions about levels of involvement or self-disclosure there can also be much more elusive questions about, for example, how to handle 'resonance' or similarities between a service-user's situation and some issue in our own past or present concerns, how to remain focused on difficult judgements despite emotional pulls one way or the other, and how to cope with the unconscious communications which may for example leave us feeling confused or angry after a difficult exchange. The key terms here are 'how to handle', 'how to cope', because they suggest that the social worker has to be continually aware of the ways in which these sorts of personal or emotional undercurrents are operating and may be influencing her, and has to actively work out how to respond. In other words, in the midst of the encounter she needs to be monitoring her own emotional and cognitive reactions to what is happening and deciding how to modify her input accordingly.

The social work encounter

Because it often requires such close and highly charged relationships with other people, social work involves what has been called 'emotional labour' and 'emotion work' (Hochschild 1979), which means accepting that a large proportion of our work involves experiencing a range of emotions which many others do not experience at work, or do not have to engage with or actively work with. We not only experience these emotions, but we need to regard them as material, as data – they are part of what is available for us to work with.

To illustrate this point, if in our private lives we encounter someone whose life history or personal situation touches us deeply, we may perhaps feel a surge of pity or compassion and respond to them directly as seems appropriate. In the work setting we might encounter a similar experience, and we might feel a very similar set of emotions – but here we have to be aware of our professional task and the ethics and constraints around that task. For example, we have to be aware that half an hour after meeting this person we may meet another, and then another, so we have to consider how we can protect our own psyche while also remaining responsive and engaged. We may also have to rapidly change focus from meeting this individual to going into a management meeting and then perhaps meeting another service-user who may be angry and aggressive towards us so that we might need to modify a stance of soft receptivity to one of firm resistance. And yet, having expressed a lot of verbal anger that aggressive person may then crumble and reveal a much more vulnerable side so we have to shift again. All of these interactions will affect us, and we must remain receptive to being affected by them if we are to provide appropriate helping responses – and yet we also have to take care of ourselves so that we can remain as effective at the end of the day as we were at the start, as well as being able to detach ourselves from all this emotion after work and get on with our own lives.

A further complication is that we are not talking here about a neutral encounter between two random people, but a potentially highly charged encounter between a paid expert helper (who may be perceived as powerful and even threatening) and an individual who may be in crisis, under stress, or even under threat in terms of their 'self'. The service-user's life may have been disrupted or their self may have been powerfully affected by life events such as catastrophic and repeated loss, or by abusive or neglectful relationships – or by the fear of such things. They may feel rejected or despised in their own community or in society as a whole, and they may have had difficult experiences in previous encounters with social workers or other professionals.

This means that the service-user may bring powerful expectations to their encounter with a social worker. For example, they may be hoping to be rescued at last from a terrible situation, or to be told what to do in some impossible dilemma, or equally they may be fearing the worst, terrified that they are yet again going to be abused or neglected (metaphorically if not literally). In fact, they may have no wish whatsoever to engage with their social worker, in extreme cases maybe for fear of being found out to have harmed a family member (for instance). In these situations the service-user may put up smoke-screens or diversions to keep the social worker at bay – either consciously or unconsciously – and here the worker may have to be extremely persistent in recognising and then finding a way through or past such blocking devices to discover the true nature of the situation. In all cases the social worker's personal resources and resourcefulness may be tested.

On the other side of the encounter we should not pretend that the social worker's own self is without its complications. We all have our own personal history and our areas of conflict or difficulty, and indeed some of these may have contributed to our decision to work as a social worker, whether from the wish to help others who have suffered as we or our close friends or relatives may have done, or from the need to continually re-work tensions or conflicts that we have not fully understood. We might also be seeking – perhaps unconsciously – to fulfil our own or someone else's expectation that we should commit our working lives to helping others, sometimes at unreasonable cost to ourselves or to those close to us.

We also all have our own weaknesses, blind spots and areas which we may find too difficult or threatening to contemplate and may therefore be likely to avoid, sometimes unconsciously. However, these are not necessarily the weak spots we may imagine them to be, nor should we necessarily be ashamed of them. They may in fact be regarded as a potential source of strength (Skynner 1989), if they enable us to understand the difficulties of others, including the shame and anxiety which we may all experience at being seen to have weak areas. It is certainly important for us to be able to acknowledge these difficulties to ourselves even if not to others, and to find a way to process them so that they do not seriously distort our view of the world.

If we feel we cannot afford to recognise and accept our own difficulties, then the mental energy which goes into keeping these areas hidden or secret may also mean that we operate similar blind spots or areas of denial in relation to our practice. For example, if we had an unbearably painful experience of loss or rejection in childhood that we have never been able to deal with, we may tend to be mentally unwilling to contemplate how similar experiences may have affected children on our case load, which would be to do them a serious disservice (cf. Cooper 2005). Equally, though, with this sort of personal history we might tend to over-compensate, seeing huge loss and rejection wherever we look, if we are using the distorting lenses of unprocessed experience rather than the clearer vision of processed experience; this would be similarly unhelpful to those we may be working with. The lesson is that it is not so much the *type* of experience we have had that matters, but the extent to which we have been able to acknowledge and work at understanding that experience. The aim here will be to be able to work in the conscious sphere with material which may also have unconscious resonance (Collie 2008), and sometimes to allow this to surface in ourselves without too much defensiveness, so that we will be better able to afford to recognise and respond to equivalent or relevant experience in others.

It is probably more common than we might imagine for social workers and others to feel unable to really see others' pain and distress

— how else do we explain the fact that in so many child protection enquiries we hear of professionals, including social workers, not even literally seeing the child — or even when they do see them, somehow not noticing the cuts and bruises and other indicators of abuse?

USING REFLECTION TO EXPLORE UNCONSCIOUS FEELINGS

A social work student on placement, Yasmin, had visited a family where everything appeared fine and positive on the surface, and yet when she came away she still felt instinctively that something was seriously wrong, although she could not identify why she felt this. She took the case to supervision the next day and her practice educator asked her to go back through the whole process of the interview systematically recalling every detail. When she did so Yasmin could eventually identify the cause of her anxiety: she realised retrospectively that she had noticed – but only subliminally – that one of the children had a dark mark on his face just under his eye. She said afterwards that she must have unconsciously decided that she did not want to be aware of the possible implications of this mark, which might have indicated that the child had been physically abused. She was relieved to recognise the source of her anxiety and to realise that it had a rational basis after all, and she was now able to act on this realisation and return to the family to ask the mother about this bruising.

In this example, by going back through the detail of what she had actually seen, the student was helped to recognise not only the vital detail which she had blanked out but also (crucially) she was helped to realise that it was possible to overlook such details, and thus perhaps be less likely to do so in future.

This discussion has referred to the idea of understanding or 'processing' our own experience so that it does not distort our view of the world or of other people. This raises a big question as to what this processing means and how we can do it, and this is a question which I will address more fully in Chapter 10: 'The Learning Relationship: Learning and Development for Relationship-Based Practice.' It certainly involves social workers learning how to understand themselves, especially in terms of how their own personal history may resonate in the present.

This section also suggests that there is an overlap between the use of self in relationship-based practice and the more widespread concepts of reflective practice. Reflective practice, with its familiar distinctions between 'reflection in practice' and 'reflection on practice' (Schon 2000) can be interpreted in many ways, but has increasingly emerged as a central element in social work practice (Ruch 2005). However, one can be reflective in many ways (e.g. reflecting on one's efficiency) without necessarily focusing as clearly on the relational element as the relationship-based practice model involves. Equally, as we shall see later, the version of relationship-based practice proposed in this book often involves reflecting on the unconscious as well as the conscious elements in the relationship, which is not always the case in other forms of reflective practice. In other words, relationship-based practice definitely draws on many aspects of reflective practice, but also adds its own layers and emphases.

What is 'self'?

What I am seeking to establish in this chapter is that our self is our primary tool of practice – it is the means through which we experience and conduct our practice, including the psychological and emotional demands which practice entails. I would argue that this remains true whether or not we think of our work as specifically relationship-based. However, this raises several questions including, first, what do we mean by *self* in this context, and then what do we mean by the *use* of self?

We might initially assume that our self is a single, fixed quantity, because we all know roughly who we are and what we are like (we would not have got far in this work if this were not the case). 'Self', in this set of assumptions, represents continuity in our personality, security in our identity and reliability and consistency in relationships – it is our human nature. However, while this view has its appeal, self is more complicated and elusive than it may seem, as I hope to show.

The term 'self' is also often used as shorthand for a whole set of aspects of personality and identity, including our personal beliefs and values, our anxieties and 'constructs' – a combination of our rational and intuitive views on the way the world and other people operate and therefore on how we can interact with the world and other people. It may be seen as being not so much the *sum* of our experience as the continually evolving *process* through which we experience, grow and act. Each of us evolves our own unique character and self through our own individual pattern of experience, feeling and thought and we also develop a '*sense* of self' in which we become aware of and protective of our own self. This is true not just of our personal lives but also of the professional world.

This does not mean, however, that self is a fixed single quantity. We all know that we may behave and relate differently in our personal relationships than we do in our work or study relationships, that others may see different sides of us in these different contexts and may know little or nothing of our other sides. So self may be said to be to some extent contingent upon environment and context, and adaptable or at least selectable according to our strategy. Thus I may be (or attempt to be) a different self in my interactions with my boss than I am with my friends, or I may find I am quite a different person within my own family or towards my partner than I am with my clients. Some of these decisions about shifting self/selves may be made at a conscious and deliberate level, while others are probably more unconscious.

Self may also shift over time – I may develop my self as I mature in my life and my practice, so that (hopefully) I become more responsive, less insecure or more confident. Experience may teach me not to worry so much about what may happen if I make a mistake – or perhaps that I should worry more! As I evolve I may also feel more able to draw on certain aspects of myself in different situations, and more able to leave behind anxieties which troubled me before. So self may be said to be mutable and selectable over time – I can begin to choose more about my self in order to use different parts of myself as I wish to. It is partly through this variability and the ability to select and employ different aspects of our self that we start to develop the capacity to actively 'use' the self in practice.

However, self is not a purely internal quality, solely dependent on our immediate family environment. We are all also located in our community and society as a whole, and our sense of our own identity and potential, our self-worth and self-belief, are further contingent on the extent to which we feel we can identify with others and feel valued and respected by them and by the extent to which we find we have genuine opportunities to assert and achieve for ourselves within society. For many people, however, including some of those who find themselves in the position of becoming service-users, there may be a struggle to feel accepted or heard, known or valued within society, and they may feel ignored or despised or actively conspired-against by those in authority. People may feel excluded or devalued because of negative stereotypes about their ethnic origin, their gender, their sexuality or just about the particular part of town they live in. They may feel that these negative stereotypes are almost branded on them, making it impossible to be heard fairly or treated equally. As social workers we need to know about such stigma and to understand something of what it means for people, as well as understanding how we and our agency may be contributing to it.

Furthermore it is not only the service-user who may have such experiences of conflict between self and society. We may all have ways in which we differ from the imagined norm and may thus have been subject to negative stereotyping and the consequent threats to or impingements on a sound sense of self. See Kumsa (2007) for a powerful example of the ways in which such experiences may inform and affect our assumptions in practice (in this case in working with refugees). As social workers we will need to reflect on our own self in similar terms: what experience do we ourselves have of feeling oppressed, overlooked or rejected by society, and if we cannot identify such experience, how can we be sure that we will be able to understand the full range and depth of the service-user's experience? As with other aspects of this theme, questions such as these need to be continually asked in respect of each new encounter, rather than assuming they can be put aside after brief consideration in a training exercise.

There is finally a sense in which the whole concept of self can be seen as contested and elusive in a post-modern world in which there are few fixed entities and no absolute certainties, and in which competing ideologies and discourses put everything in doubt. In particular, while in much of the earlier literature on the use of self there are echoes of the white western Christian 'soul', firmly located in historical certainties about good and evil, 'normality' and 'abnormality', all of that now needs to be seen in a different light. The self is a much less solid and secure concept than it may have appeared even 50 years ago. Although we do need to think about self in social work as if it is an identifiable and perhaps core aspect of personality, we may also have to accept that this is shifting ground and that ultimately when we think about what we mean by 'self', we can perhaps say rather as St Augustine said about time: 'so long as nobody asks me what it is, I know, but as soon as I am asked, it disappears from my view'.

The *use* of self: visualising an elusive process

As an example of these shifting grounds, the whole question of the *use* of self raises an unexpected issue – if *I* am using my *self*, what does this imply? Who or what is selecting and employing the self and what is the process of selection? Is there a central processing facility – a core self which sits in the middle like the blobby brain in a sci-fi monster and deploys aspects of self from within a known range? And if there *is* some kind of core self, then what does it consist of, how does it relate to the other parts of self which it deploys – and what about the *un*conscious aspects of self that we have been thinking about throughout this book?

Lest this debate becomes too abstract, it may be helpful to try and visualise the use of self through the idea of seeing it as a process. One helpful metaphor is found in Ruch's image (2002) of the 'spiral' process in which we continually reflect and review, adapt and act, reflect again, and so on, gradually moving forward in a self-reflexive process. The suggestion here is of a professional self which evolves and adapts over time and which grows with experience and learns from that experience. This image is especially useful in terms of the process over time in which self has both continuity (we remain primarily the same person throughout) and flexibility (we respond and adjust over time), and yet we still manage to gradually move forward, rather than just going round in circles as might be implied by Kolb's Learning Cycle (Kolb 1984).

A second way of visualising the use of self may be to think in terms of mapping out the main components or constituent selves which are involved. Thus we might begin by drawing three intersecting circles, representing for instance the personal, the professional and the political (or for some perhaps, the religious) aspects of self. This visualisation immediately enables us to consider those areas in which, for example, the personal and the professional overlap, or where our political beliefs may either illuminate or conflict with our professional responsibilities. Figure 3.1 shows these overlapping circles and includes some of the questions which arise from visualising the components of the self in this way.

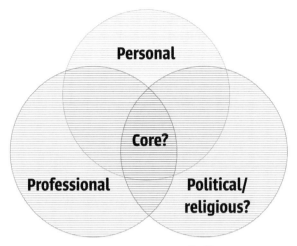

Figure 3.1 Aspects of self

Draw a map of your self – divided up into a number of circles, for example, personal, professional, political or religious. Now reflect:

- How did you decide upon the categories, and how firmly would you draw those boundaries?

- How much do the areas overlap with each other, and can you influence the extent of the overlap?

- Are other people aware of your categories and of your views about the boundaries between them?

- Are you aware of managing these boundaries, and which part of your self makes decisions such as this?

- Is there a central overlapping area and does this represent your 'core' self?

The image also enables us to think about how we might ideally wish to position these circles in relation to each other and to the whole. Would we wish, for example, to maintain clear distinctions between our personal and professional selves? In this case we might do well to avoid working in residential care or other settings in which we may be exposed to a great deal of personal–professional overlapping in the everyday life-space. It also enables us to think about the issue of these boundaries – how permeable or otherwise are they and would we wish these to be any different? It can be argued, for example, that in order to be an empathic and responsive social worker you may need to have quite permeable boundaries, so that you are sensitive to people's anxieties. However, if your boundaries are *too* permeable and you soak up all of the anxieties around you, or have no way of dealing with them, you will be of little use either to others or to yourself, as you risk becoming 'flooded' and then (to mix the metaphor!) experiencing burn-out. We might conceptualise this issue as the need to monitor and control the boundaries between the personal and the professional.

We might also look at these overlapping circles as a whole, and consider how we would wish to envisage the process of the use of self. Is it, for example, a case of having a *professional* self with which we choose to deploy (or not) aspects of our personal self – and if so, how do we wish to patrol the boundaries? Alternatively, is it a case of placing the *personal* self at the heart of the process, deploying professional skills and technical expertise according to a process of reflection? Some people, meanwhile, will wish to prioritise the political area, or a religious belief system, which may drive the whole system, inspiring our work with the spirit of change, reform or even redemption – though again we will have to monitor any possible collisions with others' selves or their belief systems.

There is no single right answer to these questions: there are some people whose circles seem to overlap almost completely, and who appear thoroughly integrated and congruent, and others who keep the circles far apart and yet still manage to appear whole and thoroughly engaged in their work. This suggests a further observation – what matters is not so much *how* you manage your own use of self (or, as it is perhaps becoming, *uses* of *selves*), but that you do manage to do so, that you take it seriously and pay continual attention to it, because it is not a single, one-off event but a cyclical and interactive process. What we are really talking about in professional practice, after all, is always not just use of self but the use of self *in relationship with others*.

Below the surface: the unconscious self

Having come this far, however, we need to take a further metaphorical step back and consider another dimension of self. This discussion has mostly proceeded as if the self is always conscious, rational and within our control. While this is the best premise to start from, it is by no means the whole story, as we saw in the case of Yasmin and her 'blind eye'. If it was the whole story, then we would never have the experience of being taken by surprise in the strength of our reaction to certain people and events, and we would perhaps always be able to avoid work-based stress and distress by safely compartmentalising it in the 'professional' sphere.

The reality is, however, that there is much more going on than the elements of which we are consciously aware, but that we may become aware of these other elements through the unfolding of events and the developments of thoughts and feelings in the course of our experience. We will now look at one way of conceptualising these other less conscious or rational elements, using a simple diagram which demonstrates where they may be located (though not necessarily what is within them). The aim is to enhance our capability as practitioners by increasing our awareness and by placing more of the dynamics of relationship and exchange in practice within our available range.

Mapping the mind

We will attempt to locate these less conscious and rational parts of our experience not by moving straight to Freud's view of the unconscious, but through a diagram which itself takes a more rational approach. As noted above, we started with the assumption that the self is always conscious, rational and completely within our known range: the interesting thing about using the Johari Window (below) is that it draws upon rationality and logic to demonstrate that there is more to the self than logic and rationality.

For instance, there may be things about my self which I may not be fully aware of, but of which you are only too clearly aware – such as the way in which I react when someone in authority tells me to do something, to take a common example. I may carry on with this mode of operating in ways which may be evident to everyone around me though apparently not to myself. In everyday life this sort of pattern may not matter too much, but in social work, where the way in which we interact with others may affect their well-being and outcomes as well as our own levels of job satisfaction or stress, such patterns may turn out to be of critical importance to our practice. If I am unintentionally aggravating or alienating some of my clients or colleagues by the way in which I interact with them, I will be doing nobody any good. It would therefore be helpful if we had a way of acknowledging such patterns, discovering what they may mean in relation to ourselves, and perhaps thereby discovering how to modify some of our own patterns so as to produce better outcomes for ourselves as well as for others.

Moreover, if there are things about me which *you* can see but which I can't, then there will also be things which *I* know but (hopefully) you don't. These may be my own private thoughts and experiences which mostly need to remain with me and under my own control – except that, again, in social work I may find some of my experiences powerfully echoed or mirrored in others, for better or worse. While I am working with a service-user I may discover that some aspect of their experience has some connection with my own: either a direct parallel, or perhaps a strong contrast. In either case, I am likely to have some feelings about these patterns. It may well still be appropriate to keep my own private experience private, although by being more aware of the connections I may be able to more readily and accurately empathise with the other person, and more likely to remain in control of my responses to them. Equally there may be aspects of my personal self which I decide I want to share with colleagues in the workplace, although as we have already seen I may need to reflect on the extent to which this is appropriate.

So far, then, we have acknowledged that there may be things about me which you know but I don't, as well as things which I know but you don't. But what if there also things about me which I don't know and you don't know, but which are nevertheless real and having an effect on my thoughts, feelings and patterns of interaction with others, and therefore on my effectiveness as a practitioner?

It might be objected that if neither I nor you (nor, apparently, anyone else) is consciously aware of these factors, why do they matter, and how can we ever know directly about them? The answer is that the fact that we are not aware of them may be partly that we are not being observant enough, or have not yet learned how to make sense of some of the more puzzling or painful aspects of practice. For example, (as in the case of Yasmin) it will occasionally happen that we will come away from a piece of work feeling unaccountably angry, anxious or distressed – strong feelings which may have been lingering somewhere in the back of our mind during the work but which have never quite come to the surface. It may only be later in the day or week, when we are safely ensconced in the security of home or in supervision, that such feelings come roaring back, reminding us that there was something about the session which seemed to affect us powerfully, but which we cannot really pin down, even though we know there was *something* odd going on. It is the kind of situation in which we might start asking ourselves, 'Is it me or is it them?' Here it may be helpful to ask ourselves not so much what the exact feeling is, but where the *strength* of feeling comes from. Sometimes we will have been unsettled for reasons which eventually tell us something useful about ourselves rather than about our clients, but sometimes these feelings will be telling us something vitally important about the client or their situation which they have not been able to tell us directly, and of which they may not be fully aware themselves, but which may nevertheless be of critical significance.

The next question is, if this area is so elusive and so unknown either to ourselves or to others, is it really possible to access it or to take account of it in our practice? The answer is probably that it will always remain to some extent elusive and difficult to work with, although there are certainly things we can do to increase and improve our awareness in this field. In Chapter 10 on 'The Learning Relationship' I will discuss some of these approaches.

The diagram

The first step in working with these different areas is to be able to map them out, and this is where the Johari Window (Luft 1984) is helpful in offering a diagrammatic representation of those aspects of self which are known and unknown, and thus also enabling us to visualise the boundaries between them and the ways in which we may aim to adjust those boundaries (see Figure 3.2).

Joe Luft and Harry Ingram (thus JoHari) not only mapped out these areas, but gave them each descriptive names. The first is the *'Open' area*, the area representing those aspects of self of which both I and most others are aware: my basic disposition, my ability to look people in the eye, for instance. The second is the *'Blind' area*, representing those things of which I am blissfully unaware but of which others *are* aware, such as my unintended frown, or my short temper when crossed. The third area is the *'Hidden' area*, my private thoughts and feelings, my memories, fears and hopes: perhaps in practice such examples as my anxiety about working with potentially violent people, or my ingrained prejudices against certain groups. This is quite a mixed bag, and we certainly have to be careful in drawing directly upon such factors, and yet they may be affecting our practice and it will sometimes be helpful to disclose some aspects of self to clients or colleagues. Finally there is the *'Unknown' area*, representing those things about me which I don't know and you don't know but which may still affect our communication. This area equates more or less with the Unconscious, and to a large extent it remains unconscious, although we or others can sometimes become aware of it in unexpected and indirect ways, such as slips of the tongue, dreams and day-dreams, as well as through other processes which we will explore later.

	Data known to self	Data unknown to self
Data known to others	(a) The free or open part of me	(c) That about me to which I am BLIND but which others know
Data unknown to others	(b) That about me which I keep hidden from others	(d) Unknown Area (no one knows - the unconscious)

Figure 3.2 Johari Window
adapted from Luft (1984)

The real value of this diagram is in helping us to visualise what can otherwise seem abstract and elusive. In particular it raises questions about the boundaries between each of these areas: how aware are we of these boundaries, for example, can we control and adjust them, and do they vary in different circumstances or in interaction with different people? The diagram suggests some ways in which the boundaries may be adjusted, through processes such as feedback and disclosure, and implies that effective communication with others may be enhanced if we are prepared to use these means to expand the proportion of the *'Open' area* compared with the other areas. At the same time the diagram highlights the difficulty of working with awareness of the possible *'Unknown' area*, representing the unconscious factors within the self.

We have now looked at two visual metaphors – the overlapping circles and the Johari Window – which illustrate different components of the self and which suggest some factors which social workers will need to consider in using the self in their work, in particular the issues of the boundaries between these components and the question of which part of the self it is that uses the rest of the self. We now look further at this last question by considering one particular model which has been proposed.

The internal supervisor

A further answer to the questions about the ongoing process of using the self is suggested by Patrick Casement's idea of the 'internal supervisor' (1991). It can be argued that we learn most about the use of the self in practice though our use of supervision, by which I mean actively *using* supervision through bringing for discussion and reflection not only the facts of the case but also the feelings, and not only the client's feelings but our own feelings – in fact every aspect of our experience in relation to this piece of practice. This means, in other words, bringing our *self* for supervision: meeting with the supervisor in as undefended a manner as possible and offering them as close a view as we (and the supervisor) can tolerate of the nature and experience of the helping relationship which is unfolding between us and our client. It is through actively bringing *that* (social work) relationship into *this* (supervisory) relationship that we can be helped to examine our practice and learn from it, and especially to recognise the personal and inter-personal dynamics which may arise and to work with the relationship (Mattinson 1970).

However, even the best supervision can only last for a limited amount of time and can only cover a small proportion of our total workload, and it is Casement's argument that out of the good experience of this sort of supervision we can develop the capacity to do some of this reflection and realisation for ourselves, as if we were continually supervising ourselves. Ultimately, he argues, we will internalise the experience of supervision and develop our own capacity to do much of the work of supervision here and now in the midst of our practice: observing ourselves in relationship with the service-user, monitoring the nature and quality of our work and continually reviewing how our self is both contributing to the work and being affected by it. We are presumably more likely to successfully internalise this capacity for supervision if we experience our supervisor as 'good enough' – trustworthy, attentive and bringing positive results in terms of our understanding of our work.

Much of our concern through this process of internal supervision will be to ensure that we provide the service-user with the most appropriate help, fully attuned to that person's needs and situation, and that we do so from within a helping relationship. At the same time it is right that some of our attention will also be directed to monitoring and preserving our own sense of self, including our integrity, our safety and even our sanity at times. For example, those working with people with extreme states of psychological disturbance do have to pay special attention to the impact of such disturbance on themselves. Even in less extreme circumstances we still need to pay attention to our own levels of stress or distress and to prevent ourselves becoming overloaded emotionally.

This process of cultivating and using our internal supervisor should eventually become thoroughly integrated into our practice, becoming the primary means through which we continue to actively use the self. Even for the most experienced, however, it is not something which should be left to chance or intuition, but something we need to continually work at. It is also important to note that using an internal supervisor is not an *alternative* to continuing to have regular supervision with an actual supervisor – which remains essential – but complementary to that. Finally we need to remember that (at risk of sounding pedantic) there still remains a 'core' self which needs to activate mechanisms such as the internal supervisor. It is to this idea of the core self that we now return.

The core self

Having acknowledged the complexity of this topic of the use of self, and having allowed for the many components of self and even for the fact that some of it may be elusive if not almost illusory, I want to return to the concept which I have been hinting at throughout this chapter: the idea of the practitioner's 'core self'.

We will all have met colleagues and/or friends who strike us as particularly grounded or centred, and who seem to have a quiet and level-headed confidence in their work which somehow also conveys itself to clients and others and which may have an effect of calming and reassuring those in distress without resorting to a false pacifying. Such people are not necessarily any more intelligent or contented than the rest of us, but they do have an air of being in touch, not easily knocked off course – and able to help others to feel similarly. In its full form this is perhaps a rare and impressive quality, though I would suggest that at a more everyday level there is something of this quality that we can all achieve. My suggestion is that what we are seeing here is someone who has developed an especially solid and reliable core self, an ability to handle the sorts of emotional and psychological challenges and setbacks which we may all encounter in social work without feeling too much under personal attack or at risk of suffering.

On the basis of the earlier discussion this well-developed core self presumably plays a central role in monitoring the individual's professional and personal experience, in 'internally supervising' the working self, and in deploying the other aspects of self involved in engaging with the service-user and others. I am not arguing that the sort of people I have identified as having a sound core self do not experience stress or doubt – far from it – but that they have developed the art of living with stress and doubt without being consumed by it, and of remaining sensitive to others' needs but without taking this to the point of vulnerability. Nor am I idealising such people or suggesting that they have some kind of super-hero strength and can handle any situation, but I do suggest that what they have developed (perhaps intuitively) is a personal quality which overlaps with professional skill to create an effective persona, a base from which the individual can communicate securely. Equally I would not wish to confuse this core self with the cultivation of the different personal trait of charisma, or some kind of personal magnetism. By contrast, the core self has an unmistakably authentic quality to it, rather than anything showy or in other ways false.

How do we achieve this state, what means do we use to get there? I am suggesting this is more art than science, more a question of growth and development than merely of training. My proposal is that it is through a combination of supervision and educational processes, including specific attention to self-knowledge and self-awareness, that we gradually learn from experience how to work with aspects of self in practice, and in Chapter 10 I will say more about this learning.

More than simply *using* the self we might call this '*working with the self*' to emphasise that it involves continual work, in a conscious and deliberate process, even though it may also involve drawing upon whatever hints we can derive from the unconscious and unknown aspects of our work.

Conclusion

In the context of looking at the use of self in relationship-based practice we have looked at different ways of visualising the self and its elements and at how we manage the boundaries between these elements. The context is that it is not just self that we have to consider, but *self in relation to others* – self as affected by others' needs and expectations, and by their expressions of these things. The emphasis here has been on knowing yourself and understanding yourself and we have touched on some examples of this, although there is much more to be said, especially about the less conscious aspects of self. Perhaps the key relationship to be considered is our own relationship with our self: how well do we know this self, how aware are we of the ways in which it is called into service in our practice, and how conscious are we of the decisions which we have to take about using and taking care of this self? Finally I have also emphasised that use of self is an ongoing process rather than a simple one-off event, or something which can be 'fixed' while training and then left to run itself. This is a theme to which we will return in Chapter 10.

● Section 2 ●

WORKING WITH THE RELATIONSHIP IN PRACTICE

Chapter 4

Brief Encounters

Working in Complex, Short-Term Relationships

RAVI KS KOHLI AND JANE DUTTON

Introduction

Imagine you are by the sea, trying to understand what makes the sea what it is. You have a bucket in your hand. By the sea's edge, you lower the bucket into the water, and fill it. You only have a moment or two to do this. Looking at what you have captured, you try to decipher the ways in which the waves around you are similar to and different from the water in your bucket, and whether in any sense you can say that you've 'caught' the sea. The challenge you face is to understand at least some of the breadth and depth of the sea by studying the seawater. There are many layers of thinking that you do, and many filters that you use, to come to some of the answers. You may reach a number of conclusions, not least that while there are limits to how tides can be measured in a bucketful of seawater, there is something of the essence of the sea that remains.

In brief work, an opportunity to hold a little bit of the ebb and flow of people's lives evokes similar opportunities and challenges, and it is these that we consider in this chapter. We propose that people who move in and out of the sightlines of busy practitioners are hard to understand, because the tides governing their behaviours are only sometimes visible. Their movement can create and sustain a sense of them being blurred, poorly lit and partially visible. This challenges those who try to understand their trajectories, and to see them as having substantial, clearly delineated forms. Given such fast-moving lives, how are we to know what to do for the best in brief encounters?

For refugees coming to richer nations such as the UK, encounters with public authorities are likely to span immigration, health, education and social care. After getting through national borders, they have to cross professional and cultural borders in order to access resources. These borders are difficult to cross in the context of contemporary pressures on public spending, as needs increase and resources diminish relative to those needs, particularly in places where migration is relatively high (Sachrajda and Griffith 2014).

This chapter, framed within a context of working systemically with refugee families, considers ways in which workers can think about all vulnerable people on the move, and through attempts at sense making, help to sustain relationships that are purposeful, even if lived within short capsules of time. The challenge that immediately faces us in practice is how to find quick ways to distil rather than sieve people's experiences so that we catch their hopes, talents and needs together, and do something about these in respectful dialogue. In this sense the clinical work with refugees that we use below illuminates, we hope, ways of working that have resonance across different encounters where people are only momentarily visible, no matter where they have sprung from or are going to. We suggest here that refugees, like many service users, come to seek our assistance prepared for encounters which are an amalgam of hope and distrust, with stories that are bleak, sometimes tragic, not just in relation to their past experiences, but of bruising and ambivalent encounters with those in authority within the territories where they have sought sanctuary. Often from positions of liminality, they boldly echo some of the fundamental worries and concerns that all vulnerable people may have about those who hold resources, who judge them and influence their lives. In meetings where speed and distrust co-exist, we discuss how brief encounters can be managed in ways that allow us to understand people who use our services, and enable them to understand us. We propose that even in complex, short-term relationships, there are ways of generating light that lets both parties be seen in fuller form than simple ciphers of 'good', 'bad' and 'needy'. We propose that through honesty, clarity, reliability, kindness, warmth and precision – the cornerstones of generating trustworthy relationships – we can systemically construct ways of working that distinguish enquiry from interrogation. In this chapter we look at short-term work through two stories of refugee families within child and family social work.

We begin by outlining some important theoretical ideas about life on the move.

Life on the move

Maintaining the analogy of a sea of movement, Bauman (2007) refers to 'liquid times' that we live in, where the velocity of encounters between people generates a great deal of uncertainty about who we and they are, what we are becoming together, and where all of us are located, psychologically, politically and practically. There is a storm of living, and the shapes, rhythms and patterns of our lives are determined by our engagement with forces that range from the global and trans-national to the local and particular. Within this context, encounters can be experienced as collisions, as people glance away rather than remain together over time. As these encounters gather speed, a particular danger arises – seeing those on the move as artefacts, capturing their status and ways of being within categories of administrative utility, and using snippets of information in mechanical ways within increasingly bureaucratised contexts, to make collages of people's lives in the records we create about them. The social and relational aspects of human exchanges diminish, creating a rudimentary sense of gathering information rather than understanding 'the other'. In practice this is reinforced in two ways within social work. First, Ferguson (2008) sees social work itself as being on the move, being delivered at great speed with fractions of time apportioned to contact with service users, while at the same time becoming immobile through a thick forestation of regulations and procedures that seek to solidify and make systematic the approaches social workers are expected to take in uncertain circumstances. Within the space created by the push and pull of liquidity on the one hand and administrative solidity on the other, he suggests social workers need to slow things down, so that they can 'create stillness and moorings while on the move' (Ferguson 2008, p.576). Secondly, and in a similar vein, Parton (2008) makes an eloquent point that social work's embrace of information technology has reduced its capacity to understand people's narratives, and the proliferation of forms to gather data, in a context of increased regulation, has divided 'us' as social workers from 'them' as users of services. It is not the case that Parton (2008) sees or argues for a division between the social and technical – indeed he refers explicitly to the emergence of a techno-social culture within which we are located and work. He invites us to not confuse tools with skills, and to allow ourselves space within which, no matter the speed of interactions, we can develop an understanding of others and ourselves that links us as people trying to make sense of our encounters together. So the first question in relation to people on the move, in considering relationship-based practice within contemporary social work, is not just what we come to know about them, but what we understand about each other when we meet. In effect, what joins us to them?

Us and them: relating to people who become refugees

Citizenship of a safe country is comforting. For people that have it, it brings two distinct advantages in relation to movement. They can be still when they want to, and more or less go where they want to go, and come back home when they choose. Moreover, being still and choosing to move signal a sense of who they are and their status and position within the land where they live. Citizenship also allows them to move within their memories. In visiting places where they grew up, rooting about in families and communities of origin, and creating shapes and patterns of living through rituals or narratives all provide a reassuring foundation. Here they can move backwards and forwards along the routes of belonging that connect them to others. Over time, their emotional geography begins to echo their place within their territory, and the lands that they live in connect in deep ways to what Urry (2005) refers to as their landscape of experience. As we have noted elsewhere, citizenship can offer us continuity where:

> Within our day to day lives, we can experience ourselves as individuals, as well as members of communities that through luck and perseverance have achieved a level of stability. Our world is ours, and we [are] ordinary people, enduring the rough and tumble of our lives without being blown away, because many pegs hold us in place, whether they are people, owned spaces, belongings, or documents that confirm our entitlement to remain and prosper within our territories. (Kohli and Mitchell 2007, p.xiii)

The picture for refugees and their families is much less stable. Within a range of situations that result in forced migration, from war to natural disasters, the boundaries of citizenship in the country of origin fragment or atrophy, and ordinary life collapses. Over a period of time, or sometimes suddenly, people who seek refugee status have to make decisions about movement that will get them out of harm's way, and heading in the direction of sanctuary. Moreover, as they pack their bags and belongings, their appeal to the worlds they enter is very carefully constructed within the terms of the 1951 Convention Relating to the Status of Refugees. Here a refugee has to show that he or she has to move:

> owing to well founded fear of being persecuted for reasons of race, religion, nationality, membership of a particular social group or political opinion, is outside the country of his [or her] nationality and is unable or, owing to such fear, is unwilling to avail himself [or herself] of the protection of that country; or…is unable or, owing to such fear, is unwilling to return to it. (UNHCR 2007)

Given this legal definition, people seeking sanctuary have to create a compacted identity in order to negotiate the terms of entry into host nations, both consciously in terms of what they remember to tell, and unconsciously in containing what they need to forget (Papadopoulos 2002). By doing so, they move from a detailed life to a labelled existence. Here stories are constructed and managed in ways that attempt to maximise the chance of being allowed to remain and resettle within a new land, and the common currency of exchange between those seeking assistance and those in charge of distributing it, becomes one of presenting and reading the label of 'refugee'. As we have written elsewhere, while labels have an administrative utility, it is through their usage that individuality and ordinariness are compromised, and 'thick' lives reduced to 'thin' descriptions (Kohli 2006). Here, mechanical and technical categorisations simultaneously displace as well as attempt to respond to people's more wayward organic lives in ways that fit whatever limited resources are thought to be on offer. In observing the ways in which refugees respond to those in authority in such circumstances, Bertrand (2000) comments that:

> Throughout their lives, refugees have masked a certain part of their story, or highlighted their professional experiences (in order to be selected) or persecutions (in order to get refugee status), in an imaginary and creative way [and] even…social workers find it difficult to get a story that remains the same…over time. (Bertrand 2000, p.96)

Stories themselves can change shape, even if at the core they remain faithful to a thin version of events given to those in authority (Herlihy *et al.* 2002; Bögner *et al.* 2007). Paradoxically, some 'thin' stories can begin to sound similar to those who listen, as if they were cut from the same cloth of suffering (Goodman 2004). They can appear rehearsed, as if refugees, like dolphins swimming in the same narrow straits, were skilfully echo-locating pitfalls and opportunities when moving through the asylum phase. For listeners they carry a number of consequences. First, they can raise the issue of whether refugees ever tell 'truthful' stories. Second, they can generate a sense of 'sameness' where individual stories coalesce into bigger homogenised narratives and stereotypical images of refugees, bundled together into packages of victims and charlatans. In turn, as Turton (2004) suggests, there is a danger as we absorb and use the language of water and refer to migrant trickles, waves and floods, that individuals are perceived as molecules in the liquid flow of particular forms of a mass experience and as a consequence are at risk of being seen to be less than who they are. The container categorisations that they present and live through as they are processed into host countries reinforce a leaden view of their mercurial lives. So in delineating what 'we' think of 'them' and what 'they' think of 'us', an intricate dance comes into being, shaped by mutual preconceptions, needs, expectations and positions. It has a few variant steps, depending on the context within which each step takes place, yet it requires us to listen to what is said, what is obliquely referred to, and what remains in silence as refugees open and close their narrative accounts in their exchanges with perceived helpers.

Setting the context

The agency from which the examples below are derived is a multi-disciplinary child and family mental health clinic working with a range of family problems such as marital violence, eating disorders, children experiencing educational difficulties, and families being assessed in relation to the abuse of children. Referrals come predominantly from the formal networks of care and protection – social workers, schoolteachers, solicitors and medical practitioners – as well as from the families themselves. The staff group is ethnically diverse and multilingual, reflecting a context of diversity within the communities that the clinic serves. Work may be short or long term, involving one individual, a group, or a complex family and professional network. The clinic staff members are explicit about using systemic ideas to inform practice.

In focusing this chapter on brief encounters, we have chosen to think about what the phrase 'short term' means to us. Within the service we refer to, it carries a number of meanings. It can mean engagements that are limited because of the nature of the referral from organisations (for example, looking for brief assessments or interventions). Equally it can be limited because people using the service are sojourners within the locality, and due to move on. For example, they may be in temporary housing or staying in a refuge before moving to another place. Work may also be defined as brief, but occur in a short and intensive burst over an extensive period of time, with its pace and trajectory fashioned according to what is negotiated with each stakeholder as the most suitable process and hoped-for end. Whatever meaning is ascribed to the term, preparation in each encounter involves the service defining an initial framework of roles and responsibilities for stakeholders that the work can be built around, depending on the nature of the referral and the expected outcomes. It provides the scaffolding for the work and supports its progress and evolution.

This local approach is mirrored in wider attempts to encourage systematic practice. For example, in an effort to standardise approaches to assessing families, the use of the *Assessment Triangle* has been heavily promoted in social work (Jack and Gill 2003; Department for Education 2013; LSCB 2017). This aspect of social work assessment has the basic premise that three-dimensional assessments can be made through placing the development needs of children alongside the capacities of parents or care givers to respond to those needs, within an understanding of the impact of wider family and environmental factors on parenting capacity and children. These are described as three interrelated domains. The interactional influence of these domains on each other pick up on the long tradition in social work of thinking ecologically, linking children's health and well-being to the environments within which they grow and grow up. Less clearly signposted within this thinking is the relationship of the worker to these domains, and the influence of this relationship on how the assessment is conducted and understood by both worker and family. So although the *Assessment Triangle* encourages workers to be systematic, its lack of emphasis on the worker's impact on the domains underplays an essential element of the process of sense making. In our view, systemic thinking, so vividly used in a broad sweep of therapeutic interventions, has a contribution to make in emphasising that there are different types of action required from professionals according to context, and that the lived experience of the encounters within these actions are co-constructed by worker and service user, acting out of their different positions.

What has this to do with short-term work? The complexity of the brief encounter, in which both worker and service user are travellers together, requires the worker to take responsibility for the encounter as determined by professional and agency contexts. Also, the worker needs to clarify what the service user may know about the referral, how they understand it, what they think the worker's role is in this encounter, and the expectations both have of what should happen. Through conversation drawing forth layers of descriptions and explanations a space is created within those domains, within which the meaning of the encounter for all participants can be considered. Here, in joining together slowly and methodically to construct a relational space – working together from within rather than working on a problem from the outside – we generate understandings where 'mutual influence and change is possible' (Flaskas, Mason and Perlesz 2005, p.xxi). We now turn to considering how these ideas are applied in practice. In the examples that we use below, the participants and their circumstances are annonymised.

Brief encounter 1

A local authority Children's Services Department requested a viability assessment for contact between a father and his three children within the broader context of a parenting assessment.

The father in this situation, Mr Tuah, was a refugee in the UK from a country in West Africa. The following is his story as relayed initially by those referring him for the assessment.

> In his early twenties he had come to the UK as a refugee. He met a young woman with whom he had three children. During this period he had no formal employment but was thought by professional agencies to be dealing in drugs and possibly receiving stolen goods. He was said by the referrer to use alcohol excessively quite

regularly. His relationship with the mother of his children was punctuated by episodes of domestic violence from him towards her, witnessed by the children and neighbours. Due to this, and serious episodes of neglect by their mother, the three children were accommodated whilst a parenting assessment was carried out. Initially their father had supervised contact three times a week. On one of these occasions he hit one of his children (aged nine), when the child did not obey him, dragging him from the room. As a result of this, contact was suspended and an assessment of his parenting capacity began. There were three sessions available for this work to be completed and reported on.

Preparing the ground

The information workers may have about someone prior to the first meeting may be minimal or extensive. There may be the flexibility for a professional choice whether or not to read extensive information prior to the encounter; there may not. Whatever choice is made, any information creates a response, and thinking reflectively about that response allows the preparatory thinking to take place. 'How do I reflect on that information?' 'What impact does it have on me?' 'What reverberates within me?' (see Bachelard 1969) are questions which create a starting point for thinking about the context of events, widening that context to consider the positions of all actors: in this instance father, children and supervisor. The latter had reported the behaviour, as required by her professional responsibility to maintain the protection of the children from physical abuse. The children told their social worker that they were upset by what had happened and that it had been unexpected and shocked them. Yet they wanted to continue seeing their father. Mr Tuah was reported as saying that he knew he would not now be able to see his children any more, that this was what the authorities had wanted all along, and that there was no point in talking about it.

Part of the first task of the worker is to think about how to create a context for conversation. Mr Tuah's history would undoubtedly be filled with people questioning him: about his right to be where he was, about his activities, about his identity. A way of talking had to be found that was based on enquiry, not interrogation, and an agreement for talking reached in a context in which talking might be seen as dangerous.

A telephone conversation with Mr Tuah started the talking about talking. 'What do you think about the suggestion that we meet?' 'What are your views about what has been said about you?' 'Do you think it is worth talking about these – putting these views to someone like me?' In talking about these questions Mr Tuah agreed to meet to put forward his views about what had been said about him.

Doing the work

In brief work we have to move from 'thin' to 'thick' description quite fast. As we have noted, this speed of movement can unhelpfully reflect the professional context and lived experience of the worker, and the lived experience of the service user. Agreements to meet to talk can allow, as Ferguson (2008) says, opportunities for stillness for both worker and service user, to co-create a reflexive experience which can open up new avenues of thinking, description and choice, even in a short space of time. Yet this is not a given, it has to be made, in the sense that the worker needs to think about speed, and slow down sufficiently so as not to be blurred by the encounter, or to appear as a blur.

It is tempting in a brief encounter to rush to talk about the problem. Relational reflexivity, however, creates together a foundation and rules for talking which allow an exploration of meaning and understanding to thicken the thin description of the problem behaviour – in Mr Tuah's case the allegation of physical abuse during contact with his children. A pressure for quick solutions deprives both service users and worker the opportunity to question themselves, reflect on these questions and find new possibilities. Such pressure also encourages competition for the 'best' description or interpretation of a situation. This can in turn swiftly move to someone claiming the 'true' explanation. In order to avoid colonising conversations, how can we as workers maintain what Cecchin (1987) refers to as a *state of curiosity* – a state which leads us away from cause and effect and the shutting down of conversation to generating kaleidoscopic perspectives to open conversation?

In this instance, in coming to the service, Mr Tuah's views about talking together needed to be understood; without this talking, his contact with his children would not be reinstated in the foreseeable future, but the talking might be experienced as talking with the enemy. Thinking about choices and the consequences of different choices from a position of respectful curiosity seemed a possible way forward; one of these choices might be to choose not to talk when confronted with the reality of the worker's presence in the room. 'There may be some things you do not want to talk about with me…how will you know if I have strayed into territory you do not want to talk about?' 'How will you let me know?' 'Can we agree that we talk about what we have discussed and what I will write about it at the end of each of our three sessions?'

In taking account of Mr Tuah's status as a refugee, the manner and tone of talking needed to communicate respect while being clear about the parameters of legal acceptability of his actions. The worker asked the following questions:

- Is there anything about your story of coming to the UK that you would like me to understand more about?

- I imagine that your story has been quite tough. All I know at present is that you came to the UK in your early twenties. Is there anything more that you would like me to know?

Mr Tuah described his childhood as hard but content until the age of 14. At this point his country was engulfed in civil war, and his village attacked. He witnessed his mother's death in this attack and his father and two brothers were lost to him. He escaped alone, and made his way across country on foot to a more stable region. Here he made contact with other displaced young people and together they made a long and perilous journey to Europe.

Examining how explanations fit together gives an understanding of that 'fit' for both worker and service user. The worker may have a legal obligation to take a position of control if there is harm to self or others involved, but the use of curiosity can respectfully thicken the story of events, and allows the service user the opportunity to be the 'primary interpreter of their own experience' (Freedman and Combs 1996, in Fredman 2004, p.33), even if the actual outcome cannot be what they would have asked for. Use of curiosity also potentially opens a reflexive space for professional networks as in the following questions addressed to other professionals involved in Mr Tuah's situation:

- How does seeing Mr Tuah mainly as an angry person help the process of assessment?

- Are there ways in which this description can get in the way of the assessment?

- Are there other ways of describing his behaviour?

- If you chose another description, what would it be?

- What effect might that have on your views of Mr Tuah?

Thickening the story of rage to create other descriptions of Mr Tuah brought forth, for example, stories of his punctual and regular attendance at contact, always bringing food for his sons, and his concern that they did well at school. Deconstructing the different stories allows both worker and service user the opportunity to be reflexive, relationally reflexive, in that both can question themselves in conversation with the other. In working with Mr Tuah there was much questioning of the talking to create 'shared meanings' (Burnham 2005).

- How could we talk so this isn't like a repeat of previous experiences you have had with people with some legal power over you?

- How is it going?

- What would you have liked me to have understood by now?

In talking about the talking, Mr Tuah started to talk about the ways in which children who disobeyed an instruction would have been treated in his village at home. Leaping to his feet he demonstrated standing on one leg, leaning forward with one arm resting on the ground, a position he said would have to be held for up to two hours. Tears streaming down his face, he shouted, 'What is wrong in this country – how can they say I am harming my son?'

The feelings generated in a worker in such a situation will vary according to their own experiences, both professional and personal. Maintaining curiosity questions these feelings, opening the space for conversation rather than banging it shut and closing the lid on emotion, which would mirror Mr Tuah's experiences in a range of contexts. Questions such as 'What might have led them to say that when you care so deeply for them?' allowed him to start to think about how his own behaviour might have been experienced by the supervisor and his children, in the context of his own pain being acknowledged and contained.

Developing an emotional language in the room allowed further conversation about not being respected, the profound meaning this had for Mr Tuah, and his guilt about the way in which he was leading his life. Talking about the kind of guilt he had, how he would describe it, how he felt it physically, how it came out of him and how this affected those around him, particularly his children, helped to create a relationship in the room in which something therapeutic could occur. Mr Tuah showed how he could put himself in others' shoes, including those of his children, even though his own so often caused him pain.

Comment

Ending the work with Mr Tuah involved writing a report. As each session had been recorded together at the end, including different views, this would not be new information. However, putting this talking together into a report allowed an opportunity to show clearly the emotional content and meaning of events, and Mr Tuah's subtle movement of position in relation to them. It allowed him to be the primary interpreter of his own experience, without minimising his abusive behaviour towards his son. He had been able to show his realisation that it was not responsible parenting to do what he had done, as part of his parenting had to take account of the context in which they were all living. As the responsible adult he had to make this work for himself and his children. In this instance, on receipt of reports, supervised contact was re-established by the court.

Brief encounter 2

A referral for the Azzam family had been made by a primary school of six-year-old Ali, who was consistently starting violent fights in the playground and classroom with other boys, the same age or older. Ali was not responding to the teachers' authority. The referral said that the family were members of a minority group, who had experienced persecution and violence in their country of origin. They were seeking asylum in the UK. Ali lived with his parents and four siblings, three older brothers and a younger sister. The school had invited the parents to meet with them on several occasions but they had not done so. The school was concerned about Ali's home circumstances, and was seeking some help for him and his family. The family knew the referral had been made.

Preparing the ground

Referral information rarely indicates whether a piece of work could be defined as short-term. As indicated above, the worker's own context may dictate the length of their relationship to it, but emphasising the importance of thickening the experience of worker and service user in each encounter allows each to have meaning. Sometimes the information a worker receives immediately indicates different levels of context overlapping and intermingling; a complex tapestry of life in which the referred person is situated. So it was with Ali. Thinking about the *reverberation* from the initial information leads the worker to consider a family with a contextual story of persecution, loss, transition and uncertainty. The 'how' of the engagement became crucial. The school had indicated that Mr Azzam's English was good, and that Mrs Azzam's was limited. On this basis negotiating the possibility of conversation would need to be done with Mr Azzam. We thought that it would also be more usual in this cultural context, and in the absence of any information to the contrary, to negotiate with the male head of the family. The work involved three meetings just with the family, and two further meetings with family and school.

A telephone conversation with Mr Azzam began the work, to start the talking about the talking. He was asked:

- What did he know about the school's referral?

- What did he think about this?

- What did he know about our service?

- What was important for him to know about it if we were to meet?

- Did he think it was worth meeting to see if this would be helpful?

Respectful questioning to create a reflexive space allows the potential for someone in a refugee position to claim a territory of understanding in the absence of territorial rights. Part of this initial negotiation was where to meet: on whose soil? Mr Azzam chose a home visit.

DOING THE WORK

The home visit revealed that Mr and Mrs Azzam were caring for four other young children in addition to their own five. These were Mr Azzam's cousin's children; the cousin had been murdered in their country of origin and his wife had died. Mr Azzam's father had also been murdered, and he himself imprisoned. Mr Azzam said he was the authority figure in the household, the disciplinarian. There was an occasional use of corporal punishment (smacking), but essentially discipline was maintained through threats, including threats of withdrawal of affection. Thinking about territorial rights provoked a conversation about the parents' concerns.

We asked, 'From what you have told us of your story there seem to be many things you could talk about today. What is the most important thing right now you would like to talk about with us?'

Mr Azzam wanted to talk about Ali's behaviour, because it was shameful that this was happening at school. Mrs Azzam agreed and both said this did not happen at home. They were then asked, 'What do you think the school is most concerned about? How would that have been the same or different for you at Ali's age?'

Mr and Mrs Azzam both said they thought the school was concerned about the fighting, but that they were not. They thought this was normal for young boys. In their country of origin the school would not try to speak to the parents; staff would deal with all problems that happened in school and had permission from the parents to do so.

The conversation continued: 'Ali is clearly a loved boy in this family – how can he be helped to be seen as successful in school? What are the things that might help him to settle more, to belong enough not to have to fight?' Mr and Mrs Azzam thought Ali did well at home because he wanted to be there with his family, especially his father. They thought he felt safe when they were all together. They did not know what was happening at school because Mrs Azzam's English was limited, and Mr Azzam said it was not acceptable for him to be in the company of many women without their husbands being present.

Mr Azzam thought it would be helpful to have more communication with the school, but he did not know how to go about it, particularly as he also felt ashamed. We asked, 'Would it be helpful to have daily reports on Ali's behaviour from his teacher, that Mrs Azzam could bring home for Mr Azzam to read and return with comment the next day?' Mr Azzam thought it would. 'Ali seems to have responded well to your praise. Could this be used more? If so would it help him to be more successful in your view?' Both parents thought it might, and they would amplify this way of being with Ali. 'Should we arrange a meeting at the school, with a male interpreter also present, so that Mr and Mrs Azzam could attend together?' Both parents thought this was a good idea.

Finally, Mr and Mrs Azzam were asked, 'What have you heard someone say today which was useful to you, or which you might like to think about more?' Mr Azzam thought the idea of needing to settle and belong in school was something he would think about more. Mrs Azzam said she was pleased her husband would come to the school with her. Ali said he was pleased his father was going to come to his school.

Comment

Resettlement is a costly endeavour no matter what the gains. Loyalties to home and to those lost and missing can create a reservoir of unspoken feeling. Different family members may express sensitivity to this reservoir in different ways. There are many stories held in the Azzam family, which for the worker can seem overwhelming. However, taking the position of this family as an ordinary family reacting to extraordinary circumstances (Woodcock 1995) allows a conversation to determine what the most important concern is for the family at that time, in the context within which they live, as they attempt to reconcile the past with the present and future.

Whilst this piece of work was short term, the worker was invited to three further family reviews and a school review over the next 18 months. Both family and school requested this, which was seen by the worker as an important witnessing of progress and achievement (Kohli 2007). Ali's fighting in school had stopped, and his learning developed with some individual support. His parents were proud of his achievements and the family's story could start to encompass aspects of success in resettlement, guided by the parents' choice to work to make this happen.

Demonstrating good citizenship at a time of public scrutiny of citizenship through asylum application contributed to the process of resettlement. Connecting homeland expectations with a newly formed way of carrying out these expectations in a different cultural context is a complex endeavour. Mr and Mrs Azzam were able to do this, maintaining their authority and connecting this with the authority of the school, enabled the past to be contained for Ali, so that his loyalty could look to the future.

Concluding observations

Undertaking short-term work suggests high speed. This can in turn result in working with thin linear stories, where the focus on behaviour discounts the importance of the actors, the stage and the play itself. There is a danger that with families on the move colliding with professions making haste, little is made into too much, and that too much is left invisible and compressed into too little. This is rarely of benefit to any of the stakeholders involved. While we have focused here on refugee lives, the implications are clear for any short-term engagement with service users. For example, we have suggested that short-term work offers opportunities to develop thicker descriptions of people's lives by addressing context through respectful curiosity, and for creating a reflexive space in which a therapeutic relationship can occur. We have also affirmed that many referrals contain some information about a process of change, transition and liquidity in people's lives. This inherent momentum can generate a gravitational pull in family or individual circumstances, and movement itself needs to be understood as part of the problem and part of the resolution. Within the stories of forced migration, movement is part of living. Yet in these liquid times, there are many other stories that will only allow brief encounters as people step into and out of each others' frames of reference. Our invitation in this chapter is for workers to slow a little, take layers of meaning into account, and to work collaboratively in charting journeys that ensure continuity, coherence and clarity, not just for themselves, but also for those whom they join in practice.

Chapter 5

Sustaining Relationships: Working with Strong Feelings

Part I: Anger, Aggression and Hostility

MARTIN SMITH

Introduction

I was looking at a book entitled *Flower Fairies of the Summer* (Barker 1986) with my young daughter. She was showing me her favourites – Buttercup, Foxglove, Wild Rose, Forget Me Not. When we came to the picture of Deadly Nightshade she said, 'That's a horrible one – I'm going to tear it out of the book!' 'No, don't do that', I heard myself replying. 'Why?' she challenged. I can't remember my response precisely but it was probably something like: although it can be distressing and upsetting to think about negative, unpleasant things compared to positive, pleasant things there is a value in doing so. If things might harm us or work against us it is in our interests to get to know them and understand them so that we can reduce their negative possibilities and gain useful lessons from them.

It was this thinking that contributed to my interest in undertaking research into social workers' experiences of distress and fear (Smith 2005). I reasoned that, as anger, aggression and hostility featured so frequently in the experiences of social workers and others working in the caring professions it is preferable to attempt to engage with and think about these powerful influences at some level rather to deny and dismiss them.

A social worker might be working through a busy day of commitments, making a visit to a service user they know to have been mentally unstable in the past. On approaching the service user's door they find it open. The worker senses all is not well, something seems out of place, odd, discordant. However, there is nothing *obviously* wrong and there are too many other things to think about. The worker calls out to the service user, who answers. The worker crosses the threshold of the doorway to find the service user highly aroused with brightly staring eyes. Before the worker has time to think the service user has crossed the room, gone behind the worker and locked them in. The worker feels threatened, unsure, and wishes they had paid more attention to the importance of letting colleagues know where they would be. The worker can't be sure where their mobile phone is. They look up at the service user who is standing in front of the locked door with their arms folded tightly across their chest. They seem to be staring *through* the worker.

Throughout the research, I discovered many workers have experienced something similar to the above. The main fears described by participants were: (1) fear of assault, (2) fear of death, (3) fear of being 'overwhelmed'/losing control, (4) fear of being cut off by/from the organisation participants worked for. In this chapter I will give examples of these responses highlighting the impact of anger, aggression and hostility on workers and show ways in which they attempted to process and learn from their experiences. Particular attention will be paid to the 'use of self' and the chapter will conclude with some thoughts on how practitioners might sustain working relationships with service users when the essence of these relationships comes under attack.

Fears of assault and their repercussions

One participant in the research into fear told me:

> A man was being verbally abusive, pointing his finger, f'ing and blinding. I wanted his child to be examined. I was afraid that he would make complaints about me and afraid of the reaction of management if he did. I was also afraid that he was going to hit me; or something worse – kill me. It was intensely difficult for seven weeks. He was a violent man with a criminal record and I would dream of his family threatening me. I began to dream that the man was following me, that he held me prisoner, at knifepoint and stabbed me. The family made complaints about me that

chipped away at my confidence. It wasn't the complaints they made as much as the way they were handled that made it difficult. I'm more frightened when I'm in my work office than I am when I'm out visiting people. It's the criticisms of your practice internally that are the most difficult. You feel you can't do anything right. The people who deal with complaints haven't got a clue about what we're doing. It's got worse recently. I'm happier when visiting clients, even that difficult one, compared to the fear that I feel in the office. I went off work for five weeks with stress and fear.

I have started with this participant's response as within it are contained many of the fears and their repercussions that featured throughout the study. She begins by describing the kind of situation that many social workers working with involuntary clients will be familiar with – workers have statutory duties, such as undertaking a child protection investigation or an assessment under the Mental Health Act, clients do not want to cooperate with these and will attempt to avoid doing so. Sometimes non-compliance is passive, such as not keeping appointments, or sometimes, as in this case, the worker's would-be authority is challenged by direct opposition and hostility. When the worker is challenged she does not feel strong and confident in the face of the opposition but begins to doubt herself. She imagines the challenges getting worse. The client complains about her to her manager, and she pictures a physical assault escalating to the point that she is killed. When the client does complain about her she does not feel defended or supported but that 'management' have aligned themselves with the service user and, instead of 'rescuing' her, have become an additional persecutor to contend with (Karpman 1968).

The worker has valid grounds for her fear as the service user has a known history of violence. The fears get bigger so that not only is he regarded as a source of fear but so too are his family who now join him in posing a threat to the worker's sense of security and well-being. Not only does the worker picture him assaulting her in her mind's eye but these pictures also spill over from waking life into her dreams. A common finding of the research in answer to the question about the impact of experience was that participants would often distinguish between an immediate impact – 'there and then', in the room – and a longer-term impact that they realised later – particularly by way of dreams or subsequent reflection on the experience. One of the reasons why it is important for social workers to recognise and share the profound effect of distressing experiences is that they *remain*. Because really important experiences are never entirely forgotten they can build up to have a cumulative effect on the worker's mental health. Freud (1991, p.256) puts this memorably: '…in mental life nothing which has once been formed can perish – everything is somehow preserved and in suitable circumstances can once more be brought to light'.

The service user becomes like a character in a horror movie as the worker's imagination gets to work and she dreams of him following her, imprisoning and then stabbing her. These are fundamental, pervasive fears and have been triggered by the worker's response to the threat she perceives. She returns to talk of how the complaints were used to further undermine her practice and goes on to say that she found the management of the complaints and the threat they entailed more difficult to deal with than the threat of physical assault. This was another common finding in the research – workers frequently found complaints about them more difficult to deal with than threats of physical assault. While complaints procedures have their place in organisations they can also be used for purposes that are not intended and have profound consequences for workers (Smith 2009b). The worker's comment – 'You feel you can't do anything right' – sounds like a phrase a child would use and acts as a reminder that experiences of fear often have their origin in childhood experiences. These experiences, with their accompanying fears of powerlessness, being judged and found wanting, often re-surface as adults attempt to grapple with the consequences of re-awakened childhood fears.

What can we do when 'nothing happens'?

Another participant talked of his fear that he would be stabbed when he was working as a senior residential social worker in a childcare setting:

> I had got involved in an altercation concerning a client not getting out of bed. I dealt with the matter through appropriate channels. Some evenings later I was on night duty. The place was an old, large, rambling house and I was the only person on duty, all the other staff had gone home. All of the clients were supposed to be in bed and I was coming along a dimly lit hallway and was met by

three of my clients aged between 14 and 18, dressed in anoraks with hoods up. One guy had a knife. They advised me that they didn't like the way that I had handled the situation with regard to one of their peers and that they were going to carve me up. They were stood there with knives.

I did a double-take when I saw the knife. In my military career previously I had been a physical training instructor and taught unarmed combat so being faced with knives was not an uncommon scenario but in this totally different context I had no skills. I turned to go up the stairs and was waiting for this knife to go into my back. I just kept walking and the fear... I went up the stairs 'on auto' but felt a kind of giddy blacking-out fear – a white haze, seeing the wall coming and going. People had said to me since that had the knife gone in I would not have felt it because of this giddy feeling. I can't really recall what happened but nothing happened and then I felt immediately that I wanted to share what had happened but there wasn't any one around.

Once again, the incident arises from an ordinary enough typical encounter between social worker and client as the worker feels the need to enforce a boundary that the client does not want to adhere to. The event is recalled in the context of a horror-movie setting with the worker alone at night, in an old rambling house, seeing hooded people approaching him with knives, down a dimly lit hallway. He does not believe what he sees initially (denial) and needs 'a double-take' to check. Fear frequently prevents people from accessing skills and knowledge that they have. In this case, because of the participant's previous training in the military, in theory, he was well equipped to defuse the situation he was confronted with. In practice, it was as if his knowledge and skills had deserted him, leaving him feeling he 'had no skills', although this was not true. This repercussion of fear poses a question for those providing training courses intended to help workers deal effectively with challenging behaviour. If we know that what we know will not be available for us when we need it in fear-provoking situations, then what is the point of knowing it in the first place?

The worker does not confront or challenge those threatening him buts opts for the 'flight' response instead. He decides to take a risk and turn his back on the young people and carry on walking up the stairs. While doing so his imagination 'runs riot' as he expects to be knifed in the back. The 'on auto' state he describes is a form of dissociation commonly experienced by people experiencing traumatic events (Van der Kolk *et al.* 1996). His vision and balance are affected and the fear seems to be affecting even his physical surroundings as the walls 'come and go'.

The worker reaches a point when he realises that the young people do not intend to carry out their threat and he will not be stabbed. Another feeling then kicks in, probably a combination of elation and relief, similar to that experienced when people survive a 'close shave', for example, while driving, which could have left them dead. There can be a feeling of omnipotence, of 'cheating death', leaving people feeling overly convinced by and unrealistically confident in their capacity to survive. In any event, the worker feels that something extremely significant has happened and that he wants to share this with someone. He then thinks further and reasons that actually nothing has happened after all: he was threatened, the young people did not carry out the threat, he walked up the stairs and life goes on.

This confusion of feelings as to whether or not something has actually happened is indicated by what the worker says at the end of his account: 'I can't really recall what happened…but nothing happened…and then I wanted to share what had happened…" While it might be true that 'nothing happened' in the external world, there have certainly been changes in the worker's inner world. Within a few seconds he has gone from thinking usual thoughts on an everyday shift to contemplating the possibility of being killed by those he is there to care for. It is this that he wants to share. Fear is arguably more profound in the inner world than the outer (as the first participant quoted above says, 'It's the criticisms of your practice internally that are the most difficult') and workers and their supervisors need to be aware of this. Participants in the research talked frequently about having experienced some extremely frightening possibility in their mind's eye to be told by their busy manager, 'Well, nothing happened, did it? You weren't assaulted, were you? You're still here, aren't you? What's the problem?' Such responses are heard as a cruel and unthinking dismissal of an awful possibility.

In the two examples cited so far the participants feared assaults which did not materialise. The difficulties posed for them were as a result of their imaginations 'running riot' and producing disconcerting possibilities in their mental life. In the following example a male social worker tells of a time when he was assaulted.

Being assaulted: the need to get back

I was in a multi-storey block of flats visiting a woman with an alcohol problem. I was trying to deal with her aggression and intoxication. She punched me and I went down. I knew that I should use her first name and try to calm things down. There were local hoods and glue-sniffers in the flat who all had chips on their shoulders and saw me as 'part of the system'. She was saying to them that this was their chance to get their own back. There must have been about eight or ten of them by several doors. They were half spaced out and treating it as entertainment. I was thinking that I needed to get back. I got into the lift and it stopped. The doors opened and she was there. I tried to get down the stairs and she came down the stairs. I was trying to rap doors to get into other people's flats to get help. She was trying to get into the lift with me. I was holding on to my diary and knew that if those lift doors closed with her inside them then I would have to do something. I would have to react. It's her or me and it's going to be me who comes out...I would have thought, 'To hell with the job – this is jungle stuff – I'm going to come out.' There would only have been the 'fight' option left.

The fear extends and projects onto everything. On the way I passed two girls who I had seen when trying to get out of the building earlier. My eyes must have been like saucers. I don't remember the drive back to the office at all. At its most extreme it was a fear of death, of non-existence, of having to survive. I fled like a rabbit. It was so primal, so gut. I haven't looked at the police statement I made at the time. You don't want to go back. There was a loss of control. It was like a cheap video. Once out of the building I didn't know which end of me was up. It was overwhelming, incapacitating, it affects your brain. There's still gaps. I sat down with the police to make a statement but I couldn't remember. There was blood over my shirt, skin off my knuckles. Fear cripples. I remember holding on to my diary – my professional role – but by the third time I'd lost it.

Again, the memory of the event and its relating is like watching a horror movie (the metaphor of watching a film through a dissociative state is acknowledged by the participant when he describes his experience as being like 'entertainment' and 'a cheap video'). One minute the worker is in control as he is the one instigating the visit, the next minute this control is taken from him as he feels at the mercy of the antagonistic service user and friends. The dis-inhibition of the service user's friends makes for more frightening possibilities.

The participant says, 'I was thinking that I needed to get back.' This 'need to get back' was mentioned by several participants in the research into fear and has interest on at least two levels. On one level there is the 'need to get back' to the office, away from the frightening experience. On a deeper, more existential level, there is the need to get back from the traumatised self to the coping self and this aspect of experience is considered later in this chapter.

Wherever he goes in attempts to escape the service user, she follows – like the dream figures in the first account above, who track the participant down until they kill her. He asks for help which is not forthcoming. He is like certain people described by Bowlby (1988) who feel acute separation anxiety as they are unable to access dependable attachment figures or return to a secure base at a time of need. Whereas the residential social worker cited above turned his back on his would-be assailants and walked away, thus demonstrating the 'flight' option to stress and fear, this worker sees that he only has the 'fight' option available. Whereas the residential worker pictured himself being attacked by service users, this participant sees himself as the attacker who will forcefully subdue the service user if necessary in order to ensure his survival. Both are profoundly sobering thoughts.

This participant mentions his diary twice and several participants in the research referred to their diaries. In one sense this is a factual supplying of detail since social workers frequently carry their diaries with them. In a deeper sense the diary contains the worker's past and future and is thus symbolic of their life to date and that planned for the future. This provides another example of how profoundly experiences of anger, aggression and hostility can impinge upon identity.

An example of the fear 'extending and projecting into everything' can be seen in the account by the residential social worker who talked of the walls 'coming and going' (a terrifying possibility frighteningly conveyed in Roman Polanski's film *Repulsion*). This participant shows signs of dissociation as he relates his account as he imagines himself looking at himself: 'My eyes must have been like saucers.' He refers to fear as animalistic, 'so primal, so gut'. A common dilemma for those health and social care workers who have been assaulted by service users is whether or not they should report such assaults to the police. This participant tried to share what had happened with the police but does not seem to have made much sense in giving his statement. While he previously acknowledged the 'need to get back', he goes on to say, 'You don't want to go back.' The different uses of the same phrase are interesting here as the worker acknowledges his need to 'get back' to his office and his pre-traumatised self while also recognising his preference to avoid 'getting back' to the pain of the event he experienced by remembering it. These subtle nuances of use of language illustrate the ambivalence people feel when invited to talk about their fears. They want to talk about their fears in the hope of understanding them more fully and they do not want to talk about them because they are frightening. They want to 'go back' to them and they do not want to go back to them at the same time.

Being assaulted: loss of faith in human nature

A female participant working with a mental health service user told me:

> I was a senior social worker and had been working for quite a while with a woman in her early sixties who had an alcohol problem which she didn't acknowledge. She was also histrionic. I'd been helping to get her re-housed. She had an old flat on the fourth floor. On this particular day she'd phoned the secretary shouting, saying that she had got problems. Entering her flat I found her not to be her usual self. She was very aroused. She was a powerful, big-built, stocky woman. She was shouting at me, shaking her finger, saying, 'You've got to sort this out immediately.' It was a rainy day and I had a plastic mac on.
>
> As usual, I was clutching my diary in one hand and a handbag in the other. We went to the kitchen to see what she was bothered about. She was very aroused. We bent down under the sink and she showed me the earth wire. I turned up, smiled and said, 'That's perfectly all right' and she thought I was laughing at her. She absolutely boiled over with rage and got me up against the kitchen wall with her hands around my throat. The whole thing probably only took a matter of minutes although it felt very much longer.

> I've got all sorts of visual memories of it, like a video with images that stay. That plastic mac I had on – I always felt it protected me. Looking back, it's totally irrational. I can't remember if her hands were around my skin or around the plastic and she couldn't get a grip but I felt a sense of protection at the time. I thought, 'I don't know what to do.' I wasn't going to try and fight back because she was stronger than I was and absolutely raring to go.
>
> I can remember her stopping as if she thought, 'Oh, bugger this!' – a dismissive thing. I said, 'Let's not talk about it like this.' We went into the sitting room and I said, 'Why don't you light a cigarette?' The moment her eyes were down and her hands were occupied I rushed out the flat, absolutely terrified. I shook. I could hardly hold the diary. I was very shaky and was surprised that my legs did not give way. I do remember that I went home crying and it was as if I had lost something – something about faith in human nature – something as silly as that. It perturbed me as I'd always thought that I'd had a good relationship with her. It's not an issue for me now, but if I press the button I can get the memory.

This worker notes that the service user was 'not her usual self' and was very aroused but it is interesting that this observation did not lead to her re-evaluating whether or not she should proceed with her intended visit. Participants often talked of 'warning signs' that were apparent when they looked back on traumatic experiences but which they did not evaluate as prevailingly significant indicators of risk. In his book *The Gift of Fear*, de Becker (1997) argues that intuition should always be listened to carefully as it always arises in response to 'something' and always has our best interests at heart. Like Bowlby, he suggests we learn from ethology:

> Can you imagine an animal reacting to the gift of fear the way some people do, with annoyance and disdain instead of attention? No animal in the wild, suddenly overcome with fear, would spend any of its mental energy thinking, 'It's probably nothing.' (1997, p.30)

De Becker argues that the primary evolutionary purpose of fear is to protect and, as such, it has our survival and sustained well-being at heart. Although fear is not generally regarded as a pleasant emotion it is fundamentally 'on our side' which is why De Becker claims it is frequently a gift rather than a curse. A careful openness to and evaluation of workers' intuitions might prevent them from crossing thresholds they later regret.

Again the worker mentions her diary and draws comparison with being on a video. Smiles can often be subliminally interpreted as snarls by people in highly aroused states (both are teeth-baring communications) and while the intention may be to convey a friendly, reassuring manner, the received communication might be one of hostility. It is advisable for workers not to smile or laugh when in fraught and tense situations as these communications frequently make things worse. Although no one response can be guaranteed to work effectively in all situations, generally speaking if service users sense a reaction of calm, quiet, understanding authority they are less likely to let loose their potentially aggressive instincts.

The worker talks of an almost magical sense of protection she thinks was conferred by her plastic mac rather like the protective cloaks used by mythological figures (Campbell 1993). Even though she was under threat the worker retains a capacity for clear thinking which eventually helps ensure her safe escape and survival. She evaluates the 'fight' option and dismisses it. Rather than make an abortive and unsuccessful attempt at 'flight', the worker pieces together a strategy and leaves when the service user is looking elsewhere and her hands are occupied, thus succeeding in her aim.

Unfortunately workers are sometimes attacked by service users with whom they think they have a 'good relationship'. This proves no defence if service users are dis-inhibited or unwell enough to not be constrained by a previously mutually enjoyable working relationship. Like De Becker, the psychoanalyst Bion (1990, p.5) suggests that fear is a gift that functions essentially in the best interests of the worker (and the service user). He claims:

> Anyone who is going to see a patient tomorrow should, at some point, experience fear. In every consulting room there ought to be two rather frightened people: the patient and the psychoanalyst. If they are not, one wonders why they are bothering to find out what everyone knows.

Bion's point is that the right degree of fear sharpens the mind and heightens concentration. When we are somewhat afraid we are not comfortable or complacent and we do not believe that we know. We are watchful, keenly alive to new possibilities and do not fall back on a misguided belief that things will be as they have been.

The worker's tears for a loss of innocence are an indication of the extent of the repercussions that a relatively brief exposure to a fear-provoking incident can have. From this one experience the worker feels as if her opinions about everyone (human nature) are called into question to the extent that they will never be the same again. This raises the question of how workers can be helped when an encounter with anger, aggression or hostility raises profound and far-reaching questions for them.

Use of self – the traumatised self and the coping self

The case study just discussed shows how the worker is aware of at least two aspects of herself. There is the coping self that thought sufficiently clearly and soundly to get her away from the threatening situation and there is the traumatised self which weeps for its loss once the worker is away from danger.

I was talking about this aspect of the research with a colleague who told me of a time when she was in her garden on a pleasant sunny afternoon when she heard her neighbour calling to her in distress. The neighbour's baby was choking and turning blue. The neighbour seemed at a total loss about what to do. My colleague found herself taking charge of the situation in an assured, confident manner that she did not recognise in herself. She told the neighbour to call for an ambulance while she went to care for the baby. My colleague said she did not really know at the time what she intended to do with/for the baby but just knew that she could manage the situation. She stayed with the baby until the ambulance arrived and does not remember what she did or how she did it. On arrival the ambulance crew congratulated her on her efficient and timely responses that had kept the baby alive. They told her she did 'everything right' and that they would now take over. Having handed the baby over to them my colleague dissolved in floods of tears as she allowed herself for the first time to feel the anxiety and fear she had been repressing in order to cope. The coping self does its work admirably but when this is completed the traumatised self pushes the coping self out of the way and needs time and attention as it uncovers feelings and responses denied at the time. There is a sense in which sustaining relationships with service users is made more likely by establishing a dialogue between the coping self and the traumatised self within the worker in which both selves are given a fair hearing without either being allowed to dominate the discussion unduly. Much of this discussion is likely to concern feelings of anger, hatred and other strong negative feelings experienced by the worker.

Hate in the counter-transference and the wider social system

One residential social worker told me:

> You are dealing with very powerful emotions when you have been assaulted…you feel so angry that someone has hit you when you are trying to help them and it's this real anger that you cannot deal with. Yes, you can understand it, yes, you know why, yes, you know it's transference – but it's the feelings of real *rage*…you cannot bring that to supervision. I have wanted to kill – I have felt so angry – that if they were here now I would really want to do them damage… this is the bit that is not addressed…there is no reason good enough in my mind for hitting somebody. I do not care whether you look like their mother or whether you have said something that slightly upsets them.

This participant is demonstrating what Winnicott (1992) has called hate in the counter-transference:

> However much [the psychiatrist] loves his patients he cannot avoid hating them and fearing them, and the better he knows this the less will hate and fear be the motives determining what he does to his patients… Above all he must not deny hate that really exists in himself. Hate that is *justified* in the present setting has to be sorted out and kept in storage and available for eventual interpretation. (pp.195–6)

Winnicott claims that we should accept the emergence of hatred as an inevitable possibility arising from work with service users in the caring professions. His comment about emotions that need to be 'kept in storage' provides a basis for the interaction between the coping self and traumatised self described above. The traumatised self needs to be 'kept in storage' while the coping self does its work. Later there needs to be 'eventual interpretation' when the needs of the traumatised self are recognised and understood. Winnicott argues that if hatred we might feel towards service users can be acknowledged and understood then it is likely to be far less damaging than if we try to deny or repress it in favour of more acceptable-sounding sentiments.

While the worker and Winnicott quoted above are considering feelings of hatred which might exist and pass between two people, Sharon Shoesmith (2016) widens this consideration to analyse the social and political contexts in which hatred might be expressed to and at social workers. In her book *Learning from Baby P,* Shoesmith demonstrates that although approximately one child dies each week in England and Wales as a result of familial child homicide (2016, p.27) the case of Baby P was given concentrated and specific attention which ignored this wider context. In this age of 'post-truth' and 'fake news' she shows that the establishment of a compelling 'narrative' (composed and delivered by the politicians and the media) had far greater influence on the public's imagination and responses than the (mere) facts. In this narrative, which is conveyed by way of a cultural trope, social workers and selected others are seen to be responsible for what happens when a child dies while others (in this case the police and Great Ormond Street Hospital) are seen as being relatively blame-free. Shoesmith argues that as social work is seen as the weakest and most vulnerable of the professions involved it is therefore most susceptible to and least able to defend itself against attack:

> The different power dynamics between agencies makes social workers the most vulnerable of these welfare agencies to vilification by the media. Increasingly the social care profession has been positioned outside of 'proper' professions, occupying the lowest position in the symbolic order of welfare professions, compared with doctors, nurses and police. In the case of Baby P, Great Ormond Street Hospital and the Metropolitan Police Service were each able to yield much more power and influence not only to avoid blame when Peter Connelly died but also to evade immediate publicity of their own errors in the case. (p.210)

Shoesmith suggests that it is as if, in working to support the 'moral underclass', social workers have become outside all that is 'civilised' and thus come to be seen as a 'polluting underclass' themselves (2016, p.107). Because of this the public feel justified in pouring hatred and scorn on 'their failures' to prevent children from being killed by those who are in positions of care and trust in relation to them. Shoesmith refers to a growing number of abusive, threatening and obscene e-mails, texts and letters sent to her personally and to Haringey Council. Postings on social media included, with reference to Shoesmith: 'you fucking bitch, I hope you die, break her back and see how she likes it, fuck off and die you bitch', 'evil fucking bitch, i swear if i had seen her i would have decked her one. She is evil through and through, not much better than the scum who did this' and 'I think special hatred should also be reserved for Sharon Shoesmith. She felt she and her department had nothing to apologise for. What a callous evil bitch' (2016, pp.176, 166, 167). The wording of these extracts bears examination. Shoesmith and social work colleagues are not merely considered to have made a mistake or been subject to the human error of which all human beings are capable, but to be 'evil'. The use of this word elevates the nature and extent of perceived wrong-doing from that of mere 'error'. The phrase 'special hatred' is particularly revealing. Not only is 'hatred' considered to be eminently justified but there should be a 'special' version of this 'reserved' as a response to this tragedy.

Winnicott's writing about hate in the countertransference provides a valuable contribution to and contrast with the more 'positive thinking/strengths-based' responses to difficulties encouraged from social workers and others who encounter challenging relationships. Shoesmith extends this to the wider social, cultural and political stage and offers valuable and sobering insights into the difficulties (and sometimes impossibility) of sustaining relationships in the face of hostility which turns social workers and others into socially sanctioned hate figures.

Conclusion: sustaining relationships through complaints about 'dirty work'

Another possible explanation of why some workers, undertaking particular roles, attract criticism and condemnation more than others is provided in the construct of 'dirty work' (Morriss 2016). This concept posits the existence of 'in' groups and 'out' groups in society. Someone has to work with the 'out' groups and this is seen as 'dirty work'. Society needs it to be done, but wants to distance itself from, and sometimes turn on and reject, those who do it. One way of rejecting such workers is to complain about them, sometimes repeatedly and vociferously.

Earlier on in this chapter I mentioned that many social workers report that they fear complaints processes more than physical assault. While these processes can offer service users and others an appropriate right to make justified complaints when services or responses fall short of what they ought to be, they can also function as a vehicle for and even perhaps an encouragement of people's anger, aggression and hostility. Kearns (2007, p.2) writes that there are primarily two fundamental types of complainant:

> The first seeks to challenge what they believe to be bad practice, often just wanting to be heard and for the 'wrong' to be put right, sometimes they also want an apology. The second type wants more than this, they want sanctions to be imposed, the therapist to be punished or 'struck off', increasingly she wants money. I became concerned that our complaints procedures themselves seemed to support what in some cases appears to be an almost insatiable thirst for 'justice' or even revenge.

The influence of this second type of complainant can be that those complained about felt 'like their lives were being "poisoned" or "destroyed"; they also believed that they were not the "intended victim" but, rather, felt as though they were copping what belonged to an earlier significant other, usually mother' (p.4). Shoesmith's book provides a lucid and moving account of how a life might be poisoned and (nearly) destroyed as Kearns claims. On a lesser scale I have come away from what ought to have been conversations with complainants feeling less than human, as if I had not been considered as a person at all, but rather an object of derision, scorn and contempt that needed to be stepped on and/or stepped over in order to progress to the next level of the complaints procedures.

Recent writings (Clarke *et al.* 2016; Grant *et al.* 2015; Keinemans 2015; Sheppard and Charles 2015; Skivenes and Skramstad 2015) exhort social workers to learn and develop skills in applying emotional intelligence and to cultivate resilience (Grant and Kinman 2014) as a means of surviving tough working environments and sustaining relationships in difficult conditions. These skills might go some way in helping social workers retain sufficiently robust mental health to continue working in contested situations. However, if they are trying to do this in a social system which is essentially loaded against them as Shoesmith claims, their individual efforts can meet with only limited success. A farther-reaching and harder-to-get-at question is why social workers continue to passively accept the role of container of the blame, fear and denial which others refuse to share.

We have seen some common features of social workers' responses to exposure to anger, aggression and hostility in this chapter. Experiences have frequently burst unexpectedly as if 'from nowhere' into participants' mental lives. They have been recalled with a cinematic eye for detail as if the participant is an actor in a horror movie. This entails a degree of dissociation. There has been a reversion to child-like states and a loss of innocence. People have been confused as to whether or not anything significant has happened and the extent of this. Experiences of fear go to the heart of people's identity, they lose skills and are faced with options of fight or flight. All of the experiences related happened when participants were working alone. When help was sought from would-be attachment figures this was not forthcoming. It has sometimes been hard for workers to retain a sound sense of their own mental health, let alone sustain relationships with service users.

By reflecting on painful experiences alone and with trusted, appropriate others, applying insights from emotional intelligence and building resilience, social workers and others will sometimes be able to sustain working relationships despite experiencing anger, aggression and hostility from those they are attempting to help. It might be that the extent of strong feeling against social workers is such that relationships cannot be sustained. In such instances, wider social and political responses need to be considered alongside whatever any individual can cultivate and develop for themselves. To return to the illustration with which I began this chapter, this does not mean that we tear out the pages from *The Social Work Book* that we do not like. Rather, it calls for pages to be added that show in a more complete light the difficulties and multi-faceted complexities that social workers face in the context of the wider social systems in which they function. As Konrad Lorenz wrote over 50 years ago:

> Even if one is only trying to explain a petrol engine it is hard to know where to begin, because the person to whom one seeks to explain it can only understand the nature of the crank-shaft if he has grasped that of the connecting rods, the pistons, the valves, the camshaft and so on. Unless one understands the elements of a complete system as

• Chapter 6 •

Sustaining Relationships: Working with Strong Feelings

Part II: Hopelessness, Depression and Despair

CLARE PARKINSON

Sustaining a relationship where there are strong feelings of hopelessness and despair is the focus for social workers engaging with someone who is prone to depression. With depression being the most common type of mental illness, there can be no doubt that social workers regularly encounter these feelings in their work. Such encounters may occur within the full range of social work roles and settings. These settings include community mental health, criminal justice, homelessness and substance use, as well as hospital work and social work with older people, with people with physical and learning disabilities, with children and families, including those safeguarded or in fostering and adoption.

Social workers are drawn to empathise with service users. Learning about the importance of empathy and how to differentiate empathy from sympathy is an early aspect of most social work training. To empathise with someone who is themselves feeling desperate requires preparedness from the practitioner to be alive to a burdensome, suffering state of mind. It is no small matter to commit, for the length of time that this is helpful to them, to maintaining contact with a person who is in anguish.

Sustaining a relationship poses many challenges to the practitioner. This is particularly so when working with feelings and mood states that are painful and, because of the risk of suicide, potentially extremely dangerous. One particular challenge is that depression is a psychological and emotional state which is difficult to grasp. The meaning of the depressed mood lies below the level of consciousness, and therefore it may not be directly available either to the practitioner or even to the person themselves. If we are to be helpful to our service user, it is essential that we are able to recognise the characteristics of depression. We need to know how depression is experienced by the individual and also how to bear the implications of the depressed outlook within ourselves. This will include being able to tolerate the strong feelings involved for the person and for ourselves as practitioners and/or supervisors. Over potentially long periods of time, we need to be able to engage in practical ways that will be of value to someone who is suffering in this way.

Forming an enduring relationship with a depressive service user is central to making an effective intervention. This is because, as we shall see in what follows, the medium for therapeutic help is the very same site on which the depressed person tends to have a problem: the sustaining of relationships. We will be engaged in a process of helping the depressed person to see again, themselves and others including the practitioner, more or less as they really are.

Social work approaches to understanding depression

If a social worker can be helped to make their own sense of the possible origins of feelings of hopelessness, depression and despair, she or he is then less likely to jump into pathologising or labelling a depressed service user and more likely to set out to establish a relationship with them.

The *Diagnostic and Statistical Manual of Mental Disorders* (*DSM*) is the reference that most mental health practitioners refer to for definitions of mental health categories. From the current (Fifth) edition, we learn that the features of depression include: the presence of sad, empty or irritable mood, lethargy, withdrawal from activity and engagement, disturbances in eating and sleeping, a sense of low self-esteem, a sense of guilt and often a feeling of free-floating, all-encompassing anxiety. Despair represents a powerful sensation of hopelessness and readiness to give up, give in and get out of the situation and/or out of one's life (American Psychiatric Association 2015). Although someone prone to depression is not usually in a depressed state all of the time, social workers need to expect and be ready to work with periodic recurrences of depression, along with the intense disappointment and sense of failure that these may bring both to the service user and to those who are trying to help.

There are different available models from which to consider working with depression. Of these, the medical model tends to have considerable prominence, especially in the multi-disciplinary approach to community mental health. Social workers located within mental health teams find that they need to understand the medical approach in order to engage constructively with their colleagues in such settings. It is, however, the psychosocial model of mental health that most social work training emphasises, and social workers do their best and most valued work when they operate firmly within the boundaries of this approach.

What helps the individual social worker to relate to service users who are depressed?

A social work student, Marcus, arrives for the first day of his practice placement at a hostel for homeless people, where substance dependence is endemic. On this day, he witnesses two mental health assessments resulting in compulsory hospital admissions.

A month or so later, when Marcus is on a night shift, Paulo, one of the residents with whom Marcus is working, takes an overdose after a row with his girlfriend.

Paulo is a 36-year-old man who arrived from Portugal five years earlier. He has been unsuccessful in his attempts to find work and has developed a drug and alcohol habit. Now, he has to be rushed into hospital. Marcus reaches Paulo's room with the staff member on duty at the time of the crisis. He is told by the staff member to leave the room. He waits for a while outside, then goes downstairs and tries to busy himself in the office. He observes the medical team arrive and take Paulo on a stretcher to the ambulance. When the staff member returns downstairs, Marcus notices that he does not include him in any of the discussions about the case on that or subsequent occasions.

The challenge for Marcus is to make sense of what has happened for Paulo and how this relates to his own experience of the incident.

Marcus takes the scenario to supervision. In the course of this session, Marcus shares with his supervisor that this experience made him contemplate walking out of the placement then and there and giving up on social work completely.

The supervisor is aware of the following. Marcus arrives for supervision seeming to be a bit down in his mood. He relays the details of the above incident with an uncharacteristically flat tone of voice. He emphasises that he felt shut out by the co-worker on the shift, who asked him to wait outside while he entered Paulo's room. Marcus points out to his supervisor that he is himself trained in crisis intervention techniques. When he returned downstairs Marcus shares that he was feeling rejected, redundant. To the supervisor, this reported feeling of dejection, and Marcus's impulse towards walking out and giving up on social work, seem connected.

The supervisor muses. Marcus feels both that he had no clear role in this evident crisis situation and that the skills he does have were not wanted or appreciated. He speaks in a detached way about the incident with Paulo. He says he was told that the paramedics administered an injection to Paulo before transporting him to hospital. 'And that's it.' It is as if, on hearing later about this injection, Marcus invests this knowledge with considerable significance. Was it for the administering of the injection that he was excluded, and asked to wait outside? With 'and that's it' Marcus conveys to his supervisor the bitterness of feeling left out of the action, prevented from helping. Perhaps it is also, the supervisor ponders, a means of minimising the significance of what was, after all, a life-saving intervention.

The supervising tutor, knowing Marcus usually to be tuned-in and sensitive in approach, shares her associations with him. First, though, she suggests they think together about what Paulo might have been feeling that could have led him to take an overdose at this time. As the basis for this they consider some aspects of Marcus's presentation that may offer clues as to what was going on for Paulo that day, what Paulo may have been feeling. The flat presentation hints at a depressed mood. Marcus's sense of being rejected by the hostel worker might also link to Paulo's disappointment that he has been unable to find regular employment. This too could help explain the intensity of Marcus's feeling that he is redundant and that the skills he does have (such as in crisis intervention) are not valued in this setting.

Marcus's sense of having no clear role may indicate how Paulo feels too. Paulo is an adult male who has left his country of origin. He is alone in a big city where he can find no work. He has numbed himself through his use of drink and drugs. Paulo appears to have lost touch with what and who is important in his life. Outside the closed door, Marcus, powerfully if momentarily, loses contact himself with his own motivation for the social work course and feels like giving up, killing off his ambition to qualify.

The supervisor, knowing something of the work of Janet Mattinson (1970) on 'mirroring' in supervision, was alert to this aspect of Marcus's presentation. Mattinson suggests that a supervisee, behaving in an uncharacteristic way, may be conveying a dynamic that actually belongs to their relationship with their service user. If so, this is likely to be a dynamic that the supervisee is finding difficult and could use some help with. The supervisor sensed that Marcus's lack of interpersonal connectedness when he talked about the incident with Paulo was just such a communication. This could therefore legitimately be explored as another way into thinking about the relationship work with Paulo.

The supervisor now learns from Marcus that Paulo is typically known to make some progress in facing his difficulties with himself and with the hostel staff but then, as he begins to get in touch with painful reality, he tends to back away. He cuts off and impulsively resorts to drugs and alcohol as a means of escape.

Some weeks later, Marcus reports on the development of his work with Paulo. This includes some impressive reflections on the possible relevance of Paulo's age and stage to his current anxieties. Marcus has learned of the psychodynamic take on the 'mid-life crisis' (Jaques 1965). He considers that Paulo, as a middle-aged man, may be currently in the throes of his own mid-life crisis. Paulo has not yet been able to find a way to use the skills that ensured he had employment as a younger man in his country of origin. He does not have a life partner or robust friendship network. He was recently rejected when he proposed a more intimate connection to a friend. Paulo's drug use makes it difficult for him to face and get help for his depression. As a practitioner, Marcus now feels a new connection to Paulo. He notices that, having begun to think about the likely trauma for Paulo, he can consider a number of practical ways in which he might engage with

Paulo, who wants to find work and secure community housing. He recognises the value of helping Paulo to find a more rounded, realistic sense of his current circumstances while working towards these self-defined goals.

Paulo's depression had seemed unavailable to conscious awareness both in Paulo himself and in the workers who wanted to help. It was Marcus's feelings about Paulo's near-death experience, as explored in supervision, that gave oxygen to an idea of what was happening for Paulo. The feelings are apparent, even though the source of the feelings, to an extent, remains hidden. Getting hold of a conceptual model that tells us what to look out for in work with a depressed person is something that we will now address.

Theoretical concepts as a way of containing painful psychological, emotional and social phenomena

We can consider an application of what Cooper and Lousada (2005, p.19) refer to as theory as 'a project of revelation' and Marion Bower (2005) calls the 'containment value' of theoretical concepts. The idea, for our purposes, is that good-quality theory can equip social workers and their supervisors to make constructive interventions with service users who are suffering from depression.

It has to be said that psychoanalytic ideas, for which the originator is Sigmund Freud, are not easy to grasp at first encounter. They are, though, in our experience, well worth struggling with for the understanding and insight into human psychology that they offer. Conceptual understanding makes it possible for us to name the feelings experienced when we are with someone who is depressed. Having named the experience and, with the help of explanatory theoretical concepts, understood something about it, it then becomes possible for us to communicate this understanding to others.

As social workers, from our qualifying period onward, we apply our learning from one context and one service-user group to another. We are often called upon to report and share our findings in inter-professional contexts. If we have a named and communicable understanding of the experience and origin of depression, we are more likely to be able to hold on to a coherent, psychosocial perspective within a multiprofessional context of work with a depressed service user.

What do we know about the origin of depressed states of mind?

> Mourning is regularly the reaction to the loss of a loved person or to the loss of some abstraction which has taken the place of one, such as one's country, liberty, an ideal… (Freud 1917, p.243)

In a wonderfully rich paper published one hundred years ago entitled 'Mourning and Melancholia', Freud (1917) notes that mourning always involves an experience of loss. This is usually in relation to the external world. Whatever the practice context, in social work we think of the loss that our service users may have suffered as including not just loss through the death of a significant other but also the loss perhaps of a home (in the case of migration, forced or voluntary), the loss of a job or house (increasingly in current times) or a lost love (in the case of a failed relationship). There might be, for children in care (or their parents), the loss or reduction of contact with their families (or children). Around the birth of a baby with a disability, the loss may be felt by the parents of the 'normal' child they had imagined and were expecting.

Working with grieving service users, we know that people often struggle with multiple losses. Complications in the grief process can mean that an individual may get stuck or overwhelmed and face particular challenges for recovery. Bereavement may be lifelong, as when parents mourn the death of a child. Social workers become aware from early on in their training of the usual course that mourning takes. We soon learn that, however strange the grieving process might seem, this is personal to the individual mourner, and it is generally a process that calls for a protected space and a respectful stance, at a distance appropriate to the wishes and needs of the person.

However, grieving a loss is not the same thing as suffering from depression, which is what Freud and others refer to as melancholia. This is so even though these two experiences – mourning and depression – do have, as we shall now see, many features in common.

In 'Mourning and Melancholia', Freud explores the nature and origins of melancholia, including in its manic form. He compares melancholia to the processes of mourning following a death. He comments on the evident similarities between the two experiences. With regard to melancholia, he notes that the following characteristics can be found: a profoundly painful dejection, cessation of interest in the outside world, loss of the capacity to love, inhibition of all activity, and a lowering of the self-regarding feelings to a degree that finds utterance in self-reproaches and self-reviling, and culminates in a delusional expectation of punishment (p.244).

Of these characteristics, all are common to both mourning and melancholia with just one exception. It is the lowering of self-regard with associated self-reproaches that Freud suggests marks the difference between the two in terms of the identifiable affect or feeling. The presence of this lowering of self-regard in melancholia is pivotal.

> Shola is 15 and lives in a children's home. The staff group finds it difficult to keep her within the safe limits of the home. Shola is using drugs and socialising with local gang members associated with violence and police involvement. Following a visit to her mother's over the holiday break, Shola's behaviour changes. She no longer goes out and becomes withdrawn and lethargic. She stops eating regularly. For once, she allows the staff to care for and about her. They are attentive and responsive. Then one night she cuts her wrists. When asked, as she begins to recover, what has prompted her to attempt suicide, she tells the social worker that she feels completely worthless.

For Freud, in both mourning and in melancholia, there is initially a turning away from reality and a wishful clinging, usually to a significant person. Eventually, though, in mourning, the respect that we have for life and for reality generally asserts itself, and although we resist it at first, gradually, over time, we give up the lost, loved person and begin to let go. Freud suggests that we expect mourning to be painful, that we accept and take in our stride the experience of 'painful unpleasure' then 'when the work of mourning is completed the ego becomes free and uninhibited again' (Freud 1917, p.245).

Although melancholia also involves a response to the loss of a loved object, this loss is probably not through death. For Shola in the situation above, a visit to her mother meant she was confronted with the fact that her mother could not meet her needs for care and closeness. Freud gives a parallel example of the jilted lover or the person who feels let down, slighted or betrayed by their loved one 'so that the object-relationship was shattered' (p.249).

It could be that it is clear to the person themselves what or whom they have lost, but often this is not the case. In melancholia, knowledge of the loss of an important relationship may be withdrawn from conscious awareness. So, for the melancholic person or for anyone trying to work with or understand them, the source of the loss may not be apparent. It is, instead, the effects of the loss that are evident. This was the case for Paulo and Shola in both of whom we can see the low mood, lack of self-regard and thoughts of death by suicide. Although, in mourning, the process is more likely to be obvious because it is a conscious one, seeing the suffering of the melancholic may be puzzling to us because we don't know why the person has become so withdrawn or what it is that is preoccupying them so completely. Just when the staff felt most connected to Shola, she cut her wrists.

Freud emphasises the impact of the lack of self-regard in our understanding of melancholia. What has happened is that the melancholic person has severed their loving attachment to the dis-appointing person. In order not to lose them, the melancholic person has then identified with them and, through this identification, has installed the representation of the now rejected and hated person in their mind. With the critical part of their mind (the superego or conscience) the melancholic has then immediately begun an attack on that part of themselves that is in identification with the one they have rejected:

> If one listens patiently to a melancholic's many and various self-accusations, one cannot in the end avoid the impression that often the most violent of them are hardly at all applicable to the patient himself, but…they do fit someone else, someone whom the patient loves or has loved or should love…we perceive that the self-reproaches are reproaches against a loved object which have been shifted away from it on to the patient's own ego. (Freud 1917, p.248)

Freud notes that the reason the melancholic feels no sense of shame in front of others is that when they appear to be berating themselves for their utter worthlessness, they are really denigrating the loved object with which they are now so identified as to seem to be one and the same.

Depression and the ability to relate to another separate person

An important aspect of Freud's paper, with which almost all subsequent work on depression continues to resonate, is Freud's exploration of why this internal process should have taken place at all. He proposes that what the melancholic is doing is regressing to an earlier, narcissistic time. Narcissus is the youthful god who falls in love with his own image in the lake. In Freud's view, before we are able to love someone else, just like Narcissus, we take ourselves as our first love object. The depressed person withdraws from their connection with the significant person in the external world and instead sets up a preoccupying drama inside themselves. The driving force in melancholia is that through identification with the rejected love object, the depressive person ensures that 'the love-relation need not be given up' (p.249). The problem shown here is that the depressive person is actually not able to face the loss of the loved object.

'Narcissistic identification' happens because the person cannot tolerate losing their love, or it might be their ambition or being let down by someone significant. The internal conflict that now ensues leaves the person feeling empty and exhausted. Their ordinary resources, needed for coping, are no longer available to them. Freud suggests that, in mourning, the external world feels empty to the bereaved person. In melancholia, it is the ego that is empty, leading, as we have seen, to a lowering of self-regard and a depletion of personal resources. Even so, it does seem clear that this is something active and urgent being played out within the relationship between the depressive person and their internalised object.

Suicide and 'sadistic impulses'

Shola evokes deep sadness and distress in the staff who are around her and (possibly) in her mother too. Those working with Paulo also feel distressed and Marcus is affected by a sensation of pessimism when he connects with Paulo during a suicidal phase.

Freud suggests (1917, p.251) that the melancholic often has a strong wish to get even with those who are close to them:

> The patients usually still succeed, by the circuitous path of self-punishment, in taking revenge on the original object and tormenting their loved one through their illness, having resorted to it in order to avoid the need to express their hostility to him openly.

He examines the place of sadism in melancholia to explain further the tendency towards suicide. In melancholia, there is ambivalence (hatred as well as love) felt towards those in the external world. Through regression to a 'narcissistic object choice', the significant person has been got rid of. Within the mind of the person, however, the representation of the significant other may nevertheless prove more powerful than the ego itself. It is in such a situation that 'the ego can kill itself'. Another way of describing this scenario is to say that the life instinct is overwhelmed by the death instinct. We would also say that, when this is the case, the person feels utterly hopeless and is in despair.

The powerful hatred emitted, Freud suggests, is an expression of a battle going on within the melancholic person between actual life and death. Sleeplessness, refusal to eat and suicide attempts or completions are expressions of this battle, with the 'death instinct', at such times, in the ascendancy.

Depression as vulnerability in forming and/or sustaining relationships

The literature on depression shows that cognitive behavioural therapists, psychotherapists and relationship-oriented social workers all start with the same assumption. It is that someone who is prone to suffering from depression is likely to have a difficulty in the way that they perceive their relationships with others, particularly those on whom they rely.

Thomas Ogden is a contemporary author and psychoanalyst. In his reading of Freud's 'Mourning and Melancholia' (Ogden 2005), the focus is on why it is that one should experience melancholia instead of staying with the process of mourning in the face of a loss. His proposition is that melancholia occurs precisely because the melancholic subject is suffering from a relationship disorder. That is, the melancholic person has, at an early stage in their development, not succeeded in differentiating themselves so as to be able to recognise 'self' as distinct from 'other'. The consequence is that the mechanism by which one becomes capable of loving another separate person is in some way faulty. The love that one may feel for another is not sufficiently free of the other person to be able to allow for the independence and separateness of both.

The difference, then, between the mourner and the melancholic is explained like this. The mourner is able, gradually, to face the loss of their loved object, to accommodate their associations to this person in their inner world, and carry on with their life. For the melancholic, Ogden notes (p.33), the process is first to abandon the object in the external world and then, through identification, to preserve this object as a means of avoiding the painful feelings of loss. In exchange for the evasion of this pain, the melancholic is doomed to experience the sense of lifelessness that comes as a consequence of disconnecting themselves from a large part of external life. 'In a sense the internalisation of the object renders the object forever captive in the melancholic and at the same time renders the melancholic endlessly captive to it' (Ogden 2005, p.34).

But why does the melancholic person regress to this (narcissistic) way of relating in the face of the expected or actual loss of a loved object? By way of explanation, Ogden emphasises the importance of Freud's 1914 paper on narcissism. Its premise is that, although we take ourselves as our first love objects, we then, gradually, become able to relate to and know the separate qualities of a significant other, usually the mother or primary carer. This achievement of gradually getting to know the other is key. Ogden (2005, p.36) suggests that: 'The movement from narcissistic identification to narcissistic object tie is a matter of a small, but significant shift in the degree of recognition of, and emotional investment in, the otherness of the object.'

This process of getting to know the other is developed most fully in the work of Melanie Klein (1935) and followers, especially around her concept of 'the depressive position'. In this idea, 'depressive' does not refer to depression but rather to grieving for an outlook from which everything seemed more certain (Britton 1989). Within the constructive outcome of this grieving, guilt is implied, and regret too, for the aggression dealt to a loved one and the hurt we may have caused. In the depressive position there is a sense of responsibility for damage done and concern to make things better. Klein places the baby's first experience of the depressive position at four to six months of age. Britton (1989) points out that Klein views the baby's struggle to accept the autonomy of their primary carer as simultaneously one aspect of the Oedipal struggle. He proposes that Klein's work represents a development from Freud's thinking in 'Mourning and Melancholia'. According to Britton (p.39), 'Freud linked the preservation of sanity and reality to the relinquishment of the idea of the permanent possession of the love object. But he did not apply this to the dissolution of the Oedipus complex.'

Can the baby tolerate being in a three-person relationship? The baby is aware that when their beloved person is not with them, it is likely that they are with a third person, perhaps their father. The enormity for the baby of facing and enduring this painful jealousy-inducing reality may not always be managed. It can be seen that failure to navigate this step in development is significant. For our purposes, it may account for the melancholic person's refusal to allow for the separateness of their primary loved object. Is it this refusal to accommodate a close person's distinct and separate existence that is re-enacted each time an individual, who has not yet worked through this struggle, succumbs to an episode of depression?

Britton (p.40) sets out the connection that can be made between the two processes. 'Just as in the depressive position the idea of the permanent possession has to be given up, so in confronting the parental relationship the ideal of one's sole possession of the desired parent has to be relinquished.' The implications that flow from Klein's development of Freud's notion of the Oedipal struggle is that an adult, prone to depression, is also likely to be someone who has difficulty accepting the love object's right, as an autonomous person, to come and go as they please, and that this struggle may be considered to begin in early infancy.

Implications for practice

What can we learn from this exploration that is applicable to work with people suffering from depression? One thing to stress is that, however helpful a conceptual framework might be, there can be no substitute for the practitioner getting to know the individual person and developing a relationship with them.

As was apparent from Marcus's work with Paulo, short-term interventions can assist with a specific episode of depression. However, even short-term encounters require the practitioner to present themselves in a way that enables trust to develop. There needs to be the opportunity to listen and really hear about the experience of the depressed person. This is necessary for assessment purposes and because of the suicide risk that is likely to accompany expressions of hopelessness. In supervision, Marcus was sharing what he had learned from Paulo. What were his current social circumstances and how do these relate to his depressed state of mind? How did the recent rejection in his romantic life affect matters? In what way was Paulo vulnerable?

If there is to be the possibility of making sense of an individual's susceptibility to depression, a longer time frame will be needed, probably in the context of multi-disciplinary work including with medically trained colleagues if medication is sought. How does the depression link to the person's developmental experiences? In what way might the relationship that the person makes with you, and others in the team, inform you of their potential and of their support needs? What happens to the dynamics with your supervisor when you think with them about your depressed service user?

In Freud's 'Mourning and Melancholia' paper, the proposal is that a period of depression will end only when one of two conditions has been met. It is either that the rage (against the significant other) has been satiated or that the rage has abated because the rejected object has been declared to be worthless.

It was because Marcus's supervisor noticed that he was behaving in a way that was out of character that she was able to begin to hypothesise with him about the mental state of his service user, Paulo. In order to continue to be effective, what is of particular importance for social workers to think about in supervision is the impact on the interpersonal relationship of their work with someone prone to depression. This is because, as we have seen above, the depressive person is likely to have a specific problem with sustaining relationships. The fact that this is so offers both a potential obstacle and a therapeutic opportunity. The opportunity is that an attuned, well-supervised practitioner may be able to observe, within the relationship constructed between themselves and their service user, the themes that have trapped and troubled the depressed person in their past, and to work with this relationship to achieve change. We know, from the canon of research on attachment (such as Bowlby 1979; Ainsworth 1991; and Main 1991), that relationship themes from childhood are likely to be played out and represented within the current relationship context. The direction of change then is in helping the person to let go of, and indeed to mourn, lost expectations and to accept a fuller, though less certain, reality.

The potential problem or challenge in this relates to the states of mind that the social worker could encounter in their professional relationships with depressed service users. Along with hopelessness and despair, they may meet expressions of derision, contempt, rejection and disgust. They are also likely to experience aspects of the exhausting battle that the depressed person is waging between forces that are loving and life-giving and those that are hateful and death linked.

Social workers may attempt, in various ways, to evade the experience of staying in touch with a depression-prone service user. It is essential for the effectiveness of the work that such defences are spotted by the supervisory pair so that they might be worked with as they arise. As Cooper and Lousada (2005) point out, most expressions of avoidance by social workers are, after all, human and understandable responses. In this instance, a social worker may be asked to bear the apparently unrelenting hostility and grief presented by the depressed service user.

How might a social worker's reluctance to engage with a depressed client be shown? We could perhaps avoid making direct contact with someone we know to have had some disappointing news which might trigger a depressed response. It may be that a social worker, in the context of community mental health work, fails to visit their service user in hospital following another admission. Does one social worker look too quickly to transfer a depressed service user to another member of staff, when it would be better for all if the work that had begun could continue? If there is a risk of suicide or another kind of urgency, such as a manic episode, a social worker may defend against this by minimising the significance of what they hear.

Practitioners and their supervisors are not surprised to discover that we ourselves construct a variety of defences in response to ongoing work with depressed service users. Such defences may be categorised collectively as turning a blind eye to the evidence of depression and risk. This is what John Steiner (1993) refers to as finding a 'psychic retreat' from the pain involved in who and what is in front of us. It is a way of turning off our thinking. Of course, an essential aspect of supervising social work with depressed service users involves attending to the possibility that this defence is holding sway within the wider professional team.

There is a further responsibility implied in all this for the social worker and their supervisor. That is for the social worker to find and retain access to a *meta* model for safe engagement with their depressed service users. Effective, creative social work requires a containing conceptual framework and a work context that ensures the availability of reflective and accountable supervision. It is as a contribution to such a framework and context that this chapter is offered.

Postscript

As I write, the National Institute for Health and Care Excellence (NICE) 2017 guidelines on the treatment and management of depression are just out for consultation. Changes in the recommendations since the 2009 guidance are summarised. NICE guidance is, as the document states, intended for health and social care professionals, for commissioners, and, last on the list, for adults with depression, their families and carers.

The emphasis on cognitive behavioural therapy (CBT) and its derivatives continues from the 2009 NICE guidelines. The approach taken, as before, is prescriptive in tone. Treatments proposed favour those of a behavioural or pharmaceutical kind.

The language and communicating style is perhaps a little more open than in the 2009 iteration. There is explicit mention of the significance of social factors and a nudge towards a systemic approach. There is a shift too in the communicative style towards being somewhat more inclusive of the person with depression.

There is mention of psychodynamic psychotherapy (p.19) to be offered if a person with depression 'would like help for emotional and development difficulties in relationships'. But, this is to be short-term and considered only after the medley of behavioural and pharmaceutical treatments have been tried and have failed or been rejected by the person.

A stated intention for the NICE Guidance (p.1) is that of updating recommendations for the treatment of 'chronic, psychotic and complex depression'. It seems to me that this treatment, however, is narrowly conceived. The possibility that psychoanalytic psychotherapy may work best in the face of severe, long-standing complex depression is not considered. Research based on randomised control trials (see Fonagy *et al.* 2015) demonstrates the success, sustained over time, of psychoanalytic intervention for adults with severe depression. This is as compared with the short-term gains from 'treatments as usual'. It is relevant to note that such promising research is not yet included in the evidence base for this policy document nor is psychoanalytic psychotherapy recommended even as one possible choice of response among many.

Chapter 7

Sustaining Relationships: Working with Strong Feelings

Part III: Love and Positive Feelings

DANIELLE TURNEY

The previous two chapters have considered some of the powerful emotions – anger, aggression, hopelessness and despair – that are frequently encountered in social work relationships. This chapter now moves on to look at emotions that are generally construed more positively – for example, liking, affection, warmth, love – and explore their meaning and place within professional relationships.

The elements of a positive relationship

The importance of the relationship, and the practitioner's capacity to work in and with the relationship to bring about change have been the themes of this book. What service users say they value in the professional relationship has been extensively discussed (Biestek 1957; de Boer and Coady 2007; Howe 2008; Mayer and Timms 1970) and there is some consistency in terms of the characteristics of the person and/or the relationship that are deemed to be important. As others in this volume and elsewhere have pointed out, the literature is clear that an empathic, warm and friendly relationship is highly valued by service users. The qualities of the relationship create the environment within which the work between the service user and social worker takes place. If the service user feels valued, understood and secure in their relationship with the social worker, it is more likely that they will feel able to grapple with the distressing and painful parts of their life.

But the development of a positive relationship is complex and, if not given sufficient attention, risks creating an insecure foundation for the work ahead.

Although the importance of the relationship as a vehicle for change is widely recognised, the evidence as to which factors are most effective, in terms of impact on outcomes, is less clear (Roth and Fonagy 2005). Within the related disciplines of psychology and psychotherapy, studies have explored the helping or 'therapeutic alliance' – defined as 'a partnership in the service of understanding the patient's [sic] difficulties' (Keval 2005, p.41). Variables associated with the practitioner (for example, experience, theoretical and technical competence and personal attributes) have been examined, as well as the factors that the service user brings to the relationship: their motivation, capacity for psychological thought and the degree of service user/intervention match. But deciding which of the different contributory factors is having an effect has not proved easy; furthermore, although both social work and therapy are complex and challenging to practise, they are not the same and so results from one may not apply to the other.

Given that there are no ready answers to this question, it cannot be taken for granted that the relationship will work and contribute to the process of change. Rather, it needs to be subject to rigorous examination and thought. This is most likely to occur when there are obvious difficulties in the relationship – for example, when practitioners feel that service users are angry, non-cooperative or evasive, or service users are finding their social worker difficult to work with. Equally, it may occur if the supervisor suspects that the social worker has become stuck in an unhelpful, possibly even punitive, relationship with a service user. But are relationships that appear to be working well subject to the same scrutiny? This may seem a strange question, but an absence of attention to 'good' working relationships and interactions with 'co-operative' service users may mean that we fail to recognise situations where the positive aspects of the relationship have become almost a hindrance: when they can perhaps be too much of a good thing, which may then distract the worker and distort the work.

The current professional environment may well be one that is content to leave 'good' relationships unexamined. In part, this reflects the demanding, complex nature of many cases which have a significant emotional impact on the practitioner and at times can pose personal risk. In such a context, there may be little energy or thinking space available for reflecting on more apparently straightforward cases. Leaving well alone may also be a survival strategy within the current performance-driven culture, which typically measures quality in terms of outcomes rather than process. Along with the increased emphasis on measurable outputs, there has been a marked growth in the use of information and communication technologies (ICT) to systematise the way information is recorded and managed. The impact of ICT within social work has been much discussed, with many practitioners and academics raising serious concerns both about the apparent prioritising of form-filling over direct face-to-face contact with service users that seems to have followed from the introduction of computer-based recording systems, and about the nature and quality of the data that is recorded.

Without rehearsing the many critiques of the electronic information management systems that have emerged in recent years (e.g. Shaw *et al.* 2009; White *et al.* 2009) it is clear that there have been consequences that were not foreseen and that have, in some ways, distorted rather than supported the professional task (Broadhurst *et al.* 2009; Munro 2011b). Systematising and, as a consequence, over-simplifying information may not properly reflect the complexities and 'messiness' of everyday practice. Parton (1998b, p.23), expressing concern about de-professionalisation of the social work task, argues that 'notions of ambiguity, complexity and uncertainty are the core of social work and should be built upon, not defined out'. And 'good' relationships with service users are just as likely as 'bad' ones to be influenced by the complexities and ambiguities identified by Parton, but perhaps less obviously so.

Understanding and managing complexity: working in and with the 'good' relationship

In this section, I look at some of the dynamics that can occur within good working relationships and consider not only what positive emotions contribute to the helping or therapeutic process but also what may be missed, ignored or not thought about when they are to the fore.

'Being human': negotiating the boundary between intimacy and professional distance

Julia, aged 29, has been qualified for four years; she has been working in a local authority Children's Social Care (CSC) team, since qualifying, now with more complex child protection cases. She has been fortunate to have an excellent team manager who gave her regular and rigorous supervision. However, her manager is now on maternity leave and Julia has experienced a significant change in her supervisory relationship with the locum. Supervision is now much more *ad hoc* and primarily focused on whether Julia's work is compliant with the performance indicators. This is troubling Julia because she is working with a case that is causing her to worry, but she does not know how to discuss it with her supervisor.

Julia has been working with Samantha and her 16-month-old son Jack for six months. Samantha is 28 and was known previously to the department as she was a looked-after child. Samantha had been made the subject of a Care Order at the age of 11 due to severe domestic violence between her parents and her mother's physically abusive behaviour towards her. Samantha had a couple of short-term placements, but eventually settled well in her third foster home with a single female carer, where she lived from the age of 13 to 18, when she moved into independent accommodation. Samantha has a good relationship with her foster mother and they are in frequent contact, her foster mother often helping out with and babysitting for Jack. Samantha did well in school, obtaining both GCSEs and one A-level; before Jack was born she trained as a beauty therapist and worked in a salon in a department store. Jack was a planned baby, and although Samantha and her boyfriend, Steve, do not live together, they had been in a relationship for two years before Jack was born.

During the pregnancy it emerged that Steve had hit Samantha on two occasions, although she did not disclose this to anyone at the time. Following Jack's birth, the violence became more frequent and severe, eventually coming to the notice of the health visitor who made a referral to CSC. To everyone's concern, Samantha has refused to end her relationship with Steve and believes she is able to protect Jack.

Julia gets on very well with Samantha; she likes and admires both her intelligence and resilience, and feels that against the odds she has made something of her life. She also finds her 'a good laugh' and realises that they have a similar sense of humour and they will often chat about TV programmes they both enjoy. Samantha will often comment on Julia's clothes and make-up and offer her beauty tips, which Julia has found herself using and finding helpful. She is also growing fond of Jack who reminds her of her godson – and of her hope of having a baby of her own.

Julia is struggling to make sense of Samantha's attitude towards Steve's violence and her belief that she can protect Jack. She is aware that in other similar cases she has been able to take a 'tough line', but finds it difficult to take such a position consistently with Samantha. At times she wonders about talking to her 'as a friend', but realises this would probably not be appropriate. At the same time, she feels she may be turning a blind eye and making excuses for Samantha's behaviour. Julia's manager has said the situation is untenable, and Julia is dreading the possibility of the department initiating legal proceedings and of being instrumental in separating Samantha and Jack.

In many respects, Julia has been successful in establishing the kind of relationship that clients say they value: one that is based on respect, liking and a degree of mutuality. She and Samantha appear to have a genuinely positive relationship: she likes Samantha and, as far as she can tell, Samantha in turn likes her. This understanding may be based in reality and it is not the purpose of this chapter to dispute such claims or indeed to disregard the value when service user and practitioner like one another. But how do we make sense of this emotional content or experience in the context of the professional encounter that is, after all, the rationale for their involvement with one another?

It is clear that an element of genuine liking may help build and sustain the working relationship. But, for Julia, the apparent ease of her relationship with Samantha is also potentially problematic. She has identified that there are some aspects of Samantha's life that she is concerned about – in particular, her relationship with Steve and the effects of his violence on both Samantha and baby Jack – and she has struggled with how to address these concerns with Samantha directly. She says she has thought about talking to Samantha 'as a friend', but is not comfortable with that idea and seems to feel that it would not be appropriate in this context. Hem and Heggen (2003, p.106) refer to 'our ideal of the "friendly professional" who balances between intimacy and distance' and highlight the real tensions there can be in 'expecting individuals to be both intimate and distanced, "human" and professional'. So what are the features of 'friendship', and why might this framing of their relationship be inappropriate? What does 'becoming a friend' actually mean in relation to the task?

We could draw a number of distinctions between a friendship and a professional relationship, but two emerge as particularly critical in this context. The first relates to mutuality and the second to power. Looking first at mutuality, Beresford, Croft and Adshead (2008) investigated what service users say they want from palliative care social work services. Although an emphasis on the importance of the quality of the relationship between service users and social workers was perhaps not surprising and was in line with other studies, there was another finding that the researchers had not necessarily expected: the way service users highlighted friendship as 'a key positive in their relationship with the social worker' (2008, p.1388). And the features in the relationship that service users in their study identified as characteristic were 'reciprocity' and 'flexible professional relationships' (2008, p.1394; see also McLeod 2008).

Reciprocity referred to a willingness on the part of the worker to share something of herself with the service user, rather than simply presiding over a one-way process of disclosure. In our everyday interactions, perhaps it is this expectation of *sharing* information – about our lives, emotions, problems and pleasures – that distinguishes those we think of as friends from other acquaintances. We all manage the degree and kind of sharing we feel comfortable with within different relationships, but the expectation (or possibility) of reciprocity is an important element of many friendships. The value of making the worker 'human' through this kind of give and take, or swapping of information, should not be discounted. However, there is also the risk of incautious or inappropriate disclosure, which can be inhibiting or confusing for the service user, and can even become abusive or oppressive. One significant feature of the professional relationship is that it is not for the practitioner's benefit. So it is crucial to keep in mind whose needs are being met by disclosure.

Second, the relationship between professional and service user is characterised by a degree of inequality that we would probably not expect in relation to a friend. When all is said and done, both Julia and Samantha know that there is a significant power differential and that this structures their relationship. While she remains in the job, Julia's role as social worker carries with it the power and possibility to intervene in Samantha and Jack's life in a way a friend simply cannot, and it is Julia's responsibility to manage this power imbalance honestly and to 'own' her concerns about Samantha's situation.

Otherwise, there is the possibility that her positivity might be misunderstood by a vulnerable service user such as Samantha, who may say (or think) later in the piece of work – or in court – 'But I thought we were friends.' It is interesting to think back to the example of Aisha and Cathy in the first chapter, where Aisha managed to tread the fine line between, on the one hand, genuine warmth and regard and, on the other, a very real appreciation of the risks in the situation and her grounded assessment of Cathy's vulnerabilities and inability to parent her child safely.

It may be easier to see friendship as an element in professional relationships where the reasons for involvement are generally less contentious – for example, the kinds of situations discussed by Beresford and colleagues in the study of palliative care work referred to earlier. This is not to minimise the challenges of working in end-of-life care or to assume that social work involvement is always wanted or appreciated, but there is no statutory requirement to make use of palliative care services, so there is a sense in which the service user remains in control of the relationship and can opt out if they choose. The element of compulsion, immediate or hypothetical, changes the dynamic and meaning of the relationship: friendship, perhaps critically, requires *choice* about whether or not to be and remain in that relationship, and this may not be an option for people in Samantha and Julia's position.

The ability to establish rapport, to be friend*ly* and to make an emotional connection, is the foundation for effective work but, as this example suggests, the expression or expectation of friendship can get in the way and deflect the practitioner from the professional task. Julia is clearly worried about having to confront Samantha with her concerns as this could lead to action within the child protection system that could change her relationship with Samantha, possibly irreversibly. It feels like a huge risk that, once taken, would cross a line and make it impossible to resume her enjoyable and relatively relaxed interaction with Samantha. The fear of destroying or betraying a good relationship by taking certain kinds of action – in this case, by moving into child protection procedures and raising the possibility of legal intervention – is powerful, and it is easy to see how it would be possible to fall into a collusive response. When the practitioner genuinely feels warmly towards the service user, it may be difficult to raise concerns, and so a pattern develops where he or she contrives (intentionally or unintentionally) to avoid addressing the more negative/difficult/painful aspects of the person or their situation and the work that needs to be done. Alternatively, motivated by a desire to see the best in a difficult situation, the practitioner may attribute more significance to small changes than is warranted and minimise any concerns he or she may have about unresolved difficulties (the so-called 'rule of optimism' identified by Dingwall, Eekelaar and Murray 1983).

Julia seems to be aware of these kinds of possibility, and the discomfort she feels has made her question her motives in not dealing with this situation in the way she would have done with another service user, particularly someone with whom she did not have the same sense of emotional engagement or connection. In the past supervision has offered a real lifeline – a space to stop and think and to explore – but this avenue appears to be closed at present as her current supervisor has different preoccupations. Julia's worries about how to proceed and her fears about the consequences of confronting Samantha are not part of his framework. Attachment theory, as Morrison (2007, p.255) notes, 'would suggest that emotion is information, and that discomforting emotions provide signals of possible danger which require attention and appraisal'. By reflecting on her current discomfort and talking to a close colleague, Julia comes to realise that the unavailability of her regular supervisor (for reasons that she both understands and accepts) has nonetheless left her feeling quite bereft and 'in need of a friend' herself. So the possibility of also 'losing' Samantha has felt quite overwhelming.

With this insight, she is able to reconsider her position and ensure that she gets appropriate support from within her team and help to think through her response to Samantha's situation. It is clear that she has genuine worries about both Samantha's and Jack's safety and needs to address these. Although she is still concerned about the possible disruption to her relationship with Samantha, Julia realises that a lack of honesty on her part would also put the relationship at risk. Genuineness has been identified as one of the 'core conditions' for effective therapeutic engagement (Rogers 1967), and if the worker is unable to share his or her concerns, then they will end up acting in a way that is inauthentic and ultimately unhelpful or even dangerous.

As the example in Chapter 1 shows, it is possible (if not easy) to be honest and challenging where necessary, without sacrificing the relationship. Indeed, if the relationship is well founded and there is a level of trust, then Samantha may be able to accept that Julia's concerns arise from genuine care for her and Jack and are shared with the aim of working with her to find a solution. Having the opportunity to hear and respond to Julia's concerns may allow Samantha to share her own thoughts and feelings about her situation, knowing that she will be listened to thoughtfully and with respect (Turney 2012).

This section has looked at some of the complexities involved in managing a professional relationship based on genuine liking and warmth, focusing particularly on the meaning of friendship and its place in the relationship. The next section takes this discussion a stage further and considers the issues that arise in trying to understand how or whether love can play a part.

Is it in the job description? Love and the professional relationship

It does perhaps feel slightly odd to be mentioning love in the context of professional relationships. It is not, after all, a subject that fits easily into current professional discourse within social work, particularly in its more managerialist manifestations, and it may challenge some of our thinking about the boundaries between the personal and the public domains. This may be a particular issue in residential child care where workers share the 'lifespace' with residents (Smith 2009a). Over a number of years, policy statements on children in the care system from government and elsewhere (e.g. Care Inquiry 2013; Department of Health 1999; Le Grand 2007; National Institute for Health and Care Excellence 2013) have repeatedly emphasised the need for children to be 'securely attached to carers capable of providing safe and effective care for the duration of childhood' (Kendrick and Smith 2002, p.49). But at the same time, Kendrick and Smith (2002, p.50) observe that '[t]here is a danger that, in interpreting "safe-caring", there is a presumption that close adult–child relationships are intrinsically suspect and should be discouraged'. We assume, for example, that adoptive parents will (learn to) love their adopted children, but are ambivalent about the idea of love being part of a professional rather than a private/family relationship.

Other professions have responded differently: love has been discussed within the (psycho)therapeutic literature (e.g. by Klein 1952 and Winnicott 1947), and in connection with relationships of care in nursing (Arman and Rehnsfeldt 2006; Stickley and Freshwater 2002). Through the concept of 'unconditional positive regard', an understanding of the role of love is also found in the 'core conditions' outlined by Rogers (1967) in the context of person-centred counselling. So is there a place for love in social work relationships: are practitioners allowed to love? *Should* they be allowed, even expected, to love the children or adults they work with? And how close can these relationships be? This is an issue that perhaps comes into sharpest focus when we are considering the relationships that exist between children living away from their birth parents (whether in foster or residential care) and those who look after them. We assume that an adoptive parent will love and be loved by their adopted child but are perhaps less clear about the expectations on foster and residential carers and the children they care for, despite guidance from the Department for Education (2012) emphasising the need to 'ensure that children have a secure, stable and loving family to support them through childhood and beyond'. Studies by Biehal (2012) and by Meakings and Selwyn (2016) explore the challenges and complexities of establishing affectionate and loving relationships within foster families. Foster care clearly does not work for all children and young people who are placed away from their birth families; indeed, some will unfortunately go on to experience a level of abuse and maltreatment or simply an inadequate standard of care while within such a placement (Biehal *et al.* 2014). But the literature does also highlight the positive experiences for children who love and are loved by their foster family (see, for example, Biehal 2012).

It could be argued that the intensity and intimacy of family life potentially makes the establishment of loving relationships more broadly 'acceptable' in foster care. But how does the recognised need for children in care to have a secure base translate to the context of relationships between staff and children or young people in residential child care settings? The following view of the care system was offered to me by a colleague, from her own childhood experience.

> Alice, an academic in her forties, described growing up in a family where her parents were both social workers in a care home run by her grandparents. Once placed there, children typically stayed for years, perhaps for the duration of their childhood, and may have had no other significant adult attachment figures in their lives. As the children grew up and moved on, the relationship continued. Alice recalls former residents of the home coming back for significant family events and her grandparents in turn being invited to join their celebrations – with her grandfather being asked to give the bride away on more than one occasion. There was an assumption that the previously looked-after children continued to be part of the extended family, and when her grandfather died, a significant number of the now adult children returned for his funeral.

This example seems to illustrate the notion of 'professional closeness' (Kendrick and Smith 2002) in work with children and to show that love can indeed be part of the everyday practice of care in reparative relationships.

However, approaches to residential care have changed since the experience described above and it may seem like a relic of a bygone age – and perhaps to present an overly rosy view at that. It is clear unfortunately that residential care has not always been the safe haven for vulnerable children it was designed to be. There have been cases where notions of professional closeness have been seriously abused and children's lives have been undermined by exploitative and invasive relationships with adults who were in positions of trust and responsibility. Responding to well-publicised scandals in children's homes, anxieties about the possible misuse of the professional relationship have been expressed in rules and regulations that appear to forbid closeness or physical contact, leaving workers who, in some cases, have become so concerned about accusations of overstepping the mark that they are virtually unable to relate to the children in their care; the notion of love simply cannot be acknowledged, much less acted upon.

Part of the difficulty with any discussion of love is that in English this one word carries a multitude of meanings; we make it express 'an entire range of emotions' (Stickley and Freshwater 2002, p.251) which, in other languages, are more easily separated out (see also Arman and Rehnsfeldt 2006; Smith 2009a). Stickley and Freshwater (2002, p.251) show, for example, that in classical Greek, *eros* or erotic love can be distinguished from *agape*, 'a nonerotic pure love that seeks nothing in return. *Agape* can be aligned with altruistic love in which an individual can care for a complete stranger as if that stranger were family'. In a similar vein, Latin provides the notion of *caritas* from which our concept of 'caring' is derived, and which conveys this same sense of 'giving altruistic love to fellow human beings' (Arman and Rehnsfeldt 2006, p.5). We need to be clear that what writers like Smith (2009a and 2016) and others who contributed to the 2016 Special Issue 'Love in Professional Practice' (*Scottish Journal of Residential Child Care*) are talking about are the kind of affectional bonds that are part of the experience of a secure attachment and are rooted in the experience of *agape* rather than romantic or sexual attraction.

With these ideas in mind, the notion of love looks more possible – even necessary. Indeed, Smith (2009a, p.123) argues that the question should not be 'whether workers can or should love those they work with. In many respects, that question should be turned on its head and reframed as, can they not love them?'[1] The ability to manage boundaries sensitively and in the *child's* interests is critical, but the importance of close and caring relationships which allow children to form secure and lasting attachments has not changed and needs to find a place in our more bureaucratised and risk-averse care systems. Reclaiming the notion of love may start to offer a way forward. It is always going to be difficult working at what Smith refers to as the 'contact boundary', but perhaps a commitment to relationship-based practice involves trying to 'grapple with this complexity and attempt to act ethically within it' (Smith 2009a, p.123). The alternative, a situation where 'care' is reduced to something that is anything but actually caring and nurturing, offers a bleak vision for both practitioners and young people.

---

1   These issues are explored thoughtfully and in some depth in a Special Issue of the *Scottish Journal of Residential Child Care*: Love in Professional Practice (2016) 15, 3.

In the context of 'mainstream' child protection social work, these ideas about love and humane care have been less obviously explored. But perhaps they find expression in discussions about the need to rethink the way child protection systems and processes are understood and delivered (Lonne *et al.* 2015), moving from an authoritarian and often punitive approach to a social model (Featherstone *et al.* 2014) more rooted in an understanding of the 'social-relational nature of the pressures [families] face' (Featherstone *et al.* 2016, p.11).

Misreading the signs: understanding 'false positives'

One of the premises of relationship-based work is that the practitioner is using themselves in the relationship, and the particular person of the practitioner therefore matters. The worker is not a blank sheet but an individual with their own history, opinions, likes, dislikes and experiences of relationships. So skilled practice involves thoughtful use of self and a degree of emotional intelligence (Howe 2008; Morrison 2007). But this emotional intelligence is not infallible, and the worker's own feelings and emotions may have a powerful and, in some cases, distorting impact on the way the relationship is understood and managed in practice.

It is clear that some of the challenging dynamics that can arise in the context of positive relationships – the risk of collusion, avoidance of difficult situations, misattribution of strengths and so on – can also be a feature of less well-founded relationships. Fear, for example, may be a strong motivator not to rock the boat and risk upsetting a volatile or otherwise fragile relationship. However these circumstances may come about, the consequences of a worker failing to recognise and address them can be catastrophic, particularly for a vulnerable child. Therefore, effective use of self requires the capacity to reflect – on one's motivation for doing the work, on why particular service user–worker relationships develop, and what meaning these relationships have for the different participants. So in this last part of the discussion, I look at the notion of 'false positives' and how and why practitioners can find themselves in situations where they do not read the signals correctly or get drawn in to superficially positive relationships which prevent them from intervening effectively.

Many practitioners will have had the experience of making contact with a new service user and being regaled with a list of their predecessor's faults and failings, perhaps followed up with 'but you're not like that' or 'he/she was awful but you're OK'. Of course, the obverse may also occur and the worker can find themselves as the one being categorised in entirely negative terms which seem to bear little relation to their involvement, while a colleague is depicted in glowing, but equally unrealistic, ways. In Chapter 2, Ruch drew attention to the notion of 'splitting', a concept developed by Klein to explain how individuals try to defend themselves against unpleasant and anxiety-provoking aspects of their experience. Klein suggested that, in early development, the infant is not able to contain the powerful conflicting feelings of love and hate for the same person and tries to protect himself or herself from the 'bad' feelings. Splitting is seen as a defensive strategy whereby the 'bad' feelings are got rid of and 'located' elsewhere. This process may result in a polarisation of good and bad feelings. For example, a young child may idealise one parent and act as if that parent contains all the good aspects of the parental relationship, while the other parent is left with all the bad elements. A similar dynamic may occur in later relationships, whereby one worker is denigrated while another is idealised, or when 'bad' aspects of experience cannot be contained within the relationship.

These processes of splitting and idealisation may occur at different levels. Thinking back to the example of Julia and Samantha, it is possible that both worker and service user are trying to make sense of some of these dynamics in different ways. Samantha is not willing to recognise the problems in her relationship with Steve, and it may be that part of Julia's motivation here is to 'rescue' her from this difficult situation. Julia has become, in a sense, the 'good' worker for Samantha, and neither will find it easy to change the terms of the relationship. For Samantha, it may be very difficult to acknowledge the power and potentially coercive nature of Julia's role, so she focuses on the positives – the good relationship, the chat, the make-up tips – and doesn't allow the more threatening aspects of Julia's role to come to the surface.

Part of the latter's task may be to try and help Samantha come to a more balanced understanding of the different dimensions of the role – and that they can (indeed, *have to*) co-exist. But this also requires from Julia an integrated acceptance of the tensions that run through the social work role; it is one that features both care *and* control, support but also power to compel, and these do not always sit easily together.

In order to work effectively with Samantha to address the complexities of her relationship with Steve and to allow her to acknowledge both the good but also the dangerous and damaging elements it contains, Julia perhaps first needs to find a way of reintegrating the different and conflicting elements of her role. She cannot usefully be either 'friend' or 'rescuer' but needs to find a way to regain her professional and personal authority and to work honestly with Samantha, acknowledging both the 'good' and 'bad' aspects of the social work role.

As we have noted, it may be tempting to take a superficially positive response at face value, because finding oneself as the 'good' worker may initially feel flattering. The worker's own need to be needed or to be liked may make it harder to challenge the positive attributions. But taking the time to reflect on and understand these dynamics and remaining respectfully curious about the relationship is critical, to ensure that the meanings of the emotional messages are not lost and to enable the practitioner to hold good/bad feelings and positive/negative aspects of the relationship in a healthy, authentic tension. This is where good reflective supervision can be key, if it provides a safe space for the practitioner and supervisor together to question what is going on, and consider how to work most effectively with and within the relationship.

Lastly, perhaps one of the most problematic examples of misreading a 'good' relationship with a service user is when compliance is wrongly understood as cooperation. Cooperation involves a genuine collaboration between the social worker and service user, a dynamic that characterises their interaction. In the safeguarding context, cooperation has been identified as involving parental acceptance of the professional concerns, an acceptance of responsibility and willingness to address the concerns to bring about change (Platt 2007; Reder and Duncan 1995). Although denial and overt non-cooperation can be difficult to work with, they are at least unequivocal. More challenging are situations where apparent parental cooperation disguises a lack of congruence between the parental and professional perspectives (Platt 2007; Reder and Duncan 1995). Parents can give the appearance of cooperation when in fact they are simply falling into line in order to avoid further professional involvement in their lives and without any real or sustained change in their parenting. In the most extreme cases, some child death inquiries and serious case reviews have revealed how, under the guise of cooperation, parents have deliberately stage-managed the contact with the social worker, while the child has continued to be neglected and/or abused (see, e.g., Haringey Local Safeguarding Children Board 2009; London Borough of Brent 1985; London Borough of Greenwich 1987).

As stated earlier, given that social workers often deal with angry, violent service users and outright hostility, it is understandable that in some situations a more positive connotation is given to the interaction with families than is actually warranted. In his analysis of the Victoria Climbié case, Ferguson (2005) argues that, in order to understand a social worker's response in any given situation, recognition must be given to their 'lived experience' and how this shapes and informs behaviour. Specifically, he argues that 'workers bring their trauma from other experiences with them into all the work they do…[so] we must always look beyond the parameters of the immediate case and try to understand how it was affected by what workers were carrying from all their other experiences'. But this 'looking beyond' and understanding 'what workers were carrying' requires time, support and emotional energy. Not for the first (or last) time in this book, this points to the need for practitioners to have adequate thinking space and to be supported through consistent reflective supervision if they are to engage effectively with the challenging emotional realities of day-to-day practice.

Conclusion

For service user and practitioner, being in a positive, genuine relationship where warmth and affection are possible is perhaps something to aspire to; but, paradoxically, as this chapter has suggested, managing a positive relationship may also be complicated. Warmth, affection and even love may all have a place in constructive and empowering professional relationships, and workers should be encouraged to use these emotions in a thought*ful* rather than a thought*less* way (Yelloly and Henkel 1995) – to be aware of their own emotional responses and to reflect on their meaning. We all like to be liked, and it is tempting to relax into an emotionally reinforcing relationship and to avoid looking too closely at what might prove to be unsettling or disruptive. So the challenge for practitioners (and those who support them) is to be able to hold on to the positives, while at the same time maintaining 'a therapeutic position of safe uncertainty and authoritative doubt'

(Flaskas, Mason and Perlesz 2005, p.xxv) – in short, to remain curious and keep thinking alive.

Acknowledgements
With particular thanks to Karen Tanner for early discussions and case study material.

Chapter 8

Long-Term Complex Relationships

LINNET MCMAHON

Social work practice is often geared towards short-term intervention with the laudable aim of providing the minimum intervention that will help someone manage a difficulty in their life. There is often a less worthy pressure of minimising cost. However, there are some people who need a more sustained form of help. These fall into two main groups. There are those who cannot manage unaided the task of independent living in a complex society because they have a disability, whether physical disability, learning (intellectual) disability, or a long-term mental illness, or because they are experiencing the frailty of ageing and perhaps dementia. Then there are those, both adults and children, who have serious and continuing difficulties in their relationships within or outside their family arising out of previous damaging emotional experiences, often going back to infancy, of particular concern when care of children is inadequate. Of course, there is also overlap between these groups. Similarly, in terms of practice, although there are differences in aspects of practice, there are some common themes arising from the long-term dependency needs of both groups of people.

This chapter looks at some of the challenges involved in long-term complex relationships. Above all, it is about the use of self of the worker who has the task of finding an appropriate stance so that they are sufficiently involved to be a real person in someone's life, while still retaining the capacity to think about the situation, and so provide emotional containment and a helpful response. To do so over the long term can be immensely rewarding but also extremely demanding.

The holding environment provided by the organisation and team (or network) is crucial. A practice example shows how a thinking team can together overcome some of the barriers to effective work.

Knowing someone over time and holding on to knowing

Over time peoples' needs change. For example, someone with Downs syndrome might actively go on developing literacy and independence skills well into adulthood and with support may live reasonably independently, perhaps have employment and a partner. Yet early onset dementia may later mean a need for a more intensive form of care. Appropriate provision depends on a long-term partnership involving the assessing social worker, those directly providing services, the service user and their families and social networks. Over the years there needs to be continuing communication between all concerned, making sure that those who best know the person are consulted, so that there is a rounded picture of the individual over time, ensuring that their potential for development or their deterioration is noticed, and addressed. This may seem obvious but it can present real difficulties as workers come and go, and their knowledge of the person is lost, and even the structure of services may change. It is all too easy to assume that how someone 'is' at a given point of time is how they have always been or will be.

Structures to hold on to the 'knowing' within a team, network or organisation are essential. This involves not only files and records but also systems of communication. One of the most useful is a regular meeting of members of a team or network, not only to plan but also to think together, both about what they know and what they don't know about someone they support. Staying with a feeling of uncertainty, of *not knowing*, can help a team identify less conscious processes and feelings, which in turn may help make sense of complex or 'difficult' behaviour. Once the meaning behind behaviour is understood it is more possible to find an appropriate response. This is a theme to which I will return.

Dependence and independence

There is a continuing tension between meeting needs for dependency and for independence. This is true for every one of us throughout our lives. We know that the infant's growing autonomy arises out of early dependence on a reliable attachment figure. A child with a secure attachment develops an inner working model of the world as trustworthy and of themselves as worthy of that trust and love. This enables the child to explore new experiences and new relationships with confidence, knowing that there is a secure base to return to at times of anxiety or distress. Thus independence grows from initial dependence. These original attachments do not disappear as we get older but are maintained, if at a less intense level, throughout life. We go on to develop new relationships, new attachments. Attachments both old and new sustain us at times of fear and anxiety, stress and distress, loss and grief. Their absence makes life harder to bear and to manage. So we are always moving between dependence and independence.

So it is with people we support. It would be mistaken to view someone as either dependent or independent; both states co-exist and both matter for emotional health. Some workers incline towards meeting dependency needs; they are good at looking after people. Others feel more comfortable attending to independence needs, noticing how they can help someone develop. A classic study of residential care of people with physical disabilities (Miller and Gwynne 1972) contrasts a 'looking after' people model with a 'horticultural' model, but emphasises that good care involves holding both ideas in mind simultaneously. This requires us to be observant and, like the 'good enough' mother with her infant, attuned to someone's mental state so that we can make sense of what they might find helpful at a particular moment, whether it is some comfort and nurture or an encouragement to do something more challenging. Such holding in mind provides the emotional containment that in turn enables someone to hold on to and manage difficult feelings, such as anger and fear, rather than vent them on others or turn inwards in despair.

Dilemmas in listening to the voice of the service user

Listening to the voice of the service user is often interpreted as attending to what people say about how they want to live; it is about their making choices. Certainly people need to be heard and to have what control they can over their lives. Too much social care practice in the past has been about doing things *for* people, within an often routinised domestic culture of care (Menzies-Lyth 1988) without respect for the individuality of people and their preferences, even over basic things such as what time and how to wake up or go to bed. However, there are two risks in an unthinking encouragement of self-directed choice.

One is that it may enable the worker to duck any parental care function. For example, they may allow a learning-disabled adult to eat as much as they want whenever they want, and to spend hours on the sofa in front of the television, with life-shortening obesity as a consequence, quite apart from the insult to the service user's sense of self. A more responsible function might be to provide more structure for daily living, including the management of food and mealtimes (while still taking account of individual preferences and avoiding routine care) and offering some activity that requires physical effort. Above all, there needs to be real attention to building a warm, open and honest relationship within which some encouragement to create a fuller life becomes possible. This is hard work, and made even harder if other members of the support team settle for a quiet life. Similar courage is needed by the unsupported foster carer who makes demands or sets limits with trepidation because the child threatens, 'I'll tell my social worker.'

Another risk is that we might be hearing only the *expressed* choice, while the unconscious voice may be saying something very different. Much communication is non-verbal but always has meaning. It is up to us as workers to unpick this meaning. In the previous example about over-eating, it might be that the service user is feeling 'hollow' and 'empty', 'hungry' for affection, in desperate need of something 'to get their teeth into'. These are metaphors for feelings as much as they are about food. Another example is the traumatised child in yet another foster or residential placement who angrily rejects any kind gesture with 'go away' – or 'I can look after myself.' What the child might also mean is 'I am frightened you won't like me and will send me away again.' One child being put to bed on his first night shouted, 'Don't put the duvet over me.' His worker intuitively understood that he meant, 'Do put it over me' and gently covered him up and stayed until he went to sleep (Ward and McMahon 1998).

The worker's stance – finding a place between 'too close in' and 'too far out'

The difficult work I am describing here makes emotional demands on the worker. It goes beyond providing good basic care to something needing more involvement. It also requires a reliable continuing relationship over a long period of time. It is only possible to provide this within an organisation and team where the nature of the work and the demands it makes on the worker are understood and supported. We shall return to thinking about the organisation. First let us consider the worker. Many of us are drawn to the work of meeting the needs of more dependent people because we have memories and feelings about unmet needs in our own lives. The more aware we are that taking care of other people may also be helping us meet our own needs the less likely we are to fall into the trap of rescue and collusion, of becoming so involved in caring for someone that we lose our sense of perspective and become unable to think, with a rising level of stress, perhaps followed by dismissal for 'losing it' in the heat of the moment. A rescue stance is also ultimately unhelpful to the service user because it affects their sense of being emotionally held by a thoughtful and containing person. The more emotionally damaged person may momentarily revel in the emotional collusion, which is probably a familiar pattern from family experience, but opportunity for growth is lost.

Of course the opposite stance, of too much distance, is equally unhelpful. The worker who keeps an emotional distance has no way of really knowing someone and fails to make the most of any opportunity to engage, with at best loss of opportunities for the supported person's development and at worst (when such care is ongoing), some angry acting out (often by a group), or by depression, despair and dissociation. We need to work at finding a stance between these extreme positions, somewhere more involving and concerned than so-called 'professional' distance which is nothing of the kind. We need to be close enough to be attuned to someone's mental state, recognising their different moods and feelings, and engaged – even preoccupied – in a way that demonstrates that we really care. At the same time, we need to be far enough out to be able to think about what is being communicated, whether by words, body language, actions and so on, and to respond helpfully to difficult feelings, providing an emotional holding that helps someone in turn manage their own feelings.

Opportunity-led work (Ward 2006) through the work of the day is what brings together the meeting of a supported person's needs for both dependence and for autonomy, responsibility and growth. Again this work needs to be managed within a team where workers can together think about what is being communicated, how this can best be responded to, and where boundaries might be needed. Such concern and involvement may on occasion mean that we are prepared to do something, to champion someone who may need provision other than they are receiving. A study of children in the mental health system (Farnfield and Kaszap 1998) showed how much they valued a social worker who would go beyond listening to *acting* on their behalf. Yet without a supportive system for staff, such action puts the worker at some professional risk, of burn-out if not attack from management.

The essential task of the organisation and the team – provision of a holding environment

People's needs cannot be met long term by even the most dedicated workers if they are working in isolation. In an immediate practical sense there is a need for active management if there is to be continuity of care for someone whose needs may vary from day to day. A worker who feels part of a team which meets for mutual support and with a manager who appreciates the contribution of each worker is more likely to feel committed to the task. The worker who feels emotionally contained, thought about and cared for is better able to do the same for the service user. This provision of a holding environment is crucial in managing long-term complex relationships. Individual supervision can provide an essential space for a worker to think and be thought about (Hawkins and Shohet 2006), provided that it is not used by management for making demands. However, there is even more to be gained by also making space for reflecting together as a team. This is not easy to organise, especially in a system based on shifts, but it can be achieved where the organisation understands its value. Well-structured handover meetings are important but no substitute for regular team meetings. There is much experience to draw on in therapeutic child care settings where the use of such meetings is seen as an essential part of the organisation's work (Ward *et al.* 2003, Ward 2006). Here is one example.

A CASE STUDY IN DEVELOPING TEAM THINKING

Fifteen-year-old Luke had spent most of his childhood in an institution for children with autism where he was heavily medicated, then sent home to his mother and stepfather when his behaviour deteriorated. At home he could not sleep at night (his mother worked night shifts), and often refused to eat. He had not left his bedroom for three months. His mother sought help and Luke was referred to a residential therapeutic home for troubled young people. The following is based on the team manager's account.

I read Luke's case history and decided to think about Luke's needs from a psychoanalytic perspective as opposed to the previous medical approach he had experienced; he had been diagnosed with eight different disorders then un-diagnosed later. His parents had separated when he was one, at which point he began to sleep in his mother's bed. He had been rejected by his father, as had his mother, so it seemed they had formed a dependent attachment to each other to fill the gap. When he was three, a new partner moved in and Luke had to sleep on his own again. He was desperate to get his mother back, rejecting any overtures from his stepfather. He began to complain of various illnesses.

When Luke arrived at the children's home he was in a state of acute panic at being separated from his mother. As at home, he was unable to sleep at night or leave the house. One night when I was sleeping in, I heard Luke screaming in terror and found him in the living room wrapped in bed clothes. As I moved to comfort him, he grabbed me and held on like a child, begging me not to leave. He was crying, talking of hallucinogenic visions, and asking me to get him sectioned. I realised that we had to understand why he needed to do this, rather than dismissing such behaviour as manipulative. His agoraphobic behaviour could be linked to his fear of total abandonment by his mother: if he ever went out she might not be there when he returned, and when he went to sleep she might not be there when he awoke.

After Luke's arrival, meetings became more difficult for the team. I noticed that certain members of the group would be ill on meeting days. Some were giving so much and doing all they could to make things better, only for Luke to tell them that they did not know how to look after him; yet they did not want to admit that they were struggling. Others wanted to end the placement as inappropriate. Luke made everyone feel inadequate. Listening to the team it was clear that Luke's presence had made them feel some very unwelcome feelings. I suggested that we were experiencing the same feelings of guilt, impotency and frustration as his mother had been feeling for years, that he was effectively making the team feel the way his parents felt. The split team were acting out the family dynamic of struggling mother and rejecting stepfather. Some of the team found this made sense although others continued their defensive rejection, fearful of not being able to manage Luke.

I knew I had to provide containment for a largely inexperienced team through helping them to express their fears, to make sense of Luke's behaviour, and to come up with working strategies to help them in turn contain Luke. Then they could feel safe and confident when working with him and think more clearly about their task. I decided to facilitate the unconscious work, while another manager addressed more practical issues such as rotas. The first task was to set boundaries and help the team take ownership of the team meeting. The idea of creating our own contract was welcomed and the team discussed how they felt about differences in attendance and time-keeping. Everyone agreed to arriving on time and texting a message to the group if they could not make it. They explored their fear of sharing, and thought about how they could make the space safer by not talking about group issues in sub-groups outside the whole group, or with others. The team appeared confident to work out concerns together.

As a team we thought about Luke's needs and together came up with this plan for looking after him. We decided to help him feel safer by setting firm boundaries – which his mother had never been able to do because he always threatened to commit suicide if he did not get his own way. We structured his day and planned it with him the night before. Before he went to bed we tidied his room (symbolically putting the order back in his life) and let him know where we were sleeping if he needed us in the night.

While sorting his clothes for washing I found a tatty cloth that was chewed at the ends. Knowing what this might be I asked Luke if he wanted me to wash it and he replied no way, that this was his blanket. I said to him the smell is really important. He took it, smiled and sniffed it. After this I noticed Luke would go to his bed with his blanket, which we later found out to be his mother's old nightgown. We understood that this was his 'transitional object' (Winnicott 1971), one he had created to help him manage the anxiety of being separated and becoming a separate person from his mother.

In the morning when he had great difficulty getting out of bed he was brought tea and fresh towels for his shower. He would take over an hour slowly easing out of his sleep and bed – his symbolic womb that smells of his mother. We slowly changed his inverted sleep pattern one hour every night until he was able to get up in the morning. We would always plan a good breakfast and eat together; then he would play the guitar and sing for 15 minutes before school. In the evening after mealtime Luke chose his reward for the day, usually a game or music or a TV programme. This thought-about approach to daily living reduced his anxiety enormously. Luke's diet improved and he started to go outside in small doses, still needing lots of human contact.

The space in team meetings no longer felt flooded with Luke and his needs. The team explored in a light-hearted way their understanding of Luke's projected unconscious feelings (his unbearable feelings about his parents that he got rid of by getting his carers to experience them instead), how they had split and acted out one or other parent – his enmeshed, preoccupied mother or his despairing, abandoning father. Through being able to recognise and hold on to feelings rather than to continue to act them out as Luke did, they were able to shift in perspective and think about Luke in a more professional way than his parents could, and they felt that they were then able to manage him much better. They discussed how working at understanding their own inner feelings had helped this process; they were able to notice which of their feelings arose from their own experience and personal history and which were put into them by Luke.

Luke had formed secure relationships with us, but could still get panicky when staff were leaving at night, needing hugs and warm milk (more symbolic mothering) to help with the transition.

He now talked about his stepfather. He would laugh and say, 'My dad has really bad parenting skills – he would ask me not to swear and does it all the time.' It was as if he was learning not to idealise his stepfather but still love him – he could hold the good and the bad together. I know from feedback from the team that if we hadn't thought together about Luke's projected feelings, about how to make daily living a therapeutic experience, meeting his most infantile needs and helping him build secure attachments with staff, we would not have been able to provide a holding environment which enabled him slowly to move away from total dependency and start to take responsibility for his feelings and actions.

This case study shows how a thinking team, supported by emotionally aware leadership by the team manager (Ward 2014), could together understand how Luke's early experience of closeness with and then abandonment by his mother left him in constant terror of continuing abandonment, in which his only strategy for getting care was to be ill or apparently mentally ill. All this, of course, was happening at an unconscious level. By thinking about the transference, the feelings they experienced in caring for Luke, workers could get some clues as to how he was feeling. These made sense in terms of what they knew of his history.

Creating a space to think – reflecting together on anger, splitting and conflict

Many people who need long-term social work help have a history of emotional deprivation and damage. Those who have had damaged attachments from infancy grow up with an inner working model of the world as one of distrust; they feel unworthy of love and care and do not expect the world to provide it, although they long for it. Their feelings of pain, of anger and fear, shame and envy, are so overwhelming that they are unable to become a container for their own emotions. Instead they get rid of their painful or 'bad' feelings by dumping them (projecting them) onto and into other people who then feel these emotions for them. Such a process of projective splitting is not limited to this group; it is a normal tendency, especially at times of stress, to respond by blaming someone else. It can always be a useful exercise to ask ourselves, 'Whose feelings am I feeling?' (Shohet 1999), trying to sort out those that come from our own personal history (personal counter-transference) from those that belong to the person we are working with (diagnostic counter-transference). When we are experiencing an emotion that we would not normally have in a particular situation it is a useful rule of thumb that this is likely to be a transference.

Members of a team will have a range of different relationships with and feelings about someone they support, and the detail of these can illuminate aspects of behaviour that are not otherwise understood. Often workers will find themselves enacting different aspects of the relationship difficulty, as in those working with Luke. A common experience is that the team will be split between those who feel comfortable working with a particular person and those who feel angry and fed up, 'can't bear them' and want them gone. As a team tries to make sense of this conflict together, they may realise that each is experiencing an unconscious projection of a different aspect of the person, one worker perhaps being the 'good' internalised parent and another the 'bad' one (see Mattinson's 1970 Reflection Process). This makes it possible to build up a fuller picture of the person's inner world which can help in finding productive ways of responding (Obholzer and Roberts 1994). Not least it helps in reducing a worker's sense of an attack being personal. When such a split is not understood, the conflict within the team is not contained, which will have damaging consequences all round. The ultimate aim is that the team's emotional containment should enable the person concerned also to hold on to both 'good' and painful feelings, and so develop a more integrated sense of self, able to think before (re)acting.

There are other versions of supportive structures. In foster care, for example, the caring family can feel overwhelmed and alone with how to survive daily living with an emotionally damaged child. Their phone call to their social worker saying, 'They'll have to go' may mean 'I can't hold on without help.' A fostering agency that locates the foster carers as professional partners within a supportive and coherent professional network (including education and mental health services as well as social work), providing spaces for thinking and making sense, can minimise placement breakdowns (Whitwell 2002). Similarly, network meetings of professionals whose task is to think together about someone (much as concerned parents talk together about their children after they have put them to bed) can achieve something more appropriate than a meeting simply devoted to planning (Hey *et al.* 1995). A space to think together is equally vital for people providing long-term help to a troubled family where the task may be to provide continuing support to help their children through to adulthood and beyond. Thinking together about how the family works as a system (and about how the professional network may unconsciously be drawn into replicating this system) can help in finding more effective ways to work.

Loss, leaving and bereavement

Loss is a familiar experience to anyone on the receiving end of social work. The experience they have in common is loss, actual or potential, of their capacity for autonomy, whether through an aspect of their body or mind that has let them down or through an emotional disturbance often originating in an unsatisfactory primary attachment, which is another absence or loss. A social model of disability rightly rages against society's unhelpful attitudes and provision, producing some social change as well as increasing individuals' sense of self, a positive way of responding to a loss which is nevertheless real. A service user may feel real grief, sometimes expressed as anger, over their physical or mental condition, their loss of independence and capacity for interesting work, their inability to find a partner or to have and raise a child, their hope for the future. These are painful feelings and a worker may too quickly reassure or emphasise the positive when what is needed first is a capacity to hear and bear the pain, and to acknowledge someone's profound grief (Sinason 1992; Sinason and Hollins 2004).

Social care workers come and go, and social workers currently change with great rapidity. A long-term relationship with a worker is rare, but where it exists may be very precious. For many service users in group care settings their main sense of continuity comes from their families (if they are still alive and in touch), from the familiarity of the place where they live, and from one another, as well as from the workers with whom they are in daily contact. There needs to be much thought about changes in any of these, as we go on to explore.

Bereavement

Oswin's (1991) study of bereaved learning disabled people was called poignantly *Am I Allowed to Cry?* Bereavement such as the death of a parent – that is, the loss of a primary attachment figure – is nowadays better understood and a comprehensive literature available. A service user may be helped to attend the funeral and their grief recognised, although we need to keep in mind that grief continues over the much longer term. Because someone 'hasn't said anything' it doesn't mean their sense of loss has gone. Grief may be expressed in behaviour if words cannot be found. A sense of loss recurs with more intensity at seasonal events such as Christmas, especially when others are going home and they are not. Such recurring pain needs acknowledging although a brief recognition may be enough.

Physical needs change as people age, become more dependent, and move towards death. Services are often geared to a limited form of provision which might then lead to a demand for a move, with attendant loss of familiar relationships. An example shows how this can be minimised:

> Ian had lived for over 30 years in a residential setting for people with learning disabilities. As he developed dementia, his social worker was demanding he move to a specialist nursing home while the home manager argued, eventually successfully, that they would provide the additional care needed so that he could stay in a familiar place among people he had known all his adult life. When he eventually died following only a few days in hospital, with his care worker beside him, he was mourned by fellow residents and staff alike. Fellow residents attended his funeral, a formal recognition of his death and absence.

Another example of attention to feelings is a care home for elderly people where there is a special and very public place for flowers, photographs and mementoes of someone who has recently died. This must provide reassurance for the living that they will be remembered after their death, a very different experience from some care homes where dying and death are hidden from view; a body is quietly shuttled out through a back door and a person's death not discussed with residents for fear of 'upsetting' them. This defensive avoidance of loss, continued over time, is damaging to open, trusting relationships between staff and residents in which people feel free to express pain as well as joy. Where workers are able to be open about death they may be surprised by how different the feelings expressed are – some may be missing the absent person, others may be fearful for themselves, someone else may feel relieved (and a bit guilty) that there will be more worker time for them, while another might be envious of the attention the absent person had engendered, and so on.

> To return to the example of Ian's death. Staff had great difficulty in talking to one another about how affected they were. Because he had needed intense care in his last year they had spent much time with him and appropriately become very fond of him. They were caught by surprise by the intensity of their grief and tried to bury such feelings which they perceived as unprofessional. There were no structures within the residential setting for workers to share these feelings with one another, where they could realise that they were experiencing a very natural and appropriate grief, where it could be thought about, and the pain expressed and emotionally contained.

Denying such feelings makes it harder for a worker to risk giving the same quality of care in future; instead they may seek to avoid painful feelings by a more distanced stance. Providing a structure of team meetings where it is acceptable and expected that staff will talk about how they feel, and where they can feel heard and understood, enables workers to feel emotionally held. In turn they become more able to think about how service users are feeling, and help to emotionally contain their difficult feelings (Obholzer and Roberts 1994).

Leaving and moving

Loss occurs when someone leaves their home or household, whether the family home or a care setting. We have seen how an organisation could avoid an unnecessary move by itself adapting to provide the changing care needed, although the eventual loss also needed acknowledgement. A happier situation is when someone is moving to a more independent lifestyle. Even here their sense of loss of familiar surroundings and friends may need as much acknowledgement as their anticipation (and anxiety) at moving on (Marris 1974). Both they and the remaining residents, and staff too, can be helped by some ceremonial goodbye to mark the change and to provide an opportunity to register feelings both of progress and of loss. Together with attention to maintaining some form of contact or link, this can help those moving on feel to that they have a 'secure base', providing the basis for confidence and growth, as well as reassuring those left behind that people do not suddenly vanish but continue to exist elsewhere.

There is a similar need to mark the transition when a foster child or child in residential care is moving on, including where the placement has broken down. In fact it is probably more important to mark such a difficult transition as a way of giving the child a different, and more hopeful, experience of ending from one they are likely to have had previously. The foster carers or workers will have their own grieving to do, even if they are relieved that a particular child has gone. They may need time for their family or community to think about and come to terms with the presence and now the absence of the child, to express both positive and negative feelings. They need space and time to do this if they are to be able to provide a positive and thoughtful welcome for the next child. Again, there is a need for planned structures to enable this shared reflection.

A worker leaving

When a worker leaves, especially a long-standing member, but in fact anyone who has made a real relationship with others, there needs to be the same recognition of bereavement and loss. A worker may find the leaving quite painful and try to avoid it as far as possible by 'making a dash for the exit'. Many are self-denying enough to find it hard to believe that service users will miss them. Indeed, service users in long-term care may be inured to, and emotionally blunted by, a long succession of uncontained leavings, and this in itself needs addressing. People's need for attachment to carers will vary, but dependency does tend to create attachment, especially if other significant attachment figures are absent. The defended worker who argues that avoiding making close relationships lessens the service user's pain when they leave (and implicitly their own too) is denying their humanity and potential for emotional growth. Mattison and Pistrang's (2000) research on people with learning disabilities in residential care revealed the immense pain of separation and loss when someone's key worker leaves and explores how this relationship can most helpfully be ended. Sudden leavings without discussion, for example as in a dismissal, can be particularly damaging, as people wonder where someone has gone or what has happened, often imagining the worst or – like a dependent child – feeling abandoned and perhaps blaming themselves for not being good enough. This may then become too painful to talk about and people retreat further into themselves.

A clear explanation of the leaving is needed, whether or not it has been asked for. Where it is possible the leaving needs to be anticipated and discussed. A ceremonial goodbye occasion can be helpful. This can be painful for both workers and for service users, and needs a setting where tears or anger can be understood and emotionally contained. After the leaving there is the same need for the worker to be remembered, in occasional mention or in photographs, for example. As with any bereavement a significant aspect of loss can be the loss of familiar patterns of daily living. A team which knows about the detail of this pattern can work at maintaining it as far as possible. A succession of staff leaving is highly disruptive to the provision of reliable continuity of care in daily living. A well-supported worker is more likely to stay and to provide the valued long-term relationship which a service user needs.

Use of self

Long-term work makes particular demands on both an individual worker and on an organisation. By its nature it is complex because it is about meeting needs for dependency as well as independence, which necessarily involves close relationships involving bonding and attachment. This is the case whether or not the service user is 'officially' emotionally troubled. All will have experienced some degree of loss of autonomy and their inner worlds will be affected, if in different ways, by this loss. Inevitably there will be other losses through a lifetime. We know that resilience depends both on the quality of early attachments and on the continuing existence of strong, supportive relationships. This is as true of a severely ill or disabled adult as it is of an emotionally damaged family with children at risk. The helpful professional is one who is prepared to be involved, to get in touch with a service user's inner world and the pain they will find there, and to make warm relationships. At the same time they need to find enough distance to keep the capacity to think, rather than to lose themselves in unhelpful rescue or angry rejection. Boundaries are necessary, both to foster the autonomy of the service user as well as to allow the survival of the worker! The use of self is crucial but it can be painful to reflect on our own feelings rather than denying them. It takes mental effort to make sense of troubling or troublesome behaviour, and perhaps even more effort to notice and respond to withdrawal and depression.

As with any long-term relationship, we can easily slide into habitual ways of perceiving and responding to someone, with a consequent lack of thinking and creativity. Boredom can mask our despair that we can ever achieve useful support and change. 'Oh, no, not the Smiths again' may be heard in the office. Familiarity can make it harder to recognise projected feelings of service users' anger and despair, especially if it chimes with our own existential doubts. Long-term social work relationships usually involve finding what can be quite a personal place within the family or client system and it can be quite a struggle to retain the objectivity to reflect on the functioning of the system and see where change has occurred or where there are new possibilities. Recurring pain and loss can wear down our capacity for emotional containment.

We have seen that if a worker is to emotionally 'hold' a service user they need in turn to be 'held' both by their team and their organisation. In any case, providing long-term care usually requires a team of workers and is certainly likely to involve a succession of workers over time. Thus it is essential that the leadership and management of the organisation recognise the importance of providing a holding environment for workers (Ward 2014). This includes structures and spaces for teams and networks to come together (group supervision and consultancy are at least as vital as individual supervision) to think about the feelings aroused by the work, to feel valued and understood by management and one another, and to think about individual service users, sharing and making sense of everyone's collective knowledge both conscious and unconscious, and recording it in ways so that it can be passed on. We need to pay attention to transitions of all kinds,

Chapter 9

Endings Are Different from Outcomes

Working with Endings in Relationship-Based Practice

ROBIN SOLOMON

Introduction

I will begin with an example of the consequences of a common mis-handling of an ending:

> I was meeting with Audrey, a foster carer whose foster daughter Jane had, the previous day, shared with her further disturbing memories of the abuse that had led to her being in care. Audrey was agitated and upset. I encouraged her to phone Jane's social worker and talk it through with her and organise what to do next. She phoned, and the social worker answered; 'I'm not Jane's social worker anymore', she said. 'You will have to speak to her new social worker' and gave the name. 'She's not here now, but will be back this afternoon.'
>
> 'Oh', Audrey replied, sounding calm, 'Thank you. I'll call later.' She put the phone down slowly, turned to me and yelled, 'AND WHEN EXACTLY WAS SHE PLANNING TO TELL ME AND JANE THAT!?' and burst into tears.
>
> The following week, I learned that Jane had refused to meet the new social worker, cursing at her and locking herself in her room. Audrey, meanwhile, described angrily a late-night call by the new social worker to come to yet another meeting, adding, 'And who do they think they are to demand I do this when I already had another appointment at that time; and I have to bring

my younger children to school?', adding this to a mental list of other unreasonable demands and building what felt to me like a growing body of evidence to demonstrate that the whole social services department was useless.

Endings are different from outcomes

Little attention is paid in the current climate of social work to the social worker/client relationship. Instead there is a preoccupation with procedures rather than processes. This book has emphasised throughout how relationship-based practice depends on understanding and using the experience of being in the professional relationship as an integral and essential component of the intervention. While there has always remained in the social work literature at least some nominal concern for how professionals establish relationships with their clients – working in partnership and anti-oppressive practice, for example – less attention has been paid to the significance of the process of finishing, transferring or ending work in whatever form that takes. Whether this is about a case transferring from an assessment to a long-term team, from a commissioner to a provider, or when helping a child in care move from one placement to another, current social work discourse is more likely to be concerned with prescribed 'outcomes' rather than with actual endings.

This fixation on workload and task management has left little space for reflecting on the actual experiences of transferring or ending the work done together, and the impact this transfer or closure has on the clients and on the workers. Rather, what often gets prioritised is an organisational imperative to transfer work quickly to another team, to refer to another agency to reduce caseloads, and to meet targets or shift risk. Over time this tends to devalue the significance of planning for or using the ending of the relationship purposefully.

Current preference for brief interventions has perhaps also helped relocate interest in the dynamics of endings into the domain of longer-term therapeutic work. However, even in short-term work, not reflecting on endings is a lost opportunity. Every session, even if you only have one, also has a beginning, a middle and an end which, if observed and considered, might provide meaningful information about how people have experienced or managed previous issues of loss or separation – information fundamental to a good assessment or planning.

Many of the clients that social workers meet have experienced traumatic separations or abandonment that can contribute significantly to their presenting difficulties or can limit their parenting or other capacities. Initial evidence of attachment profiles or capacity to access help may become apparent even during one session by observing how people engage with a worker or say goodbye at the end of a session. Yet without reflection, this useful diagnostic information can be missed. Social workers have perhaps lost confidence in using these relational clues in their work.

My aim in this chapter is to identify some theoretical ideas that can help explain why termination of a professional relationship can offer a reparative opportunity, ideas that will be significant for social workers hoping to intervene effectively to make meaningful change, and to identify issues to be considered when planning for or working on this area with clients. In contemporary clinical literature, reference to the process of endings is perhaps more likely to be found in the field of psychotherapy than in the social work literature. There is much that can be drawn from that field, however, which will be relevant for social workers in all settings when thinking about how they effectively transfer or end work with clients, and especially when they find themselves in conflict with certain organisational imperatives. My aim is also to identify the skills involved in using the experience of finishing appointments with clients, not only to help in the assessment of the clients' internal worlds, but also by using this to gather evidence about the capacity of a particular client to make or use relationships in a productive way.

Returning to the illustration of Audrey above, it is interesting to notice how the social worker had lost any sense that she might have meant something to Audrey or Jane, or that, as a person, she had any significance. Perhaps she couldn't imagine that she was anything more than an interchangeable faceless administrator. There was no preparation for a proper handover to a new worker, since her unspoken assumption seemed to be that this transition would not have any meaning or elicit any feelings – or perhaps at some level she *did* realise that it would elicit such feelings, but hoped to side-step them by not addressing the topic directly with Audrey. Unfortunately, not only did the ending itself have significance, but also the pain and anger felt by those on the receiving end was greatly increased by the social worker's denial and avoidance of this pain.

This example tells us something about how some social workers have come to defend themselves against the powerful feelings stirred up in their work by acting as if there is no relationship between themselves and clients, just a set of tasks to be achieved and outcomes to be met – in this case a quick transfer to another team. But unless we have a framework to understand these feelings, or a way to reflect on them, they can potentially feel unmanageable and disturbing, leading to further avoidance and denial, and in some cases to burn-out among social workers who find themselves carrying increased amounts of unrecognised and unprocessed stress. Meanwhile for clients such as Jane, left abandoned again, it is easier to be angry and confirm that 'all social workers are rubbish' rather than being able to acknowledge that she is going to miss the person on whom she has come to rely. Already abandoned both by her mother, who had chosen her new partner over Jane, as well as by a previous social worker who had already left, this further loss confirmed Jane's internal feeling that she herself was 'rubbish' and not worth holding on to. For Audrey, with her own earlier more hidden personal grief, and left to manage Jane's hurt and anger, this abandonment quickly hardens into a potential 'grievance position' (Solomon, in press) where she turns to complaining about how badly treated foster carers are, rather than being able to support Jane in her new loss. The least powerful and most vulnerable player is usually the client, and the risk to Jane here was that she would not be able to contain her anger and disappointment and would 'act them out' in such a way as to confirm her feelings of worthlessness, possibly leading to a further placement breakdown, more loss and more pain.

Even if such a breakdown was not triggered, without some way to understand what has happened, Audrey and Jane could easily come to be labelled as difficult to work with, which could in turn exacerbate their angry, unprocessed feelings, rather than their being able to use the ending of this relationship in a developmental way. It is important to consider Audrey and Jane's responses, the impact these will have on new relationships through re-enactments and the potential for displacement of strong feelings. It is also important to think about how the anger, potentially projected on to professionals, or networks, may potentially affect the way they are responded to in turn by others.

What is the place of separation and loss in ordinary development?

In human development, our earliest experiences form internal templates for later relationships. One of the bases for relationship-based social work is the assumption that the internal model of self and other that was formed in earlier life will be manifest in the worker/client relationship (or in the transference); therefore, the template for managing separation (in both clients and workers) can be observed and identified in this relationship itself. In this way, more helpful experiences of transitions and endings can be provided through the way that these professional relationships are handled. If not recognised as such, defensive or unprocessed transitions and endings may risk becoming the site for destructive re-enactments or repetitions, and sometimes lead to further breakdowns and failures; whereas, if understood, they may offer opportunities for significant growth, development and change.

> All human relationships involve a coming together, a being together, and a separation. Each relationship, and life itself, contains these elements and the management of this painful process. The experience of these processes are mediated by the internal and external factors that bring the participants together, keep them together and separate them, and the meaning that is ascribed to these comings and goings. (Lieberman 1979, p.295)

The act of coming together, or beginning a relationship, can be planned or unplanned, welcomed or dreaded, desired or imposed. While the motive will certainly influence the quality of the relationship, it does not dictate its outcome. Unplanned pregnancies, for example, can result in joyous births or regrets in the same way that planned births can result in either happy families or abused children. So too with separations and other major transitions such as divorce, migration or other endings.

The earliest experience of the infant is usually one of total dependency and self-absorption – all about getting its own survival needs met and gratified. In the baby's world, the mother and baby are not differentiated. As the infant grows, however, and begins to realise that it is a separate individual – that there is a 'me' and a 'not me', a self and an 'other' – it is both exhilarating and frightening.

Klein (1940, 1975) described this early stage in especially vivid terms, arguing that for the baby, the mother that meets its needs is the good mother, and the one that doesn't is the bad mother. To the baby, these two aspects of the mother are as if they are separate people, one good and one bad. In order to protect the good one, and defend its own survival, the baby must keep them separate. Klein terms this stage the 'paranoid-schizoid position', which emphasises the extreme emotions said to be involved and the need to compartmentalise such feelings. Soon, however, the baby comes to understand that these good and bad mothers are one and the same person, which in turn allows the baby to experience themselves as separate from the mother. Klein argues that this move to what she terms the 'depressive position' may trigger in the baby feelings of guilt in relation to its previous rage at the mother, and thus also to the need to make reparation. The great majority of young children move through these experiences to a relatively steady state in which they are mostly in the 'depressive' or reality-oriented position, while occasionally lapsing (as we all do!) into more extreme feelings of fear or rage. Where this process is interrupted or seriously distorted however – for example, if the mother has a serious mental health or addiction problem, or is preoccupied with external stressors such as violence or competing demands which interfere with her parenting capacity – the consequences for the child may be serious. It is also worth emphasising here that, while early psychoanalytic thinkers focused almost exclusively on the role of the mother, more contemporary theories look equally at the nurturing role of fathers or other carers and consider functions rather than gender.

A significant part of the process through which the child attains this 'depressive position' is the weaning process. In psychoanalytic literature, the process of weaning (from the breast or bottle) introduces a stage of development that centres on separation of the infant from the mother. It is understood that although this shift is necessary to allow the infant to become more independent and relate to its wider environment and extended network, it can evoke many emotions in both baby and mother as this relationship becomes less exclusive. It is also suggested (very significantly for our purposes in this chapter) that this process lays a foundation for developing internal templates of how separations feel and are managed (Klein 1940; Whyte 2003).

A baby taken from the breast can feel satiated and content or put down too soon and anxious. This is dependent upon the interplay between the internal needs of the baby and the mother's responses. A mother or carer who is attuned to the baby's communications will notice movements, patterns and sounds that give clues to the baby's hunger, when to pause, try again, stop; when they have had enough, need a pause, or need more. A different mother or carer may be more motivated by her own needs, personal satisfaction or feelings; another by external demands such as other children or work needs. This is a continuum, and most parents balance these responses in a 'good enough' way (Winnicott 1953).

Both parties need to make meaning of this interplay. For example, where one mother may feel that a demanding baby provides evidence of her success as a mother, another may feel depleted and may experience the baby's demands as greedy. The issue is not inherently whether the baby is in fact a hungry baby or a baby with colic who cannot be soothed, although this is significant. It is also about how they *both* experience these interactions.

Sleep is another example of the constant rehearsal of separation. Some babies can go easily from being cuddled to being put down; others appear to imagine that this is the end of the world. Sometimes this separation is more difficult for the mother than for the baby, if for example the mother has difficulty in putting the baby down, or 'letting go'. Dilys Daws (1989) suggests that it can be just as difficult for the mother to do without the baby as it is for the baby to do without the mother.

One way in which the baby learns to deal with separation both in terms of brief separation when the mother has to leave the room, and more intensely through sleep patterns and weaning, is through attempts to gain some control over what is happening. We can sometimes see how a baby may try to cope with such emotional stress when we see it clinging on either to a part of its own body, or to an object, as it tries to cope with loss or change, or perhaps tries to avoid 'going to pieces' during a move from one place or state to another. Winnicott (1953) demonstrated how young children often use cuddly blankets or soft toys as 'transitional objects' to help them cope with these experiences of coming and going, holding on and letting go.

Babies – and in many aspects of life, children – have little direct control over the coming together and separating. Thus control becomes one of the key elements of emotional development, or the development of an internal template of relationships. How these earliest separations are understood, managed or defended against is a mixture of the sense the child makes of it, dynamically interplayed with how the adults help or hinder that process via their own understanding and explanations, and the resilience and the quality of the external holding environment – the rest of the family, its extended network and community supports, etc. In ordinary development, the baby starts to learn more about managing comings and goings, gains and losses by learning to take charge of loss and recapture through games such as playing hide and seek and peek-a-boo. This is all about learning to exercise some control over chaos or feelings of anxiety about separations and reunifications.

One can see issues of separation being worked on if one observes young children: as soon as they are developmentally able, they practise leaving and coming back by crawling and later walking away from their carer, and then returning, often to touch the person for reassurance, only to go off again. When this activity assures them of the 'object's' (i.e. the other person's) constancy, they internalise the object, by which I mean they develop a secure belief in the existence and constancy of that person, which in turn permits them to differentiate from and be without that person.

Difficulty with control is often cited in referrals as a factor that brings families into contact with professional services as children are said to be 'beyond parental control'. Foster carers and adopters often cite their children's 'battle for control' or 'extremely controlling behaviours' as a key factor in placement or family breakdown. Yet there is often little thought given to the relationship between such control-related behaviours and how each particular child may have made meaning out of their experiences of early separations.

A further struggle with separation occurs in adolescence. Blos (1962) called adolescence the second stage of individuation because again the young person struggles between separating and not separating, leaving and not leaving. These are normal processes about evolving separateness and practising separation. This is a stage heavily characterised by ambivalence. All of the young person's relationship with the carer (even into adult years) is in some way about this individuation process.

In other words, developmentally, the process involves having enough of our needs met to be able to move from a state of dependency to independence (or interdependence depending on cultural and social norms). This is not to say that dependence is bad; rather, it is about the process of gaining a state of equilibrium, or developing enough capacity to meet our own needs or to know how to get our needs met, to assure or own survival and satisfaction.

Ernst and Maguire (1987) suggest that mothers and daughters go through different separation processes than mothers and sons because of a greater identification of the mother with her daughter; therefore, females are likely to have different separation issues from males. Likewise, it is important to take account of culture when reflecting on these issues, as culture helps define the separation and individuation norms of a particular cultural group. Where some cultures place a heavy emphasis on independence and separateness, other cultures stress interdependence. However, while these patterns are culturally regulated, they are also familiarly or interpersonally transmitted.

In other words, separation and individuation are about having enough of our survival needs met to be able to move from a state of total dependence to being able to meet our needs within a culturally defined inter/independence from our own or shared resources.

Parallels with social worker/client relationships

Just as, in Lieberman's terms, all child development and all relationships are about a coming together, a being together, and a separation, so too can this define social worker/client relationships. Asking for, or getting identified as needing a service, parallels the coming together. It may be this identification of a need for help (from the client or through statutory identification) that awakens early experiences of dependency. The social work activity is the 'being together' of the relationship, bringing its successes and failures, its satisfactions and shortcomings. When the work is achieved, or it needs further or different work elsewhere, then there comes an ending to that relationship, and the need for a separation. Like the tiny baby being put down, or adolescents testing their wings, these separations will inevitably bring questions such as: 'Can I manage on my own?', 'Have I had enough of my needs met for me to function successfully without your help?' These are the questions which may be re-evoked for clients during the ending of work. For those clients who have asked for help, such feelings may be more available for discussion. For those on whom intervention has been imposed, these experiences often exist in their unconscious, as these are often the same people who have not had their early needs met and who have had to use extreme defences very early in their development to manage their feelings of panic when their needs were not met.

Practice of the 1990s informed by the 1989 Children Act, emphasised the importance of partnership and a partnership of equals – a professional and a client coming together to achieve a task. When this works, it works well, and it most often works when the client has an internal template of an available, reliable and concerned 'other' and a secure self; or in attachment terms, a secure or autonomous adult attachment profile (Main and Goldwyn 1998). However, when the hoped-for 'partnership of equals' doesn't work well, for example if such internal models are not intact or available to the person, then the relationship may be much more problematic, and the social work interventions may be unsuccessful. For many clients, the need to ask someone for help evokes the dependency position, and is therefore more likely to activate these early templates.

Social work clients are often those in society who have had the most traumatic earlier experiences with separations. This is compounded by the likelihood that the difficulty that led to the need or desire for social work help was also a traumatic experience of loss or separation. These traumatic experiences of loss could be of either social circumstance such as immigration or bereavement, or less identified losses such as those experienced through the loss of good-enough caretaking or attunement by neglectful or preoccupied parents.

Nowhere is this more evident, poignant or significant than when working with 'looked-after' children. For them, endings have very often been particularly traumatic and unprocessed. Thus it is not surprising that unplanned and crisis-based endings or breakdowns are repeated in their placements – and it is this response to breakdown, premature endings or traumatic separations that should become the focus of the intervention.

Each meeting/session has a beginning and ending too

Just as the entire work with a client or family has a beginning, middle and end, so too does each encounter. As such, one-off meetings can afford us snapshots of endings, although they can't usually be worked with in the same way as if they were more readily available for thought, as might be the case in a recurring pattern in longer-term work. However, through observation and reflection it is usually possible to begin to develop an understanding of the way the person experiences endings by how they manage the end of each session.

Isaac is a nine-year-old 'looked after' child. I saw him weekly at the same time and in the same place. It took six months for him to settle and use our time together, and it was clear from what felt like his constant 'being in my face' interspersed with sprinting out of the door, and his constant state of mindless motion and sound, that he couldn't believe that I would be a person who might be interested in getting to know him, and be available on an ongoing basis.

Isaac had been in and out of care many times. Each time he had settled in a foster home he was then returned to his parents. During those initial six months of our work, there was an extended court case and a great deal of uncertainty and ambivalence in the professionals' minds about what would constitute the best outcome. Expert witnesses, the guardian, the social worker and manager all had different views about parental capacity and ability to change. During one of the periods of rehabilitation, Isaac had disclosed further assault from his parent, although there was no further physical evidence; and yet, despite this, he continued to state that he wanted to go home. Isaac had committed and thoughtful foster carers, who brought him to see me with firm regularity despite his refrain that coming was 'boring'.

Isaac would dart in and out of the room and back to the reception area, sneaking up on his carer, but returning to the room with some coaxing. He would run out of the room, hiding in corridors and doorways. At first I would be worried and anxious that I could not find him, and feel foolish when he would reappear, darting back into the room and locking me out. Weeks later, he would still run into the corridors and hide, but it became more like a game; I was less worried, and he would laugh like a toddler when I would pretend at first not to know where he was and then act surprised when I found him. Sometimes he would jump out and want to know if I was scared.

During the height of the uncertainty about rehabilitation or remaining in foster care, when even our sessions felt to be in jeopardy depending on the outcome of the court case, he would keep asking, 'How much more time?' I would look at the clock on the wall and say how many more minutes. He would then get into an argument with me about one minute more or less – that I was wrong, and that he was the one who really knew when the session would end.

One week very near to the court hearing, when, as I regularly did nearing the end of each session, I reminded him that we had five more minutes left, he took the foam ball we had in the room, and started throwing it surreptitiously but with force at the clock, knocking it off the wall. He got a bit worried that it had broken, but being reassured that it had not, he took the plasticine we played with, and slowly and deliberately covered the face of the clock. He then put it on the table, darted out of the room, and pulled the door closed behind him, leaving me in the room.

What is one to make of this session? Without a framework that allows you to understand issues of endings, Isaac would probably be described as a disruptive and controlling boy. But with reflection there is much more to understand about Isaac from this session. I knew that Isaac was uncertain as to whether he would be staying with the foster carers he had come to trust or returning home, and that he was undoubtedly full of ambivalence. All of the adults whom he was meant to trust were unable to be clear as none of them could be certain of the outcome. Being told by me in our session that we had five more minutes left, Isaac was faced with another ending over which he had no control. I was the one deciding when it would end. The attack on the clock, which visually represented the ending and my control over that ending, was surreptitious so that I could not take it up with certainty and therefore it would not have to be directly known about. However, when he did knock it off the wall, the part of him that wanted to break the clock so that the end of the session would be uncertain became quite worried. Covering the clock in plasticine seemed to me to be a way to make the ending more on his terms as I would not then know what time it actually was so that I couldn't say it was over. He then put my useless control tool on the table and darted out of the room, leaving me before I left him and letting me know, through this experience, what it is like to be left by someone and not to be in control of the ending. This was a very powerful communication but not one that Isaac at that moment could have discussed or verbalised in any way.

In the context of many weeks of him needing to take control of the end of sessions and leave me feeling embarrassed (I couldn't manage a nine-year-old child) and abandoned, I was able to feel more confident that this was what he was meaning to communicate. In addition it mirrored the external world of the court case and his not having any control as to which set of parents he would be leaving or who would be leaving him. Had this been a one-off session, while I would not have felt as confident of my interpretation, I think it would still have offered a useful insight into Isaac's internal template, and into how he desperately tried to manage endings by taking control of the comings and goings. However, this control was an unconscious defensive control – the session still ended, but he felt in control, like the baby who defends himself against the anxiety caused by the absence of a carer by believing they were the one who made the carer go away. This had echoes in what I knew of Isaac's early life of emotional abandonment and it also mirrored his experience of coming into care, with his insistence that it had been his choice, despite the social workers having assessed the parents. Asking me if I felt scared when caught by the surprise of separation and reunion helped me to understand more about his scared anxious feelings.

Quite literally, Isaac had had to dart back into the waiting room on many occasions to ensure that his foster carers had not abandoned him while he was with 'another carer', meaning me. I think he also was giving his foster carer a taste of the experience of disappearance and reappearance in an unexpected or shocking way.

Things to observe

Clues as to how people experience endings are available in every session. If you have set a finishing time at the outset, which both people are aware of, it is important to watch what happens near the time agreed. Running overtime could be a genuine need to complete something urgent but if it is a regular occurrence, it might have a different meaning. Are endings abrupt, or does each person acknowledge preparing for the finish of the session? Has the client continually watched the clock, being the first one to note it is time to end? Nearing the end, or during goodbyes, does the client, hand on doorknob, tell you a tantalising bit of information or a quick story that demands your attention and ensures you remain longer? These ending styles can help us to build a picture of the internal world of the client.

Like the nursing baby of their early experience, do they turn away from the feeder before they have had enough, or want more because they are not yet full? Are they experiencing you as a feeder who will take away something before they are able to use it, or as one who will force-feed you at the wrong pace? If you put them down and they have enjoyed the experience of your help or interest, will you come back? Do they need to protect themselves by dismissing your help as useless? Or do they omnipotently believe that they don't need anyone's help and can manage everything themselves?

Leaving and being left

The ending of a relationship is the time when each party is evaluating its potential and shortcomings: for example, was it a satisfying relationship between worker and client or an unsatisfying one? The emotional work will be about whether the client can manage on their own – have they had enough of their needs met for them to function successfully without the worker's help? Did it feel like an experience where the worker was available or neglectful? Is the end a decision within the control of the client or an experience of being abandoned or dropped? Was there a chance to think about this, as with the toddler returning to the parent, or was there a wrenching of the links between them?

In most separations, someone leaves and someone is left. To leave and to be left are different experiences and reflect different consequences, affects and meanings. The ability to manage and use separations to enhance development rather than to feel further traumatised depends on previous experiences of the successful management of separations. In all separations other than death, both parties are potentially available for contact. However, the experience can be traumatic when the one who leaves simply abandons the other (Lieberman 1979), and the painful experience for some clients will be that even the most carefully planned and 'managed' ending may feel like yet another betrayal of hope and trust.

One way of trying to cope with the pain of feeling abandoned is to 'get your retaliation in first' by rejecting the person who is abandoning you before it actually happens; another way is to disrupt or distort the ending, or even to try to destroy the value of what the relationship has actually offered.

Denise was a foster carer in a support group that ran for a year. A woman with a history of traumatic separation in her own life, she had found the group a place where she was listened to, and where the difficulties of fostering were appreciated. She had a two-year-old girl placed with her whom she was struggling to manage. This child had been placed with her in an emergency when the foster carers she had been living with had gone abroad for a family bereavement and couldn't take her with them. These carers, the group was told, had been like grandparents to this child ever since her mother had gone to prison and thus left her abruptly when she was six months old. After eight weeks Denise had told the social worker that she could no longer look after the girl, but the social worker had said that Denise must keep her until they could find a suitable respite carer or until the other carers returned from holidays. Unrecognised, the two-year-old girl was now manifesting her distress at another sudden abandonment through difficulties in sleeping, over-eating and misbehaving.

Throughout the last two months of the group, the participants talked about ending, reflecting on a range of feelings about the experience. In the penultimate week, one carer talked about how she would have liked the group to carry on but knew she would take the group with her in her mind. Another carer said that she was ready to finish the group. It had been hard to commit herself to coming every week and while she had enjoyed it, she was looking forward to having her Thursday mornings back. At this point, Denise put her fingers in her ears and said loudly and firmly, 'I'm not listening, I'm not listening – it's not ending.' The rest of the group laughed.

In the final week, we had organised a special lunch to mark the last group. Denise arrived, with her foster daughter, saying that she had had enough, and that the child was hyperactive and greedy and stubborn. She said that after she left the group she was going to bring her to the social services office since they hadn't listened to her and found the child another placement. The group was now taken over by the crisis of the abandoned child and of Denise's distress – and the final session, which was meant to be a celebration of the group's life and learning, became denigrated by Denise as a failure as she brought up all her old grievances of the past towards an unsupportive social services department and the uselessness of anything that I or the group had been able to offer. Denise was abandoning the child in much the same way as she was feeling abandoned by the group.

Perhaps with hindsight, the group might have taken more seriously Denise's statements and gestures in the previous session, although the final session may still have been too hard for her to handle. Sometimes we don't know the extent of people's pain until they take desperate measures to demonstrate it to us.

Finding completion and letting go

The issues of ending are different depending on the stage of the work at time of separation. If the work has been completed and there has been a planned and agreed-upon ending there is the most likelihood that both parties will feel a sense of satisfaction. For the worker there will be a sense of having been effective, and the knowledge that the person can manage or can use their capacities to get further help if necessary, thus allowing each of them to let go. This is much like the parent waving goodbye at the school gate knowing that the child will not only manage but will develop through that separation, despite any sadness, while also feeling some relief that they too can get on with other adult things.

It may seem paradoxical that successful intervention leads to separation from the very relationship that nurtured the progress. Yet, as we well know, when children and adolescents move from one developmental phase to another, they must forego certain aspects of dependency to achieve greater growth and autonomy. In direct work, too, where a feeling of dependency, among many other feelings, is often present, the attainment of mutually agreed-upon goals is often, and sometimes painfully, 'rewarded' by loss. For many clients, the loss is profound because the working relationship has provided an unusual opportunity to be accepted, listened to, and encouraged to grow.

However, despite organisational imperatives to close cases, there is a yawning gap between those that are closed and those where the work is complete, particularly if we consider emotional insight and development a core aspect of that work. In these cases it often seems, despite protests to the contrary and adamance about wanting it to end, that it may feel to the client that their needs have once again not been met, which can reactivate feelings of being abandoned and left vulnerable.

This was illustrated in the example of Isaac, for whom, despite his continued 'Yeah, the session is over' or 'Hurray, we are going to finish', or 'Good – I won't see you during the holiday', the experience of not having control of being dropped from the mind of a neglectful mother, and therefore being abandoned, evoked a need to wipe away or deny any feelings of disappointment, worry or sadness. He became triumphant over the separation – in other words, telling me 'I don't need you', or 'It's my choice to be separate,' or 'I'm glad you are not there', etc. Meanwhile the need to be the one in control – the argument over the time when we finished, and the leaving the room first and keeping me locked inside – were valiant attempts to master the endings in the repetitive way which was his only means to survive such separations from a helpful adult mind.

Likewise, Denise, the foster mother in the group, became so concrete as to close her ears to the possibility of a separation, and both denied the ending as well as presenting a new situation that attempted to keep hold of the group.

Social workers have issues with endings too

Whenever I teach about endings, I always ask the group: 'Are you the one that leaves the party early or helps to clean up?' 'Are you a "waver" or a "don't look backer"?' Professionals are not immune to feelings about endings. This is not about pathology; it is about how we have all negotiated our own separation experiences in the ordinary course of our own developmental experiences. Workers, like their clients, have internal working templates of self and other, and with this comes a template of what it feels like to be together or separate from another, to leave or be left. Like our clients, we have developed defences that enable us to manage these separations. Professionalism is not about not having these feelings and defences, rather it is about being aware of them so that we do not impose them on clients, or get caught up in unconsciously re-enacting them.

The aim of ending is to review what you have been through together and what has been achieved or not achieved. It is importantly about helping the client to 'own' their own achievements. Otherwise, even a client who liked their worker and felt they were the first person to really help and understand them, might feel that any achievement was down to the worker and that when they leave, all the good work will leave as well and they will be left in the same state they were in before. This is why it is so important for the social worker to enable people to work out their own evaluation of the experience, but then also to be able to 'let go' and allow clients to make their own way into the next stage in their lives. A further aim is to deal with the feelings surrounding this separation, not just to disappear. As we saw right at the start of this chapter, many people avoid these feelings by avoiding an ending, either because they are afraid to express them or because they are unsure about how they will be received by the other person.

Conclusion

It is now the end of this chapter. As with all endings, there is the anxiety about what has been said or left unsaid, such as regret about what there was not enough space to explore, but also satisfaction about what was made available. I have aimed to draw a connection between the ways in which we all learn to handle our feelings about separations and endings and the ways in which we then need to think about endings and transition in our work with clients. We can either repeat, re-enact and reinforce earlier unsuccessful or traumatic experiences of endings, or try to use our professional relationships, brief or extended, wherever possible, in a developmental way. By observing and making meaning out of separations in the work (such as the ends of sessions, holiday breaks, missed appointments and transferring or finishing an intervention), and noticing the unconscious defences employed against the feelings elicited by those breaks or endings, we can help to establish alternative and more productive models for handling the inevitable future separations and losses our clients will experience.

SUSTAINING, SUPPORTING AND DEVELOPING RELATIONSHIP-BASED PRACTICE IN A REFLECTIVE CONTEXT

• Chapter 10 •

The Learning Relationship
Learning and Development for Relationship-Based Practice

ADRIAN WARD

Introduction

The thematic chapters of this book have all indicated the ways in which 'doing' relationship-based work makes demands upon the social worker, in terms of personal qualities such as self-awareness, resilience and resourcefulness as well as in terms of the necessary conceptual and reflective abilities. In this third section of the book we will be exploring how people may be helped to develop these qualities and skills, as well as looking at what sustains, nurtures and promotes this approach to practice, both at the individual level and at the team/organisational level.

In this chapter we look at education and training for relationship-based practice: what forms of educational process and content can be provided which will enable people to learn how to work in this way, and what does this demand in turn from the educators? The chapter will focus mostly on such learning during qualifying training, although all the material is adaptable to other settings, and there is also a section on the use of 'work discussion groups' as a means of promoting ongoing learning within the workplace.

The matching principle

The first point to be made is that education for working in and with relationships is never going to be a simple matter of learning facts and acquiring mechanical competences. If the educational experience is to

185

match up to the complex demands of the kinds of practice described in earlier chapters, it will mean moving well beyond what might be called the 'instructional' mode of education into something more attuned to developing an understanding of emotional process.

My starting point will therefore be what I have called elsewhere the 'matching principle' (Ward 1998): the proposal that in all forms of professional education the model of training should 'match' or reflect the mode of practice. More precisely, that we should aim for the 'felt experience' of the learning situation to correspond in certain key ways with core elements of the professional practice in question. I have argued this in relation to learning about practice in therapeutic child care, describing and analysing a post-qualifying course which was designed to match key aspects of therapeutic community practice including the use of 'opening and closing meetings' at the start and end of the day, an experiential learning group, and deliberately informal staff–student relationships with attention paid to the 'in between times' when significant communication might take place just as much as within formal classes. Here I shall be making a similar case in relation to training for relationship-based social work, whether this is training at qualifying, post-qualifying or other levels.

The aim of the matching principle is to explore and expand upon the intuitive view that there should be close correspondence between practice and learning modes (for example, that groupwork learning should happen primarily within groups), and it is worth reflecting on why this should be. One important reason is that this model is likely to promote the emergence within the learning context of some of the less conscious but nevertheless essential dynamics of the relevant field of practice such as the ways in which helper/helped relationships may be experienced on both sides, and the ways in which associated anxieties may arise and may be managed. In particular it may allow for 'parallel process' or what Janet Mattinson called the 'reflection process in supervision' (1970) to emerge, which will make available for learning a much richer and deeper range of experience, well beyond the formal written and conceptual material which is the basis of the more traditional view of the curriculum. The matching principle, then, emphasises process equally with content in learning – partly because it is process itself that needs to be learned. This may also allow for other aspects of practice to be experienced and learned from, and in particular the dynamics of personal, hierarchical and organisational power, such as what it feels like to experience either powerfulness or powerlessness in relationship to others.

Although the matching principle probably operates intuitively in many professional education contexts, the argument here is that in order to reap its full benefit, we should pay explicit attention to the factors that may support it, including course design and especially the nature and quality of teacher/learner relationships, as well as some of the less tangible or formal elements in education. The principle also requires us to reflect closely on the process elements of the form of professional practice in question, in order to consider how these might be matched within the learning context. By 'process' here I mean the unfolding patterns of behaviour and feeling, both conscious and unconscious, which typically develop during any form of human interaction and experience – and in this case in a particular form of social work practice – and the meaning which can be derived from reflecting upon these patterns. Process and content often interact in ways which, if closely attended to, can contribute powerfully to the development of understanding.

If we are going to apply this principle to learning for relationship-based practice, we therefore need to clarify those key elements of this form of practice which we might wish to match in the learning context. From the work described in the earlier chapters I would suggest the following as core:

- placing a premium on working with the lived experience and development over time of the helping relationship

- attending to the emotional as well as the cognitive elements in practice

- maximising the opportunities for helpful communication

- the need for reflection at a deep level

- focusing on the self of the worker

- an emphasis on personal qualities and values.

The aim in designing and operating a learning programme would then be to match these elements by consciously aiming to use them to inform the work of the programme. This will mean, for example, being open to working with process in the learning context, and attending closely to the quality of the learning relationship between staff and students, including the emotional components of this relationship. Working in this way may feel just as difficult and unconventional within the university setting as it can do in contemporary social work practice, because the working culture in each setting often places a much higher premium on attending to pragmatics, targets and achievement rather than to less tangible elements such as the mood of a group and the ways in which this may reflect external pressure on students or the emotional content of the work in hand.

In order to work in this way, then, it is not just that the work with students needs to match aspects of their work with their service users, but also that the commitment to close, supportive and relationship-based teamwork will need to be nurtured in the teaching team in order to be congruent with the proposed model of practice. Without such matching it would be almost impossible to genuinely offer the sort of modelling of good practice which is required: students soon know when their teaching staff are preoccupied with other issues, or in poor or conflictual communication with each other, just as service users know when professional systems are in similar disarray. The risk, of course, is that where there is *in*congruence the learning will be undermined, because students will feel they are being told, 'Do what I say, not what I do.'

Working with the emotions

So what do people need to learn *about* if they are to undertake relationship-based practice? I want to make it clear, first, that I am not suggesting that we can 'wind them up and watch them go' – in other words, that we can simply provide a one-off training (however substantial this may be) which will then enable people to work away without further support or nourishment. Indeed, an essential part of what needs to be learned is about the value of ongoing support and supervision – not only about the theoretical value of supervision, but about how to seek it out and create opportunities for it, and especially how to use it and contribute to it. And if that is what needs to be learned, it is also what needs to be provided and experienced as a central element of the teaching. A programme of learning for relationship-based practice therefore needs to pay special attention to the ways in which students will be supported and supervised in their learning.

There is, as we have seen throughout this book, a considerable cost in working explicitly with the relationship dynamic in social work practice: the potential cost is to the individual worker's self and morale. Engaging repeatedly and intensively with people whose lives are in turmoil or uncertainty and whose personal feelings may be full of pain and distress, anger and confusion, will inevitably take its toll on the worker. Unless the worker knows how to handle emotions such as these, the emotions will build up and take a cumulative toll, leading potentially to stress and other reactions (as we saw in Chapter 6, for example).

So how can people learn about handling these intense emotions? The first aim will be to provide opportunities for them to recognise the stress which they are *already* experiencing in their work, and to reflect upon this: how they experience it, and how they interpret what happens to them and within them. In order to provide such opportunities we need to create a learning environment in which people will feel safe to discuss their work in enough depth that they can reveal their anxieties and fears as well as simply describing the challenges and telling the story. For an example of a structured way of doing so, see the 'Seminar Method' section below.

What is needed is an environment of mutual trust and respect in which all members of a learning group will feel able to contribute on an equal footing. This may be easier said than done: it is not unknown within the learning environment for there to be all sorts of anxieties that may inhibit the development of such trust, such as mutual suspicion or even distrust between group members, personal reserve about self-disclosure, and anxiety about being judged and evaluated by teaching staff or by peers in the learning group. People may also bring with them half-remembered feelings about previous educational experiences which may have been unsatisfactory or unresolved – especially, perhaps, in relation to the management of personal feelings within the academic context, since what is personal or emotional has often been undervalued or even explicitly ruled out in traditional academic learning.

Additionally, in the professional education field, it is common for anxieties which originate in the external workplace to be imported into the classroom – and not always consciously. For example, if learners are experiencing anxiety about being made to feel somehow unworthy, stupid or awkward in their own workplace, or if they are having to operate within a hostile or critical environment in their teams, they are likely to bring with them unspoken assumptions that the same will occur within the learning environment, and they may even unconsciously create a self-fulfilling prophecy that leads to the same patterns developing within the classroom. So long as such phenomena are understood and worked with, it is not necessarily unhelpful for them to emerge within the classroom (indeed they may constitute a vital area in which people need to learn if they are to thrive as a relationship-based practitioner), although if they are not handled well they may disrupt or inhibit everybody's learning.

If these phenomena are to be successfully worked with and learned from, then we need to provide not only a safe place to which they can be brought and explored, but also a set of ideas and processes through which this exploration can be made sufficiently transparent that it can be learned from and internalised. As we have seen, the concepts which relationship-based practice draws upon include psychodynamic and systemic ideas and the use of attachment theory, so it will probably be these ideas that can best inform the learning process.

Among the methods which it may be possible to use to enhance the capacity for relationship-based work will be group and individual exercises focusing on self-knowledge. For example, it may be helpful to begin with an exploration of the 'overlapping circles' model of the self described in Chapter 3, encouraging students to locate the personal, professional and political (or other) aspects of self and to learn about the boundaries between these and thus to develop ideas about how to manage these aspects of self (see Figure 3.1). Second, the Johari Window (see Figure 3.2) offers rich possibilities for learning about those aspects of self which are either 'blind' or 'secret', as well as about those unknown and unconscious aspects which may yet hold considerable power. The aim of using such exercises will often be to trigger discussion and to promote the growth of self-awareness and especially, within the group of learners, to encourage a growing ability to make sense of the aspects of self that arise in practice, often through dialogue.

There is also a value in the use of personal development exercises, in which students are actively encouraged to reflect on their own life experiences in some detail. This can involve the use of the exercises which some workers use in practice with service users, such as 'life-lines' and genograms, as well as developments of these such as the cultural genogram: a number of relevant methods are outlined by Parker and Bradley (2007). While it is not uncomplicated to use such material within the classroom setting, raising issues of personal privacy and confidentiality, nevertheless within a facilitative learning environment they can be of great value. Indeed it can be argued that it would be inappropriate and even unethical for workers to use such approaches with their clients if they have not already experienced their use on themselves, to realise the impact for anyone of apparently simple questions such as 'What was your earliest experience of personal loss?' One of the anxieties which there may be about the use of such material in the classroom is that people may feel distressed by some of their memories. The answer to this point may be that we are all bound to encounter such powerful experiences in the lives of our clients, and some of these are very likely to have personal resonance for us, so it is better to have encountered such feelings in advance and to have the opportunity to rehearse our own ways of managing our own experience.

Some of this sort of work can be done within the group, while some aspects, especially if combined with the use of a reflective journal, can be continued individually in the student's own time. Indeed, for some people, this sort of learning soon evolves into a long-term process independently of any particular programme of learning. On the other hand, it must be acknowledged that for some people, this whole area of learning may be experienced as very challenging and even threatening, and here the task of the educator will be to work hard at promoting the culture of 'gentle teaching' (Brandon 1998) and gradual learning, working with rather than against people's defences. For further discussion of such work, see Ward (2008).

What is most important about this sort of learning, therefore, is that it is a process – a living, developing relational process in which there is continuous interaction between experience and the thinking and feeling work which transforms that experience into learning. Because it is an organic process, it does not necessarily always follow the programmes and schedules which we create, and indeed it may emerge in unexpected places and times. This may mean taking an 'Opportunity Led' approach (Ward 2006) to teaching and learning, in which we remain vigilant to those informal or unexpected opportunities to teach or model which may arise before or after classes, or which may offer learning on a theme which may not have been part of the planned content of a particular session (Collie 2008). The best learning sometimes arises not so much from instructional teaching, but rather as if there are travellers (some more experienced, others less so) who will hopefully discover or rediscover territory and make realisations, sometimes together and sometimes individually – not always about the same things, and not necessarily about what was intended or planned for.

In other words, the best learning about relational work will arise within a learning relationship. This requires something special from the educator – a willingness to be open about their ignorance as well as their knowledge, and about their difficulties as well as their strengths; a willingness to take risks and live with uncertainty within the learning and teaching relationship but nevertheless the ability to stay within role as an educator and not to break boundaries by pretending to be a friend or an equal. Just as in practice relationship-based work means managing a professional relationship, so does relationship-based teaching.

Using meetings to promote here-and-now learning

Students on professional training programmes bring with them many aspects of themselves including their personal history and concerns, their current and recent work experience and their hopes and anxieties about their future development. Such matters are of central importance to most learners, although they are not always given sufficient attention in the programme of learning – partly, perhaps, because educators may be worried about being taken off-task if they pay too much attention to the personal. However, it can equally be argued that one of the central tasks of professional education is to facilitate learning in such areas and to enable students to bring, share and learn from these concerns, which are often concerns about the boundaries between those aspects of self which we considered in Chapter 3.

One way of promoting this learning about the overlaps between the personal and the professional is to provide regular opportunities for students to reflect on how these issues are affecting them in the here and now. For example, on a course where students may spend one day per week in college and the rest of their week in practice, it may be most helpful, rather than plunging straight into the teaching, to provide some form of regular 'Opening Meeting'. Here students can reflect together on the transition which they have to make each week from the practice to the educational domain, so that they can work together at sorting out what can be metaphorically left at the door and what they can usefully bring in to the day's learning.

LEARNING ABOUT YOURSELF FROM SHARING IN A GROUP

Celia was experiencing stress on her social work placement in a refuge for abused women because she felt she was being undervalued and sometimes ignored both by her practice assessor and by the manager of the unit. This experience revived memories of a difficult phase in her own childhood, and she became not only anxious and quite depressed, even to the point of wanting to quit the course, but meanwhile she was also increasingly unsure as to whether she was taking it too personally.

She brought these feelings to an Opening Meeting at the start of the college day and was able to reflect with her fellow students and tutor on what was happening on the placement, and to begin sorting out what her personal reactions were telling her. In this case it emerged that another student had had very similar experiences in this placement and that, whatever her own history, there were also real issues in the dynamics of power and control in the management style at the placement. In the discussion group, Celia suddenly looked up and said, 'So it's not just me!' and from then on she felt able to go back into the placement feeling stronger and clearer, and to work with her personal tutor and practice educator to re-examine and improve the supervisory relationship.

What helped Celia in this case was the opportunity to reflect in a safe setting with others who were able to listen and offer constructive feedback. She was also able to learn the benefit of reflecting in a team setting on her own and others' experiences. This sort of meeting can therefore provide opportunities for learning at many levels, not only about the content of whatever themes may arise in any particular meeting, but also about the process of collaborative learning and practice. The format and structure of such a meeting can obviously be adapted for different circumstances, and sometimes just a few minutes for a brief opening 'round' can be sufficient.

Writing to promote reflection and insight

The capacity for connecting thinking with feeling which we have been discussing in this book does not usually arrive by chance, it needs to be worked at, and the skill needs nurturing and the space to grow. It might be said to be best developed within an oral culture rather than only a written culture, because it probably cannot be derived so much from reading books as from interaction, and from interpersonal experience that both challenges and supports. As we have seen, what is important in the use of self is to always in keep in mind the self *in relation to others*. The skill of the teacher in such learning lies not so much in the preparation of beautiful logical programmes, but in designing an overall approach to the task and then in providing the opportunities in which people can engage not just with the material but also with each other, and enter upon the processes in as whole-hearted a way as possible.

This is not, of course, to underestimate the value of reading and writing, but to ensure that the writing should support the learning rather than *vice versa*. One of the ways in which writing can support learning for relationship-based practice is in the use of reflective journals.

In this context I recommend the use of an intensive personal journal in which students are encouraged to feel free to write for their own benefit, rather than for an external audience. We all do quite enough of the sort of writing which has to meet others' expectations or to explain or justify ourselves in other people's eyes. If we are to develop and mature as relationship-based professionals, though, we also need to be able to explain ourselves *to ourselves*, and one way to find a path through this challenging (and unending) learning is to work at it in writing. What I am advocating is the somewhat paradoxical idea that students should be required to keep a personal reflective journal but *not* to show it to their educators or peers. By all means the educator can ask for a report back on the experience of keeping the journal, and even perhaps for an edited sample of some of the issues addressed, either of which leaves the control in the individual's hands. But the injunction not to display everything is a means of handing back to the learner the right to their personal affective reality, which must remain for them themselves to explore and puzzle out.

It is an open and largely untested question as to whether such reflective writing will *necessarily* lead to deeper reflective practice, and

I do not want to claim a causal connection. However, I would suggest that if a student can learn to make real and authentic use of a personal reflective journal, preferably on a daily basis, to record and reflect upon their thoughts and feelings in the process of their learning, they will also be likely to learn how to translate this capacity into their live practice. What the journal habit should foster within them is the discipline of valuing the detail and depth of experience and the levels of meaning and connectedness which, upon reflection, can often be traced between apparently disparate or confusing experiences. They are also likely to learn the value of returning to thoughts and feelings, reconsidering them and exploring unsuspected connections between them. This is what the metaphor concealed within the term 'reflection' actually implies: bending or turning back upon oneself and one's experience.

Another form of writing for relationship-based learning involves encouraging students to explore direct connections between theoretical learning and their own experience, to enhance the capacity for the *use* of self by expanding their *awareness* of the self. For example, in a module on Human Growth and Development, students were asked to select a life stage that interested them and to write about it from both a theoretical and a personal perspective, writing explicitly about their own (or a close relative's) experience of this life stage. Thus they were not only testing out the theory to see whether and how it applied in their own situation, but also testing their own experience against others' lives and views, and being ready to re-examine the personal narratives of their lives. The effect of this process was to encourage students to temporarily de-centre from their own experience and to attempt to view it from the outside as well as the inside, so that when they returned to viewing it from within, they might have a fuller and deeper view.

The assignments produced out of this process would often cover a wide range of personal experiences and connections with theory. One student, for example, wrote about growing up within a far-right and racist family; others about the experience of cultural difference within an African family in an impoverished inner-city borough and the impact of racism at all levels of their lives. Another wrote about the apparent contrast between the assumptions of a period of dormancy in sexual development during the so-called 'latency' period and her own experience of intense awareness of gender and sexuality issues during this stage of her childhood. What was evident in most cases was the benefit to the learner of being explicitly asked to apply the theory to their own experience. They learned not only about how other people grow and develop but also about how they themselves may be able to empathise with service users over their struggles and challenges. In such assignments it is clearly important that students' personal material is treated with great respect and confidentiality, and that they are assessed not according to the nature of the experience described but according to the student's ability to explore the connections between the theory and the lived experience of human growth and development.

Modelling

A further element in which the matching principle may operate is in the modelling effect, through which learners may seek, either consciously or unconsciously, to model themselves on the practice or personal/professional 'style' of the educators. This is not a straightforward area to think about, because it seems to imply that educators should put themselves in a position of professional or even moral superiority, as if on a pedestal to be watched and learned from, which would not be appropriate at all. Perhaps it is more appropriate simply to acknowledge that there may often be an element of modelling whether or not this is intended, and therefore that educators do need to consider whether they are able to practise what they preach, and to what extent they themselves can be consistent and congruous.

To take a straightforward example, if I emphasise in my teaching the values of punctuality and responsiveness I am unlikely to evoke much respect if I am often late for teaching sessions and slow or unreliable in my dealings with students. From the other perspective, as a learner I have more than once experienced being taught about empowerment by people whose style and whole approach is itself overpowering – too insistent on the rightness of their own views and the inadmissibility of any other view. In circumstances like these, it is likely that the 'medium' will be experienced as the real 'message' – and that people will learn, for example, that punctuality doesn't really matter (and that respect for others is not really important), or that the only way to persuade people is to overpower them. In each case, however, there would also be a deeper subliminal message, to the effect that integrity and congruence are not important, and that the personal element in practice (learning or social work) can be over-ridden and denied.

The examples I have given are of incongruity and the modelling of unhelpful or unsupportive practice. It is harder to argue the other way – to give examples of positive and congruent modelling – without sounding holier-than-thou, and the aim is after all not to set up that form of 'superior' modelling, but to be open about the struggle to be real and consistent. I have observed positive modelling by others, for example by the teaching colleague who would always go the extra mile to support a worried student, and who was explicit about thereby also modelling to the student the importance in social work practice of personal commitment and dedication (sometimes in the face of criticism from more defensive or disengaged colleagues). I have also seen negative modelling where teaching staff give the message to students of always being too busy to see them for personal support.

Work discussion and thinking space

Beyond the formal learning situation or training course, there are other ways of both cultivating and supporting people's capacity for relationship-based practice within their existing workplace. One important means of doing so is the use of regular group or team discussions of particular cases or situations, separately from the usual case conference or other decision-making meetings. What I am talking about here is the practice of developing in a team or work-group (as well as in the learning situation) the habit and capacity for sustained reflective and critical thought about the people we are working with, by working together at the skills of doing so and reflecting on both the content and the process of this learning. In addition to the benefit of the focus on which every case or situation is discussed each time, the regular use of this method also helps to help us keep our clients held in our mind – not just whichever individual or family we may be talking about today but also all the others who are always at the back of our mind even if not at the forefront.

Relationship-based practice thrives on thought and reflection, and this doesn't happen by chance, it has to be worked on and supported, validated within the organisation, and preferably also needs to spread into management and leadership – it is very hard to sustain a culture of relationship-based practice if there is not also relationship-based leadership, as we will also see in Chapter 13. This sort of thinking space also needs structuring and protecting from intrusion and disruption if it is to take hold in people's minds.

Within the group too, there does need to be an organised plan for working on the material, and preferably a structure that will support reflection and promote deep learning (Clare 2007). One way of structuring this sort of discussion is the 'Seminar Method' (Danbury and Wallbridge 1989) which uses a tight framework of presentation, discussion, observation and reflection, as follows:

'Seminar Method'

1. First the presenter talks without notes for no more than five minutes, saying something about what concerns them in the particular piece of work, and drawing on some 'live material' – a reported verbal exchange, with some naming of the feelings experienced.

2. The presenter then sits well back from the group and says no more for the next 20 minutes but observes the discussion. The task of this part of the discussion is for the group to make sense of what they have heard, to clarify what facts and feelings they think they have heard, including paying attention to the presenter – not only the facts being described but also whatever else he or she seemed to be conveying or missing or contributing to the piece of work discussed. There is a rule that the presenter is not allowed to feel persecuted during this phase, but needs to concentrate on the rare benefit of having one's own concerns and efforts attended to. The chair plays an important role in keeping the group to task and ensuring that the various elements of the task are attended to.

3. In the third phase the presenter re-joins the group and reports on the experience of listening to the discussion, including their thoughts on both the content and the process of the discussion. The task remains one of making sense of the material and of the whole experience, and of using the whole experience of the group discussion to puzzle out the material. Social work is a multi-faceted profession, and the practice

extends through many layers – individual, family, group and organisation, community, and this can all be interpreted in many different ways. This sort of group discussion can allow for the different levels to emerge, partly because the structure introduces several brief pauses in proceedings, which often seems to have the effect of encouraging both individuals and the group as a whole to re-group their thoughts, to reflect again on where the discussion is going, to think about what may be being missed. An important part of the work of the chair is to encourage people to speculate and make hypotheses about what may be going on – even if these feel like wild thoughts or pure guesswork or intuition, they may nevertheless turn out to be valuable because they move people into different and sometimes more creative modes of thinking, or connecting thoughts with the feelings which may emerge.

4. Finally in this method there is a brief period (five minutes) of further reflection, both on the content of the discussion and on the experience of it – as well as perhaps following up loose ends and closing down unfinished communications.

(This is based on a method described in Danbury and Wallbridge 1989.)

One potential benefit of this highly structured approach to case discussion is that it can occasionally allow the 'reflection process' (Mattinson 1970) to operate, unconsciously re-creating in the room some aspect of the dynamics of the case – such as fear, confusion or love – some of the themes which we have seen in Section 2 of this book. These may emerge through unconscious means such as the re-creation in the room of conflict or anxiety which the case entails, even if these have not been directly discussed by the presenter. What is happening here is that the anxiety which the case has engendered in the worker may have been communicated to the group indirectly, perhaps through gaps or muddles or confusions in the presentation, or through different group members apparently 'hearing' different facts.

In this context we need to regard everything as a potentially valuable communication, even those confusions and distortions or mixed messages, because they may relate to the underlying anxiety of the work. The skill of the chair and of the group as a whole lies in having their antennae sufficiently open to spot these phenomena, perhaps through metaphorically standing back and observing themselves (rather as I suggested in Chapter 3 on the 'use of self'). Then they need to find a way to bring them into the room, and to explore them in the group to discover whether they do indeed contain valuable clues or whether they are simply distractions or red herrings. They need to test these out against the case itself, partly through checking with the presenter, but also through other means. This will not always happen, and like certain other elusive phenomena they will perhaps be less likely to emerge if we are looking out too closely for them – we just need to remain receptive, speculative and ready to take the risk of trying out an unfamiliar idea or unlikely interpretation. The task of the educator or facilitator is to watch for such unannounced arrivals of learning possibilities and to be ready to alert group members to them – either directly or preferably indirectly, because what matters for the learners is that they themselves develop the capacity and skill for noticing and capitalising upon such learning possibilities, rather than relying on someone else to point these out for them.

What I have described is one approach to a familiar scenario – the case discussion or work discussion group. In order for a method such as this to be fully beneficial it needs to be regularly and frequently used, so that the skills are gradually learned and developed by the whole group and eventually internalised individually as a method of thinking more deeply and perhaps laterally about all aspects of their work. Thus no one particular discussion will necessarily produce the benefit, but the repeated use has the effect of cultivating and nurturing a whole approach. The emphasis in the discussion may vary according to the theme or situation, but will usually evolve into working at understanding the relationships in question. Many other approaches and variations are possible – an excellent overview of many of these is offered by Rustin and Bradley (2008).

Such regular opportunities for work discussion can of course also be used within the context of training programmes, but I am here emphasising the developmental role which they may play if used within the workplace as a form of professional development. Indeed, what many teams appear to value most in terms of continuing professional development is not only the input of new information or theory, but also the opportunity to draw upon and enhance their *own* collective understanding and potential by working closely together on analysing and learning from their existing work.

Conclusion

This chapter has outlined an approach to helping people to learn about relationship-based practice, an approach which is itself based on a relational and process-oriented model of education. It has also emphasised the importance of a process-oriented, ongoing approach to learning and development in this field, and highlighted in particular the value of 'work discussion groups' within the workplace as a means of promoting and enhancing the capacity for relationship-based practice. Underpinning all the ideas explored in this chapter is the diverse and dynamic nature of relationships and the importance of educational and professional development contexts providing spaces where they can be nurtured and sustained.

Chapter 11

Being Alongside

Working with Complexity and Ambiguity in Caring Relationships

JEREMY WALSH

Introduction

In the book's Introduction a question is posed: 'What does it actually mean to place "the relationship" at the heart of practice?' In the first edition of this book Doel (2010) viewed relationship-based social work through the eyes of service users and emphasised the importance of the service user–professional relationship being nurtured and held in high esteem. This new chapter explores this question from a new perspective, through the experiences of unpaid carers – family, friends, neighbours, work colleagues – undertaking caring activities which may entail both physical and emotional work. Doel, in emphasising how social work is not undertaken solely by the social worker and service user, acknowledged the presence of a wider system that must include the family, friends and community in which a service user resides. He identified too the value of 'professional curiosity', underlining how social workers must engage with service users as whole people, having wider lives within their community, not just defined by the 'problem' or set of 'issues' that brought them to the attention of services. Amidst inevitable legislative and organisational upheavals, social work is consistent in beginning with a human encounter between two or more people, and it is the acknowledgement of the presence of 'others' alongside service users and workers, where the role of carers fits in. This chapter examines the nature of the service user amidst the diverse relationships surrounding them, with the understanding that investing in a relationship with a service user, in isolation from their wider network, is unlikely to be fruitful. In contrast, paying attention to the wider relational system – service user, worker and carer – strengthens delivery of the social work task, rather than dilutes it.

The research that underpins this chapter came about through my diverse experiences as a social worker practising in different mental health settings and later moving into management roles where my professional life continued to be entwined with the lives of carers, and their experiences of being close to someone with a mental health condition. I also had a growing sense of disconnection in observing that carers had gained greater prominence than ever; in legislation, within the media and everyday language, while the day-to-day lives of carers remained largely hidden and were not valued in terms of financial return or social status. In a meeting that I was required to chair with the family of a mental health service user who was admitted to an acute psychiatric ward owing to severe depression and multiple attempts to take his own life, his adult son and daughter shared a list of complaints: the attitude of the staff, lack of ward activities and frustration with the rate of their father's recovery. Although their concerns were entirely founded and in some instances relatively easy to address, I was left feeling thoroughly criticised and failing in my responsibilities as a worker. Later, I reflected on what the meeting had really been about and whether the 'surface' issues had actually been a way into more harrowing issues of 'depth'. In reality, had we met to discuss the list of concerns, or had the family been temporarily enabled to unburden themselves: of mental illness, of worrying and the disturbance of caring for a father who actively wanted to end his own life? I wondered about the family projecting their anxiety about the future into me, and being able to walk away from the meeting feeling a little lighter, if only for a short time, while I was left with the feelings of failure and despair.

Taking a psychoanalytically informed psychosocial approach enables new understanding to emerge: from surface issues such as policies and procedures, to depth issues such as the emotional responses to caring for someone with a mental health condition, which may be conscious or emerge unconsciously through various defended positions such as splitting and projection. Evoking this surface and depth distinction Dartington (2010) describes the need for managers and professionals within health and social care to approach the work with two faces: one face views the necessity to be rational and clear-headed, while the other face views the complexity, emotional turmoil and disturbance that emerges from mental illness and permeates into the lives of services users and carers. As social workers, wearing either one of these relational faces also presents different degrees of risk, with the possibility of being too close to the pain that can emerge from mental illness, balanced against the risk of not getting close enough, of not engaging with the pain and avoiding the personal impact of the work which may inhibit any opportunity for change and growth.

The chapter begins by exploring what we actually mean by caring and is followed by an exploration of the psychosocial 'space' in which carers and social workers work together. A practice framework for working with carers called 'Being Alongside' is then shared, which sets out key practice principles for working with carers.

The moral and legal context of caring

Touching on what we actually mean by caring, Sevenhuijsen (1998) reminds us that care is both an attitude and an action comprising a range of qualities including: compassion, attentiveness and empathy. While 40 years ago the term 'carer' was barely in the English language, Held (2006) reminds us that the experience of being cared for is universal: 'every human being has been cared for as a child or would not be alive' (p.3). While many health conditions require specialist equipment, such as hoists and lifts, in order to provide care, the 'resource' within long-term conditions such as mental illness is the emotional availability of the carer or social worker to manage and relieve whatever disturbance emerges, and from a psychosocial vantage point, Foster (2001) argues:

> Caring for someone involves activities such as the ability to be emotionally in touch with the other person as a whole person; a readiness to consider their pain and their needs and act accordingly; and a desire to make up for any pain we may have caused them. (p.83)

Foster's view highlights the two-way nature of the caring relationship, in which emotional content passes to and fro, thereby critiquing assumptions that care travels in only one direction and conventional ideas about dependency. What is consistent is the idea that emotional and physical activities surrounding caring touch on what it funda-mentally means to be human, and are supportive of a strong role for relationship-based social work. This contention is supported by Hinshelwood (2004) in his assertion that responsibility for others is the greatest responsibility felt by people. As workers, there are a range of resources to draw on in managing the demands and anxieties associated with the caring task: professional relationships with colleagues, supervision, training courses, as well as the possibility of maintaining a boundary by leaving behind work responsibilities at the end of the working day. Carers, however, have few of these advantages and in the course of my practice I became aware that this difference added a degree of tension and complexity to the relationship that exists between carers and workers.

The thrust of the Care Act (2014) reinforces the role of carer as a category analogous to the service user, as a 'co-service user' with eligibility for assessment lowered, strengthened rights to a support plan, and to the carer's needs being met. In so doing, however, it raises a number of challenging questions. Although the legislation provides greater opportunities for carers, is being configured as a 'co-service user' the most helpful category for carers to occupy? In contrast, should we view carers and caring as something more akin to a necessary and reciprocal part of the human condition, and an inevitable aspect of the life cycle: to care for others, and when needed, others will care for me? Though successive carer-focused legislation has shone a stronger light on carers, and the scale of their huge contribution through caring activities, what actual difference does this new legislative attention make to the everyday lives of carers, faced with the harrowing experience of being close to someone whose life is marred by a long-term mental or physical condition?

Where have we come from?

In the vast majority of cases, caring for someone with a long-term condition is now firmly located in the community. In the example of severe and enduring mental illness, the outcome of the closure of the former psychiatric asylums dotted around the edges of towns and cities across the UK is that mental illness is no longer 'out of sight and out of mind'. Although community care policies coincided with advances in medical knowledge, such as the introduction of new forms of medication, ambitions to cure chronic mental health conditions remain largely unrealised. While it is largely accepted that the move of mental health services into the community was entirely the correct and progressive policy, what has emerged are the largely hidden experiences of carers who are inadequately supported, despite public awareness of carers being greater than ever. Jones (2002) reminds us that family and friends of those experiencing mental illness were closely involved with the development of the former psychiatric asylum system, and viewed hospitalisation as an appropriate resource to be drawn on in the event of a relative becoming too demanding to manage at home. Acknowledging this position underlines the possibility of a spectrum of carer perspectives, and for some families the option of 'removal' from family life was seen as the most appropriate response to a relative developing a mental health condition.

From the historical trajectory of mental health services outlined it is possible to quickly see that caring in this context is a far from straightforward task. Questioning the labels that are commonly in use, therefore, is essential, so in being described as a 'carer' or a 'person who cares' it is necessary to consider how:

> caring for others can stem from less noble motives, such as the urge to meddle or to control others. It can also simply follow from one's love or involvement with others, or from concern with their well-being. (Sevenhuijsen 1998, p.20)

Unpalatable as it may be to question the motivations of carers, adopting a realistic mind-set about how caring is understood and responded to is crucial. Of course, caring frequently takes place without any real choice being open to the carer, who assumes the role because there is nobody else who is able or available. This is the story that was almost universal in the experiences of carers that were interviewed for the research.

Understanding the caring experience: the nature of disturbance

In the course of the research informing this chapter, carers and professionals living or working with people with mental health conditions spoke about how these relationships impacted on their own lives. For Hamid caring for his wife, he experienced her as 'completely unattached from reality, doesn't want to live, wants to commit suicide'. Suleyman, the father of a service user, questioned, 'Why did he try to commit suicide by slashing his throat?' and Judith, mother of a son with a long-term mental illness, talked about how 'they always convince you that they're not ill, I've been through this so many times'. The bottom line for carers in such situations was that following the diagnosis 'life is never the same again'.

Although more guarded in their responses, workers also shared how the disturbance that emerges from mental illness finds its way into their work. An inpatient consultant psychiatrist described mental illness as 'a condition of the soul that places you at risk of losing your dignity'. For a community occupational therapist, mental illness was described as 'the beast', and a community care co-ordinator described how 'it doesn't stop at 5 o'clock. It goes on, because we worry have we done all the right things?'

The experiences that emerged from the interviews with carers and professionals powerfully illustrate the sense of psychological and emotional breakdown that sits at the heart of mental illness, which then seeps into and fractures the relationships of all those around them:

> Symptoms of mental distress manifest themselves in absent, distorted, or damaged social relationships, which are the basis of psychological nourishment and mental health. (Cooper and Lousada 2005, p.110)

The challenging relational context of caring for someone with a mental health condition is highlighted by Barnes (1997) who reminds us that there are no psychiatric beds surrounded by 'get well' cards and flowers. The stigma and fear that mental illness provokes can easily undermine and threaten relationships between carers and mental health professionals, and was suggested by descriptions such as 'hidden carers', who undertake caring but do not feel able, or want, to identify with the role. The responsibility that carers also shared was of having to 'protect' the cared-for person from harm, with the source of the harm symbolised by statutory health and social services.

What is apparent too from these accounts is the understandable need to adopt defended positions in relation to the huge anxiety emerging from mental illness, which is borne in large measure by carers. While the nature of all social work situated within the community requires defences, including a sense of boundary and a degree of detachment, these boundaries should not be to the detriment of engaging with carers, who are part of the service user's system, and hugely affected by the impact of mental illness. All too often, however, this is exactly what does happen.

Contested caring spaces: crowded and lonesome

Over recent decades a certain form of wisdom has evolved that caring for those with mental illness in the community can be understood through the image of a triangle, in which the key actors – service user, carer and professional – are represented in each corner as shown in Figure 11.1.

Figure 11.1 The Triangle of Care
(Carers Trust and National Mental Health Development Unit 2010)

Although considerable benefits have emerged from the Triangle of Care (2009) programme, including the prominence it has given to the contribution of carers, the psychosocial 'space' in which caring for someone with a mental health condition is undertaken remains fragile, fraught with anxiety, and contested by those who occupy it. In considering the idea of 'space' it is defined as: 'a continuous area or expanse that is free or unoccupied' (*Oxford English Dictionary* 2013) but for those social workers and carers who work within a mental health space, the atmosphere is dominated by the disturbance that is generated by mental illness, making it paradoxically both crowded and demanding *and* isolating and lonely, all at the same time. Despite its expansiveness the space is also 'segregated', relationally comprising the service user, carer and worker. Stefan, a carer for his sister who has had a serious mental illness all her adult life, which has led to lengthy periods of homelessness, remarked:

> I've got no contact at all with the mental health workers working with my sister, they seem to insist on me going to meetings, I turn up, they pull up a chair for me, and then I never hear from them again.

In a contrasting example, Hannah commented on the support she received:

> The care co-ordinator managed to be flexible and visit nearly every day. She was more worried than me, and that helped us to help my son to stay at home.

Within the space in which caring is undertaken, ambiguity thrives in the relationships between social worker and carer, and uncertainty abounds about what to expect from one another. This emerged in the experience of a carer who commented that they felt like they were the social worker's third or fourth priority, and from a worker who commented: 'I have hundreds and hundreds of carers swirling around in my mind.' In a focus group attended by carers and workers, the sense of disconnection and fragmentation also emerged, as carers underlined their availability 'around the clock' and then contrasted it to mental health workers who 'went home'. Workers felt attacked by this portrayal of their commitment and it provoked a defensive response: 'we go on caring beyond 5.00 pm'.

Considering the potential for ambiguity, Hoggett (2015) reminds us that aside from social defences against anxiety, social defences against many other emotions abound:

> Hope, resentment, love, envy and so forth – that can easily overwhelm us. It follows that we defend ourselves not just against anxiety, but against any experience that threatens to overwhelm us. (p.57)

The relationship between social workers and carers, part of the triangular context that must also include the service user, surfaces painful realities that are difficult to tolerate, and by drawing attention to the ability of workers to 'go home', carers highlight their personal and emotional bonds to the source of distress and disturbance which emerge from mental illness.

One way that workers defend themselves from becoming overwhelmed by the emotional experience of working with mentally disturbed people is to erect boundaries, either physically or psychically: 'madness is kept in patients and sanity in staff and rigid barriers are created to prevent contamination' (Hinshelwood and Skogstad 2002, p.8). The following experience of just such a boundary experience was shared by Lisa, a carer for her husband, who spoke about visiting him on a psychiatric inpatient unit following his becoming unwell due to a relapse in his mental illness:

When I tried to come onto the ward with things for him, I rang them and basically said I'm coming to visit and when I was coming. They were very unforthcoming with information. It's standard when he's ill that he sees his loved ones as part of a conspiracy, seriously, and I would have thought mental health professionals would understand that.

So the next time I came onto the ward to bring stuff for him they didn't let me on the ward. There's a sort of airlock so you've got an entrance and another entrance. They let me in as far as the airlock and I had to decant the stuff on a chair, and I felt humiliated and I felt really upset and distressed.

A little later in the interview, Lisa shared her experience of meeting with the care team that included a consultant psychiatrist and social worker:

Even then there was no, sort of feeling of, how on my part I was going to be supported, or informed, or looked after through the process. It was all sort of...you're here now and let's get the information from you and thanks very much and bye bye.

Lisa's 'airlock' experience provides a link to a largely unspoken 'fear of contagion' amongst workers, and suggests that carers represent an ambiguity in the mind-set of workers and a risk of the boundary with 'madness' being breached. This reinforces the notion of 'contested space' marked out by areas that segregate social workers from service users, and leaves carers confused, being neither service user nor professional. Doel (2010) reflects on the role of boundaries in the relationships between social workers and service users, noting the existence of different paradigms: one which construes the boundary as a line not to be crossed, and another as a 'penumbra' where there are shaded areas between different systems that co-exist. From the viewpoint of service users, Doel also suggests a preference is awarded to those social workers who are able to be flexible and 'human' and this resonates with the research which highlighted how carers valued those workers who were able to be in touch with distress, able to work together to respond in a containing manner, resist the urge to 'do something', and in a timely manner, take a safe, considered and measured way forward.

Within a space that is founded on 'them and us' defences that are reinforced through professional structures, the presence of carers prompts confused responses. On the one hand an inpatient consultant interviewed as part of the research stated: 'it's natural to work with carers, it's automatic, I don't even use the word "carer"'. In contrast, the sense of demarcation within the space emerged strongly from Janine, a mother caring for her adult daughter diagnosed with early onset psychosis, adding to the notion of competition for time, access, and the right to information: 'we go round and round for as long as it takes to hit a professional'. The sense of going round and round and 'hitting' a professional is suggestive of desperation on the part of the carer in their struggle to make meaningful contact within the expansive and lonely space. It also resonates with the idea of a 'transitional space' which proposes a place between the inner worlds of an individual and the outer world of society, where the key actors – worker, carer and service user – are seeking to establish a culture of living and working with each other:

> Infants and children and adults take external reality in, as clothing for their dreams, and they project themselves into external objects and people and enrich external reality by their imaginative perceptions. (Winnicott 1989, p.57)

Young (1994) stresses that the transitional space is more than the 'commerce' between the inner and outer worlds, and evolves in early child development through the infant's ability to separate successfully from the maternal figure. If a secure base is in place and there are no concerns about illness, then separation is likely. This permits the infant to distinguish the world as a separate entity or 'not me', and therefore enables an interchange between inner and outer reality, with each being enriched by the other. However, within the contested space of mental illness in the community we know that the presence of a service user with a mental health condition introduces severe limitations to the capacity to manage the inner and outer realities, with the result that disturbance can infiltrate into all relationships:

> while physical illness can be seen as separate from the person's identity (something 'one has'), mental illness is experienced much more as part of, or catastrophically affecting a person's identity. (Hinshelwood and Skogstad 2002, p.13)

How then might firm but fluid boundaries be understood and recognised?

Reconceptualising the Triangle: 'there is no such thing as a service user'

Isolation and disconnection have emerged as predicaments at the heart of the relationship between social worker and carer. However, an alternative way of reconceptualising the relationship is proposed by this research by drawing on ideas from early childhood:

> there is no such thing as an infant, meaning, of course, that whenever one finds an infant one finds maternal care, and without maternal care there would be no infant. (Winnicott 1960, p.39)

In the same way that a parent and infant must be seen as two elements within one system, the service user and carer can be viewed as aspects of one system in which there is no such thing as a 'service user', only a service user and his or her carer(s), family, friends and neighbours. This is shown in Figure 11.2 'The caring space'.

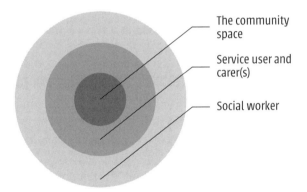

The community space

Service user and carer(s)

Social worker

Figure 11.2 The caring space

A proposed framework for reconceptualising the relationship between social worker, carer and service user puts to one side the carer occupying their own particular category, and implies that they and the service user are part of one and the same system that is affected by mental illness. This is denoted by the circle at the centre of Figure 11.2.

Surrounding, supporting and alongside the service user and carer network is the social worker who occupies the next circle, and finally both circles are located within the community. The service user and carer being co-located in a 'single system' is an opportunity to engage with the essence of the issue, which is the disturbance that arises from a mental health condition, in the context of the social network. It is also an important aspect of reframing the current arrangement which situates a vulnerable person in the isolated role of 'service user', who then becomes the overriding focus of the service.

In his reflections on community-based social work, Dartington (2010) argues that none of us are entirely independent, and the proposed framework engages with the notion that we are all in some way or another connected to someone, though with the possibility of strained relationships due to the disturbance that emerges from mental distress. An approach is therefore emerging of the social work priority being the development of relationships that encompasses the service user and their wider social network of carers, family and friends. By altering the focus from service user in one corner of the triangle and carer in the other, to service user and carer both being in the same 'space' the impact of mental illness is equally acknowledged for the user and the carer. From this premise, more meaningful relationships can be achieved that recognise there is in fact 'no such thing as a service user'.

Being Alongside – a framework for social work practice

In the turmoil and distress created by mental health conditions and other debilitating long-term physical health conditions, it is perhaps not surprising that what emerges most profoundly from the research is the importance of a meaningful relationship between a social worker and carer or as one carer succinctly put it, 'the relationship is the service and the service is the relationship'. Carers described mental health services predominantly through their relationships with social workers. This is reminiscent of Cooper and Lousada's (2005, p.110) reflections that 'whatever the modality of treatment, the capacity for relationship is, in one way or another, what informs mental health intervention'. Carers conveyed the essence of these relationships through comments such as, 'you have to "click"' and the value they placed on meetings with mental health professionals which were viewed as pivotal. In contrast, when expected relationships do not materialise, and closeness is not achieved, the sense of dissatisfaction is significant, and those moments when carers felt most burdened by caring responsibilities are equated with an absence of a meaningful relationship with a worker. For Hamid, caring for his wife, this was experienced as 'professionals come only when I really can't cope'. Maryam, a young woman in her early twenties caring for two siblings both of whom have long-term mental health conditions, referred to an absence of any sense of rapport with a social worker, or any other professional involved with her sisters. This led to a sense of her caring in isolation, with little evidence of having been engaged – as an individual carer – by services as part of the wider social system of family and friends that is affected by the presence of mental illness.

While more nuanced in their language than carers, workers spoke about how 'natural' it was to work with carers, though simultaneously they related instances of being 'inundated' with demands and calls from anxious carers, and working with families who are unreasonable, and others who were over-involved.

In understanding why relationships matter, Held (2006) argues that care must concern itself with both the effectiveness of its effort to meet needs, and with the motives with which care is provided. So, although a carer's motives and actions may be full of complexity and ambiguity, a focus on caring 'relations' enables professionals to 'value caring persons in caring relations' (Held 2006, p.38). Doel (2010) explored a similar theme acknowledging how the relationship between the worker and service user must be purposive and have boundaries that are mutually negotiated and respected, in which the relationship is both a by-product and an integral element. Therefore, in standing back from the emotions swirling around working with carers, what does caring really look like?

As a practice framework for social work, 'Being Alongside' acknowledges the distress that emerges from caring for someone with a long-term condition such as mental illness, and how the presence of a meaningful professional relationship is a significant supportive factor. Central to the framework is a relationship that is not based on an imbalance of power ('doing to' or 'doing for'). Three key elements of it are outlined below: discernment, honesty and expectations, and valuing the seemingly mundane.

Discernment

'Discernment' refers to the need to make judgements, and in the case of mental illness this is often undertaken in the context of distress and anxiety, and is illustrated through the ideas of 'servicing' and 'serving' drawn from parenting literature. 'Servicing' involves action, doing and responding, creating, as Waddell (1989, p.20) recognises, 'the illusion that needs can always be met through material or practical resource'. In contrast 'serving' is linked to the idea of thinking about thinking, and the capacity for reflecting on those emotional experiences which enable the individual to learn, 'thereby becoming a different person with different capabilities from the person of the past' (Waddell 1989, p.25). The distinction between servicing and serving is seen in the carer case studies below.

SYLVIA

Sylvia is a middle-aged woman who has spent 30 years caring for her adult son who has a mental illness that leads to manic episodes and disinhibited behaviours:

> 'I've been through this so many times with my son. I have had the responsibility of paying off his credit cards because I had the bailiffs come to take away all my stuff as well as his stuff. I have to live with this, he thinks he's well so he stops taking his medication, so he's back to square one, he's gone right down the barrel again.'

RHONA

At a similar stage of life, Rhona has recently retired and has also been caring for her adult son, diagnosed with a schizophrenic illness, in this case for around 12 years:

> 'I'm not totally watching his movements and I've even braced myself against the worst possible scenario that could be a repeat of the suicide attempt. I've braced myself against the possibility that, you know, it will be his decision, his choice. He realises something is wrong, he describes it as the left side of his brain doesn't work. And he's not very happy today because people don't understand how small things can really get to him you know, because he's really sensitive and these things happen all the time.'

DISCUSSION

Sylvia shares glimpses into the pain she has endured in caring for her son for his entire adult life. Faced with her own retirement from the workplace she fears that her previous mechanism of caring for him, paying off his debts, is no longer available. Amidst her new status, Sylvia is able to acknowledge that even when the option of 'servicing' was available, neither she nor her son were ultimately able to escape from the distress: 'I cried myself to sleep many a night.'

In contrast, Rhona seems to have arrived at a different place in her role as carer, and to be occupying a position which permits greater space to consider a response in line with the idea of serving; 'in this state of mind one is able to recognise good and bad in one's relationships, and in oneself, without forming harsh judgements' (Loshak 2013, p.50).

Rhona conveys a sense of responding to her son's mental illness through listening and taking in, rather than reacting to pressure to act in a particular manner, resonant with the idea of containment. The argument is not necessarily for 'inaction' but that non-action may at times be the most helpful response.

In Sylvia's approach to caring she has invested in elements of 'servicing' the needs of her son, and responding to his manic spending by literally paying off his credit card debts with the hope the problem will go away. In contrast Rhona appears to have reached a point where she is able to accept, and reflect on, her son's disturbed state of mind, and to ultimately live with and think about the pain and loss without reacting. Waddell (1989) sums this up as a 'responsive presence', active and transformative, in contrast from 'passivity' which could be interpreted as rejection.

In essence, then, discernment flags the importance of the professional and carer working together to distinguish between those anxieties that need an immediate response and those that benefit from a longer period of reflection before responding.

Honesty and expectations

Reflecting on the emotional work that characterises social work with all vulnerable service user groups, Cooper and Lousada (2005) argue that it is so much easier to become the patients' advocate than inhabit the more complex and conflictual role. Holding on to this challenging position is a reminder of the distinction between social workers, with their professional practice and array of assessment, support planning and risk management skills, and the position of unpaid carers who undertake caring without a similar toolkit of expertise. The focus on professionally acquired skills, therefore, distinguishes social work from 'unpaid care' which is largely based on relational commitments, often familial, friendship or partnership-based. In contrast, professional relationships are based on a set of skill-based competencies, overseen by membership of a professional body, supervision, and the employment contracts with respective employers. Acknowledging these contractual differences is important, and they are also noticed by unpaid carers, as pointed out by a partner of a service user in her remarks about the commitment she had made to her husband, when she recited her wedding vows in public: 'in sickness and in health, till death us do part'.

Amidst these differences, the importance of having regular open and honest discussions about expectations with carers is vital, recognising the dissonance that can grow between the aims of the social worker and the hopes of carers. For Maryam this was a very real occurrence:

> They never come out with a plan for my sisters, it frustrates me. They aren't ambitious, especially for people like my sisters who are confused and don't understand.

Further emphasising the mismatch, a mental health professional shared their approach:

> You go in offering not very much to begin with and people don't get disappointed. I guess you learn that through practice, but I don't know whether it's being mean with the purse strings, I've never really worked that one out.

While on one hand the prospect of recovery from mental illness is the prevailing approach, there has been limited improvement in truly curative treatments for long-term and severe mental illnesses and for many professionals they have learnt the value of setting expectations low. However, what seems to be most valued by carers is a commitment to honesty in respect to expectations that are neither inflated nor squashed. The absence of ambition is swiftly detected by carers and is viewed as letting down service users. Explicit discussion about expectations of recovery should take place at the beginning and be regularly revisited, with acknowledgement that disappointment is possible due to the inherent nature of long-term mental health conditions.

Valuing the seemingly mundane

In contrast to a specific professional intervention to promote a particular 'approach', what emerged from the research as most effective in maintaining strong relationships is for social workers to have a repertoire of skills, located within the everyday and minutiae of contacts with carers and service users. Doel (2010) also notes that service users valued social workers who were well connected to other professionals, and those workers who were able to gain resources from the agency. From the research, the ability of a worker to access resources was also identified as important, but what emerged more strongly was the ability to work sensitively, being grounded in the everyday, and cognisant of the relationship with the service user. For the worker this involves being curious about everyone's story, quietly maintaining hope, and being honest in response to carer expectations. In sharing her practice, a mental health professional based in a community team shared the story of a regular commitment she had to go out to a café, or for a drive, with a father and his young adult son, who had been diagnosed with early onset psychosis. Undertaking these everyday and often seemingly mundane activities during contacts with the service user and carer requires an extensive set of 'hidden' professional skills that enable meaningful relationships to be quietly developed as social situations are navigated together by the worker, carer and user.

In a focus group discussion between workers and carers it also became apparent that the presence of a relational context, and a feeling of being cared about in their own right, is sufficient to tip someone into the role of carer, and subsequently take on the associated caring actions. From this perspective the existence of a need in one person, matched with a feeling of caring in another, is the foundation of a caring relationship, regardless of any labels that may be applied. These qualities, which characterise all healthy carer and service user relationships, push away legalistic perspectives, and speak to an existential issue related to feelings of responsibility for a fellow human being:

> Responsibility for other people is the greatest responsibility felt by humans. Perhaps responsibility is a biological inheritance, due to becoming a social species. (Hinshelwood 2004, p.7)

From triangular to circular caring relationships

Mental illness remains highly stigmatising and carers are often hidden and isolated in caring for someone who, due to the damaging nature of their mental health condition, may be unable to maintain a personal relationship or participate in the daily rituals of life. Within this context the availability of a meaningful relationship with a social worker is seen as pivotal by carers. Although social workers recognise the support that carers provide, their focus on the service user can leave the carer on the periphery, rather than recognising that they are a major part of the system that is affected by the disturbance arising from mental illness.

Within this contested caring space there is a risk that professionals and carers experience only fragmented and partial relationships with each other, in which carers can feel rejected and unsupported, and professionals feel burdened and attacked. The professionals are clearer about their boundaries in regard to service users but are often confused in relating to carers. Carers can experience a sense of limbo, finding themselves in a lonesome and ambiguous space. Typically professionals seek ways to limit their exposure to the anxiety that carers live with, although these defences generally lead to more irritation and the loss of an opportunity to work together. When the mental health professional and carer are able to form a meaningful relationship it appears they are able to support each other, and be more effective in their shared aim of supporting the service user.

Going back full circle to the beginning of the chapter, these findings build on Doel's ideas about relationships being the foundation of strong and effective social work and, through a new but complementary perspective, question the value of the 'service user', arguing for a practice framework that encompasses both the user and carer in a single relational system as the basis for strong relationship-based social work. Because the disturbance that emerges from a long-term condition such as mental illness infiltrates all the relationships around the service user, it is necessary, as a worker, to engage both the service user and those they are in relationship with, supporting opportunities for working together. This is the environment where strong and effective relationship-based social work flourishes.

Chapter 12

Relating and Relationships in Supervision

Supportive and Companionable or Dominant and Submissive?

JOHN SIMMONDS

In the Department for Education's (2015) response to a public consultation on 'Knowledge and Skills for Practice Leaders and Practice Supervisors', the Chief Social Worker states:

> Child and family social work is complex. We need it to be undertaken by talented people whose expertise supports families, helps keep children safe and enables them both to thrive. It is only right that practitioners are supported by Practice Supervisors and Practice Leaders who are equally talented and able to provide the supervision and leadership needed for social work to flourish. (p.3)

In identifying the plan for accreditation as the bedrock for the future of the profession, the Chief Social Worker continues:

> Whether you are a practitioner knocking at the family's door, a Practice Supervisor, or a Practice Leader, holding an accreditation will say to the public 'you can have confidence in me'.

The publication of the agreed framework for Knowledge and Skills in 2015 continued a long-established struggle to improve the quality of social work practice and in turn the positive outcomes for those individuals and families that rely on the profession. Supervision has always been identified as a core component of social work practice and, typically, a high priority component for most social work practitioners. In their review of research on supervision from 1970 to 2010, O'Donoghue and Tsui (2015) identify 86 published evaluations, 59 of which were surveys. One factor that is core throughout their review is the identification of supervision as an intervention that is intended to impact on outcomes for the child and family. While this is core to the development and implementation of supervisory practice, its focus in their review does move it beyond the typical sole concern with satisfaction from a social worker or supervisor's perspective.

Jack and Donnellan's (2010) study is indicative of the general approach to supervision research in exploring the experiences of 13 newly qualified social workers and ten managers from three local authority children's services in England. Using data from questionnaires and interviews, they identified the dominance of supervision's focus on what the social workers should know and be able to do, while excluding appropriate time and space to explore the 'professional as a person' – what they felt and thought and the impact on them of doing so. These findings reflect a longer-term concern in the evolution of social work and supervision – from that of a person-centred, professional perspective to that of accountability and managerial control. A Department of Health funded study by Manthorpe *et al.* (2015) continues to identify these supervisory themes in their exploration of the views of newly qualified social workers, managers and directors.

Relating and relationships in social work and supervision

As human beings we live, thrive or suffer in a relational world. It is the world we are born into, the world we anticipate and need and the world we will struggle with. The relational will be intimate, personal and core to our being. It will also be strongly social – our sense of continuity, belonging and meaning established through the groups we become identified with and belong to. It will also be core to our learning and the transmission of knowledge. At another level we are becoming familiar with the detail of these core processes in understanding the neurodevelopmental processes that embed the relational in our brains and bodies (Mikulincer and Shaver 2014). The concept of relationships and the process of relating have had a long history in social work. Where individuals and families find themselves in difficulty, there may be a range of factors – some practical such as income and housing, or resulting from health issues of the consequences of disability – but the resourcefulness of individuals and families to work to find solutions to these problems alongside that of the state and its services requires paying attention to the relational world that enables this.

Relationships may result in people feeling connected, understood and supported, and they may be the means that bring about change in the quality of people's lives. They can also result in people feeling misunderstood and unsupported, and may bring about changes in people's lives that they do not want, such as the removal of a child into care. They can also start out with suspicion and distrust and, through hard, sensitive and insightful work, become more trusting and supportive and eventually improve the quality of people's lives. It is also the case that the idea of relationships may seem irrelevant and meaningless to those people who come into contact with services as well as those in professional practice. Each of these scenarios can also apply to supervision. Relationships and relating are core to effective supervision. They may result in the social worker feeling understood and supported, and improve the quality of the social worker's practice. They may also result in the opposite. They may also start off badly and improve significantly through sensitive and insightful work on the part of the supervisor and the social worker. The idea of relationships in supervision can also seem irrelevant and meaningless.

Describing the process of supervision and the practice of social work as parallel processes seems natural when thinking about the ways people are typically enabled and supported to work at difficult problems in their lives, whether these are personal or social problems or work problems. The immediacy of face-to-face relating, informed by human warmth and sensitive communication, is probably what the greater majority of people would identify as helpful when they are faced with upsetting, difficult or challenging circumstances. But, as understandable as this might be, the organisational context of work does not so obviously reflect these qualities when they are driven by quite different concepts such as business plans, performance management, targets, accountability and inspection. The unremitting scepticism and criticism of social work following child deaths and other tragedies such as child sexual exploitation or historical sexual abuse still impact on the identity, confidence and status of the profession when it drives a belief that control, accountability and measures are the primary solution.

Social work is not alone in this. Power (1996) argued that the evolution of a culture of accountability would fundamentally affect how organisations saw themselves and this would 'spread a distinct mentality of administrative control' (p.3). He predicted that public sector workers would become identified as 'auditees', with the danger that this would become a part of their mentality – how they saw themselves, what counted in what they did and how they were valued by the organisations they worked for. Power's predictions have had relevance for social work (see also Broadhurst *et al.* 2009; Munro 2004, 2011b). This has resulted in a serious clash of cultures between those that identify practice and the supervision of practice as a relationship-based activity and the supervision of practice identified as an audit-based activity, where the qualities of the people involved and the relationship between them are largely irrelevant. The co-existence of these different frameworks and the tension between them reflects the reality of current social work.

This issue is illustrated in the following example.

A social worker visits a service user because she needs some further information to complete an assessment. They meet and talk and the social worker fills in the missing parts of the assessment. The service user appears to be co-operative, at least in answering the questions, but he does little more than this. The social worker talks to the service user a bit more about how he has been feeling over the last couple of weeks but he seems uninterested and says no more than 'OK'. Even when the social worker suggests that the service user seems a bit reluctant to talk today, he replies, 'Not really!' After 20 minutes, the social worker leaves, objectives achieved and with relief at that, but this feels unsatisfactory – the service user has not engaged or opened up, and the social worker wonders to herself if something is wrong. Having completed the assigned objective, does the social worker put her unease out of her mind and dismiss it? It is too troublesome to think about and there is too much else to do. In supervision, the social worker says that she has got the information that was needed to complete the assessment. She also says that the service user was very reluctant to talk, and the supervisor reassures her that just as long as she has the information required, then it doesn't really matter.

The question is: does it? This is one of the very great challenges for social work now, and this has become represented as 'Just as long as you tick the boxes, then everything must be OK!' There have been many attempts over the years to clearly identify what the purposeful activity of social work is and to insist that it sticks to that agreed purpose. Yet more and more it seems to find itself in difficulty, represented by child protection tragedies like those involving Victoria Climbié, Baby Peter and others. The belief that as long as social workers are purposeful, do the things required of them and demonstrate unequivocally that they have, then all will be well. Faced with the complexity and uncertainty, as much of social work is, turn to the rules, follow them and all will be well. It is a message that makes much sense and is organisationally attractive. The audit culture may partly explain this, but, in the example given, the behaviour of the service user indicates something of his view of the social worker – 'Collect your information and leave me alone.' It may be an entirely justifiable position for the service user to take, but it needs more exploration to understand this view, and certainly this is so from a relationship-based perspective.

Supportive/companionable and dominant/ submissive relationship patterns

There are numerous frameworks that explore the nature of relationships and relating. There are two core frameworks used in this chapter and both are derived from attachment theory (Bowlby 1969). The first is that of Heard and Lake (1997) who developed a framework based on two categories of human relating. The first they term 'supportive/ companionable' and they say this is exemplified by:

> a protective, explanatory and exploratory form of relating. It is warm, unanxious and is accompanied by appropriate constructive mis-attunements. Conflict, when it arises, is handled by the recognition of the other's points of view and resolved through negotiation and compromise. (p.34)

There couldn't be a more wished-for description of how social work and in turn supervision should be! The second form of relating they term 'dominating and submissive'. This form of relating:

forces others to follow the decisions of a controlling leader. It can appear not to be damaging to others when it carries the stance of a protective and even indulgent dictator. But those who do not accept a submissive and obedient status face coercion in various forms, including being shamed and humiliated. (p.35)

There does not appear to be a more accurate description of how social work is sometimes perceived or indeed of how it can be experienced. Heard and Lake describe the formation of the dominant/submissive form of relating to be primarily defensive and arising in the context of disturbances in or loss of the attachment-based supportive/ companionable form of relating. They say:

> individuals who have been made fearful of coming under the control of others tend to be controlling to those that they assess as likely to be compliant; or they become compliant to those who they expect to greet protest and controlling behaviour by a greater display of anger or coercion. (p.92)

Heard and Lake identify these two forms of relating as applying to three basic contexts. The first context arises out of those care-giving relationships typically associated with parent/child interactions. The second are those relationships formed through mutual interest. The third are sexual relationships. Each of these three contexts may be marked by a supportive/companionable form of relating or a dominating/submissive form.

The importance of the Heard and Lake model is that it introduces the important concepts of power and authority into relationships. How power and authority are perceived and used in each of these three areas of relating may be different, but clearly power used within a supportive/companionable dynamic is very different from the way that it might be used in a dominating/submissive dynamic. It is also important to recognise that whatever intentions a person might have, in principle, to be supportive and companionable in their relating does not make them immune to being pulled into a dominant/submissive form of relating. Small and large groups and organisations, including those with the characteristics of audit cultures, may be particularly powerful in generating the context where this becomes likely. These organisations fall within the context of 'mutual interest', both in terms of how they organise themselves to deliver their stated service objectives and how they work with their service users to achieve common goals of social welfare. A supportive/companionable form of relating may be the aim, but, given the realities of loss and trauma faced by many service users at the core of their social problems, it is likely that the fears, anxieties and vulnerabilities associated with relationship-building may come to the fore with insistence and compliance dominating the process of relating. Similarly, the fears and anxieties associated with forming a relationship in supervision, where service users' dilemmas, confusions, anxieties and losses are explored, including their direct impact on the social worker, can easily become unbearable if the social worker or the supervisor fear the consequences of showing themselves as vulnerable and overwhelmed.

In the practice example above, the principle of the work taking place within a supportive/companionable relationship seems entirely desirable. There may be forms to be filled in and assessments to be completed, but both the accuracy and effectiveness of that work will depend on the service user understanding the purpose and relevance of that activity and whether there is some sense of mutual ownership of it. That, in turn, will depend on the degree of respect that both the social worker and the service user have for each other, and that is likely to have been established as a result of the work they have put in. Of course, the relationship may not have started out in this way. The service user may have felt suspicious of the social worker, but with some persistence and joint exploration and acknowledgement that asking for help or being required to accept help can be troubling and painful then that could lead to a supportive relationship being established. If this is so, then there is a question about the service user's disengagement during the meeting and the way that this might be thought about. It is also possible that none of this exploratory and trust-building work has been done and that the relationship is actually marked by misunderstanding and distrust. The anger the service user feels at having to share personal information with somebody he doesn't know and the shame he feels for not being able to manage his difficulties without having to go, as he experiences it, cap in hand to social services have led to him taking up a disengaged position where he is focused on protecting himself from any further hurt or shame. His position in the meeting is submissive, but this is a defence. Underneath, he feels angry and he just wants to be left alone. There is no advantage he can see in engaging with the social worker. The social worker is insistent that the information is made available to complete the assessment, and the service user must provide it. The social worker is angry that the service user is making the whole process so difficult; it would be easier if he just did what was required so they could all move on. There is something here which strongly suggests that this has become a dominant/submissive form of relating with a passive/ aggressive response intended to deflect the sense of the social worker's intrusive assessment.

Mentalisation

A second, complementary, framework to the Heard and Lake model has also developed out of attachment theory – that of mentalisation (Fonagy *et al.* 2002). This framework is a highly articulated explanation of the way that individuals develop representations in their mind of their own subjective experiences of self and those of others. Key to this is the acquisition of a 'language' that represents an individual's thoughts, feelings, wishes and desires in a meaningful and coherent way. This language reflects the complex nature of subjective experience – curiosity, exploration, an appropriate sense of 'not knowing' and a sensitivity to changes over time. For example, a parent picks up her six-month-old baby after an afternoon nap and finds him unsettled and whiny. Her first instinct is to soothe him by cuddling him, making eye contact and talking to him in a slightly exaggerated but comforting tone. The parent says things like 'You don't seem very happy; did you have a bad dream? Maybe you have filled your nappy; now what do I think about that? Let's see what is going on down there.' The tone of the exchange is comforting, and there is a sensitive, curiosity-driven exploration of the baby's subjective experience. The use of phrases like 'don't seem', 'did you have' and 'maybe you have' suggest the parent's respectful curiosity of the baby's subjective experience that recognises that 'unsettled' and 'whiny' are mental states that may be brought on by bad dreams or a dirty nappy, but they are mental states nonetheless. Imagination and connection in the context of a process of relating are key. But if none of this turns out to be helpful in helping the baby feel more settled, then the key issue is that the mother does not feel at fault or does not feel that the baby is at fault either. In many such experiences, this is easier said than done!

Mental states change, can be difficult to identify accurately and can be easily misattributed. A stance that implicitly recognises these qualities is the most helpful way of managing them in the course of daily living. It is important to understand that the content of one's own mind can be confused with the content of other people's minds. It is better, although difficult, for a parent repeatedly woken in the middle of the night to make some distinction between her own irritability and stress at lack of sleep and her baby's apparent irritability. She might do this by expressing her irritability at being woken again to her partner or she might say to the baby, 'I think you want me to pay some more attention to what is wrong with you, even though you know I am very tired.' It is easy in these circumstances for a stressed parent to experience the baby as a persecuting baby, and, for some parents, to experience the baby as deliberately making life stressful for the parent.

The concept of mentalisation points to a quite different concept of reality from that of the physical world. Psychosocial reality is constructed and maintained by the thoughts and feelings inside people and between them. Although this can feel real enough in day-to-day life, it is a reality that should not be confused with the physical world. For example, the reality of skin colour – black and white – is commonly used to attribute qualities to the person and their situation irrespective of the accuracy of such attributions. At its worst, it can lead to racism and extremes of racial tension and hostility commonly a part of most societies. The individual and group psychosocial processes that create racism and other forms of oppression are real enough. But the failure to recognise the misattributions of feelings of, for example, hatred in the originating 'white' group and justify them by recourse to the 'objective' physical reality of the 'black' group can have devastating consequences.

Understanding and managing psychosocial reality well – the development of the capacity for mentalisation – is based in an individual's development through the sensitive attunements and misattunements of their experiences in relationships. Being able to understand the thinking and feeling states of others and the particular nature of these states is rooted in the way that the baby's psychosocial states were responded to by his or her parents. It requires imagination and curiosity on the part of the parents and a stance by them that recognises in the course of relating to their child that their own mental states are influenced by, but different from, the mental states of their child. Having a working understanding of the nature and quality of these mental states is the basis for an individual's mental health, their ability to make and sustain relationships sensitively and appropriately, and their ability to make and become members of well-functioning social groups.

For a profession that is primarily concerned with psychosocial issues, understanding the basic nature of mentalisation couldn't be more important. The consequences of a failure to develop mentalisation can be severe. It may well play a part in many of the difficulties parents have in being 'good enough' parents to their children and, in a severe form, result in neglect and abuse. It may play a significant part in many mental health difficulties and particularly borderline personality disorders (Bateman and Fonagy 2004). The failure to relate to the baby or child as a baby or child, or the failure to see one's own mental states or the mental states of other people as exactly that, can bring about non-mentalising ways of relating. The baby's distress can be experienced by the parents as harsh personal criticism that they have to defend themselves vigorously against by absenting themselves physically or emotionally or hitting out. Such a relationship can be marked by a concreteness of thinking about the child and an impulsivity towards the child generated by extremes of emotion and consequent acting out. In such mental states, the parents have lost sight of the real 'other' child and are struggling with complex and unresolved issues located in their own childhood and the failure of their parental figures to mentalise them adequately. The failure of mentalisation can be equated with Heard and Lake's dominant/submissive form of relating – an arena where the ghosts of the past play themselves out once again in the nursery (Fonagy *et al.* 1993; Newman and Stevenson 2005; Fraiberg, Adelson and Shapiro 1975).

Implications for practice

It is inevitable that the processes of mentalisation and the consequences of non-mentalisation will impact on social work practice. The ability to practise as a social worker will depend on each social worker's developmental experience of being mentalised by their own parental figures and other developmental experiences. It can be informed by their experiences of education, training and supervision. Maintaining a supportive/companionable perspective in practice comes about through a complex and lifelong exposure to supportive/companionable relationships, of which supervision should be a part.

The previous case example demonstrates the tension faced by social workers. In order to access a service, an assessment of need and information in support of that assessment is essential. Only when the social worker has completed that assessment can a decision be made about eligibility for a service. In the name of fairness, equality, efficiency and effective use of public resources, information is key. It informs and, in many respects, determines the form of relating between the social worker and the service user. The social worker will certainly know this and the service user will quickly get to know this. But the concept of need within a bureaucratic context is different from the subjective experience of need. A mentalising framework recognises the supportive/companionable nature of child development, parenting capacity and the wider environmental context which supports it. The evolution of the organisational setting of practice has resulted in a context that can be non-mentalising and this has resulted in recording systems and particularly computerised systems that impose a dominant/submissive form of relating. There are significant risks when these become the drivers for practice as they create little space for the reflection that underpins mentalisation (Bell *et al.* 2008; Broadhurst *et al.* 2009; White *et al.* 2008).

These and many other similar developments could not be further from the kinds of relating that support human development, but their evolution and implementation is understandable given the anxiety of using mentalising processes in non-mentalising contexts. Relationship-based social work can easily be pulled into non-mentalising modes of relating, and the tools available to social workers can easily be perverted in supporting and even requiring that. This is a serious problem. Assessments are meant to give clarity and definition to a service user's problems. They are dependent on information and facts, and the concept of 'need' suggests an objectivity about this that gives the whole activity of assessment and intervention respectability. But although information and facts are usually readily available, often in volumes of files, an important component of assessment is understanding the significance of the facts: how important are they when taken together and what do they tell you? Facts need to be analysed to give them meaning. And mentalisation contributes significantly to the creation of meaning. A baby who cries a lot is a fact; its meaning to the mother or father is constructed and, at its best, needs to be mentalised. Analysis and the creation of meaningful perspectives in social work have frequently been bemoaned as absent in social work (Webb 2001). The means by which this comes about is a matter for exploration, insight and learning, and supervision is critical to this. Facts, information and analysis are no less important in this, but alone they cannot supply enough of a framework that makes good social work or good supervision possible.

So how might this happen in the case example above? In a re-imagined scenario, the supervisor does not reassure the social worker by saying that as long as she has the required information, then the service user's disengagement does not matter. Instead, he takes up a position of respectful curiosity and asks the social worker to describe more fully what she feels uneasy about. The social worker is surprised by this question as her supervisor has been preoccupied recently in making sure that assessments are completed on time and he has shown no more interest than this. The social worker has a flash of anger at this point and replies by saying that she feels that she is nothing more than an automaton – getting information, entering it in the system, not missing deadlines and arranging for others to do the really interesting work. She is surprised at herself for having been so forthright and looks at her supervisor rather anxiously. The supervisor feels somewhat defensive at this outburst. He knows he has been preoccupied with meeting timescales for completing assessments and this has driven him in his work for some time now. His initial response is to want to explain how much pressure he has been under and to ask the social worker if she understands how much is at stake and what could happen if performance targets are not met. He feels that the social worker is being naive in not understanding what is at stake.

The scene is set for a confrontation as neither social worker nor supervisor feels that their difficult position is being understood by the other. They are on the cusp of the supervisor instructing the social worker to grow up and get on with what she is being paid to do. However, the supervisor takes a step back inside of himself and, despite feeling angry, senses the social worker's distress underneath her anger. He says, 'It sounds as if you are feeling pretty fed up?' The social worker is a bit taken aback by this because it is a very accurate representation of exactly what she has been feeling. Tears start to well up inside. The social worker explains that when she says that she is concerned about a service user's disengagement in an interview, she wants to be taken seriously. It is not sufficient to be reassured that it doesn't matter.

The supervisor starts to feel under attack again and wants to defend his position. He was feeling more sympathetic to the social worker but feels now that this is not being appreciated. The pressure is mounting for the supervisor's attempt to establish a supportive/companionable form of relating to move towards a more dominant/submissive form of relating. Either the social worker gives way and backs off, because she feels anxious or guilty about the anger and dissatisfaction she is expressing, or the supervisor backs off, because he is feeling anxious or guilty about his failure to engage with the social worker over the difficulties she had expressed from the interview with the service user. The resolution of this issue will depend on either the supervisor or the social worker having the capacity inside themselves to think about what is happening and be able to express this in a way that restores the potential for this to become a supportive/companionable form of relating, rather than taking a dominant/submissive form. The capacity to do this will depend on the degree to which each can attempt to understand the way not only their own mind is working but also that of the other. Central to this is an understanding that each of them has a mind and that this conflict is not just an expression of the goodness or badness of them as people or the cause that they represent.

The ambiguity of social work and the supervisor's role

Throughout its history, social work has taken the position of providing a facilitating link between the state and the individual citizen in areas such as child care, mental health, disability and older people. This facilitating link has often been driven by the idea of the supportive/ companionable relationship expressed through the qualities of compassion, empathy, warmth and a non-judgemental attitude. Although this has been a driving force, the subjective experience of many service users is that they feel misunderstood, hurt and humiliated by the things that social workers do, defined as they are by the state and its welfare organisations. If the primary tool of social work is seen as a supportive/companionable relationship, and the service user sees it as a relationship to be resisted or avoided because of the feelings that it stirs up, then it is a tool that needs some delicate handling. Holding these conflicting images of social work in mind at the same time is a very difficult thing to do. For the social worker, maintaining a position that combines warmth, empathy and compassion, when the service user feels suspicious and hostile about what the social worker is up to, requires great emotional maturity, insight and support.

The ambiguity in the social work role is also matched by the ambiguity in the supervisor's role. They have responsibility for checking up and ensuring compliance with the organisation's requirements to follow procedures and manage budgets and, in the longer term, to satisfy inspection and audit standards. These are demanding and exacting requirements and, as Power (1996) suggests, have become a part of the 'mentality' of being a manager/supervisor. At the same time, the supervisor will need to be mindful of the complex thoughts and feelings of their supervisee arising from practice. Finding a position in supervision that combines warmth, empathy and compassion for the struggles and realities of a social worker's practice with the organisation's demands to achieve targets and remain procedurally compliant can be very challenging. As with practice, supervision is an arena where complex issues interact, which can easily lead to a collision, with the social worker being wary of what the supervisor is up to and the supervisor being wary of what the social worker is up to. Relationship-based social work may be driven by a belief in the power of human beings to work in a supportive and companionable way with one another through difficult times to resolve difficult issues, and so might supervisory practice, but a belief or commitment to do so is not the same as being able actually to do so. There are always powerful forces at work embedded in the dynamics of relating, and in social work these are highly charged because they happen at the point where the personal meets the political, organisational and bureaucratic. Relating at this boundary can stir up the strongest of feelings – heightened expectations about the possibility of problems being addressed and resolved, or heightened fears about humiliation, abandonment and loss. These expectations and fears are as alive in supervision as they are in working with service users. Understanding the impact they have on the purposeful activity of social work and the purposeful activity of supervision is critically important.

To return to the supervision session – in the second version of the scenario there was a turning point, poised at whether this would become either a dominant/submissive or a supportive/companionable form of relating. This was seen to depend on the extent to which either the social worker or the supervisor had a working concept of their own and the other's mind. The supervisor had already recognised that the social worker was feeling very fed up with the work that she was expected to do, and particularly the pressure she was under to complete assessments on time. There was also a sense that the social worker felt that, following her assessment, all the interesting work was then allocated to other professionals to do. But the social worker's accusation about the preoccupation of her supervisor with timescales was threatening the stance that the supervisor was attempting to take. If he responds to this threat by becoming defensive, then it is likely that a dominant/submissive form of relating will establish itself. In fact, the supervisor can see just how deeply upset the social worker feels by the tears that she brushes away and the pain in her expression. He says, 'You really are very upset by all of this and I think I need to try to understand this a bit better.'

The social worker is relieved that her expression of feeling has not led to her finding herself in deeper, maybe dangerous water, and the supervisor is continuing to show an interest in understanding what it is that has stirred them up. The social worker thinks for a moment and then explains that she came into social work to work with people. She hates it when service users treat her with suspicion and distrust. She knows what a difficult time so many people have had, and that is true of the service user at the centre of this issue. She really wants to support service users and find ways of getting alongside them a bit better, not just sit there with a pen hovering over a form. But she is also worried that if she tries to open things up a bit with the service user and say something to the service user about what she feels is going on in the interview, the service user will be angry. The supervisor asks, 'Angry about what?' The social worker thinks for a moment and says, 'Angry that his life has not worked out the way he thought it would. Angry about needing me to sort out his problems for him. Angry that he has to perform and meet my expectations before he can get the services he needs.' The supervisor asks, 'And what if he was to express his anger in this way?' The social worker replies, 'I would feel better for him having shared what he really feels with me, so that we could then spend some time trying to think about it.' 'Yes,' replies the supervisor, 'a bit like what we are struggling to do!'

This imagined supervision session focuses on the importance of the supervisor having a continuous internal dialogue that becomes the basis of his dialogue with the social worker. The supervisor needs to understand that it is legitimate, necessary and important to pay attention to those parts of an interview or a supervision session beyond the collection of required information. He needs to have accepted that social workers require support to be curious. In turn, the agency also needs to have accepted this and allow curiosity to develop and become meaningfully a part of organisational and professional practice. But it is important to acknowledge the pressures that exist for the supportive/companionable internal dialogue described to be replaced by a more dominant/submissive internal dialogue. There may be many contributory factors – the supervisor's own history of relationships and his internal working models, or contextual factors such as the demands of an organisation's audit culture. The advantage of the Heard and Lake (1997) model is that by introducing just one additional dimension – the dominant/submissive – to what is a familiar dimension – the supportive/companionable – they have outlined a particularly powerful idea. If social workers aspire to develop relationships with service users that are supportive/companionable and they find themselves thinking that the relationship does not feel like this, then they may be encouraged to think about what is happening. Knowing and putting this into words may then open the kind of thinking that develops insight into the processes at work with the service user.

This reflective and curious stance should also be possible in supervision. A supportive/companionable internal dialogue may help most people to quell the darkest of their feelings when they are stirred up. A supportive/companionable dialogue with another person may do the same thing. Developing supervisory practice that enables social workers to learn and develop their professional knowledge and skills and apply these in a thoughtful and relevant way means creating the kinds of space where reflecting on the powerful emotions stirred up in both the work and in the process of discussing the work is possible. The framework developed in this chapter is important because it starts where the service user is, not where we wish them to be. The more we can create a space inside ourselves that has the capacity to relate to where service users find themselves, the more effective we will be. The more supervision starts with where the supervisee is, not where we wish them to be, the more effective it will be. The greatest resource is that which exists inside us and between us, if only we can bear to look.

Chapter 13

Professional Leadership for Relationship-Based Practice

ANNA FAIRTLOUGH

Introduction

Other chapters in this book advocate for the central importance of relationship-based practice in social work. This chapter explores how we can support the development of these forms and understandings of practice within organisations and the profession as a whole. It argues that professional leadership – conceived as something that we all do throughout our career and not something that is just done by those in senior management positions – is necessary to do this. It will examine the personal and professional qualities that we need in order to foster our own professional leadership and the external conditions and relationships that best enable us to do this. The chapter takes as a case study the career development of a social worker, who is acknowledged as having achieved an exceptional level of skill in systemic-based, relationship-focused practice and has influenced others to practise likewise, and examines transformational, distributed and relationship-based approaches to professional leadership. It argues that to promote relationship-based practice we need to integrate social work values both in *what* we aim to achieve through our professional leadership and *how* we choose to exercise it.

Definitions and key concepts

Over past decades the concept of leadership, understood as non-coercive influence, has been increasingly central in management studies. Northouse (2013) provides a comprehensive overview of leadership theories and demonstrates how these have evolved from study of the characteristics and behaviours of exceptional individuals to examination of the organisational environments in which leadership takes place. Since the beginning of this century, social work management texts have also taken up the theme of leadership (Hafford-Letchfield *et al.* 2008; Gray, Field and Brown 2010). Hafford-Letchfield *et al.* (2014) use the idea of 'inclusive leadership' to bring effective relationships between people that use and provide services to the forefront of leadership practice in social work and social care. Lawler (2007) provides a useful categorisation of different dimensions of leadership in social work: promoting the public image of social work; improving staff effectiveness, social work leadership of inter-professional activities and social work leadership to counterbalance managerialism.

However, relatively little has been written specifically for professional leadership in social work outside of these management texts. Implicitly linking leadership with management has a number of disadvantages. It tends to de-couple continuing professional expertise from professional leadership and it implies that advancement in a management hierarchy is the sole route to professional leadership. It also tends to obscure the vital role of collaboration between practice and the academy in professional leadership. My own work on professional leadership for social work practitioners and educators (Fairtlough 2017) aimed to contribute to filling this gap and this chapter uses some ideas developed in more depth there. McKitterick (2015) asserts a need for 'self-leadership' – that is, consciously influencing one's thinking, feeling and behaviour to achieve one's objectives – for social workers to provide confident and skilful social work practice. Self-leadership needs to operate both on an individual basis for social workers, managers and educators, and for the profession as a whole.

The professional capability framework (PCF) introduced in England in 2011–12 provides a useful counter to the management-focused conceptualisation of professional leadership mentioned above. In this framework professional leadership is identified as one of the nine core domains of social work practice (British Association of Social Workers n.d.). It is seen as something that is undertaken by social workers at every stage of their career from novice to expert, though with growing depth, scope and degree of complexity. Although at advanced and strategic levels of practice we may specialise more in either direct practice, education or management, professional leadership is essential in all three of these areas. At the time of writing the PCF is being revised. However, the proposed new description of this domain encapsulates how professional leadership is understood in this chapter (College of Social Work 2015), so will be outlined here.

> Take responsibility for development of professional leadership appropriate to own role and status. Be proactive in selecting opportunities to model, promote or use professional leadership. Incorporate professional leadership into improving practice standards, influencing inside and outside the profession. Provide and model professional challenge of own and other's practice. Facilitate the professional learning and development of others through supervision, mentoring, assessing, research, teaching, and management.

Outside the UK context, other definitions have been developed within professional education; the University of North Carolina's definition[1] is highlighted as it adds two other important components of professional leadership: the need for 'self-knowledge' and 'moral courage'. I will return to these two aspects of leadership later in the chapter.

Two sets of concepts from the generic literature on leadership are particularly valuable in illuminating this understanding of social work professional leadership. The first draws from Burns' (1978) distinction between traditional understandings of management, which saw the management role as being to control the behaviour of subordinates with rewards, punishments and corrective criticism, which he described as 'transactional leadership', and 'transformational leadership'. Transformational leadership is involved with emotions, values and long-term change in people and organisations. Bass (1985) developed a well-known model of transformational leadership and identified four key components: idealised influence that models high ethical standards, inspirational motivation to promote commitment to best practice, intellectual stimulation encouraging creativity and innovation, and individualised consideration for others' individual abilities and needs.

The second body of ideas relates to what is often known as distributed leadership, but also as dispersed or shared leadership, which conceptualises leadership as something that can potentially arise

1   See https://ssw.unc.edu/files/web/pdf/LeadershipDefinitionandElements.pdf

in any professional interaction (Bolden 2011). Spillane (2006, p.11) understands distributed leadership to include any 'activities tied to the core work of the organisation that are designed by organizational members to influence the motivation, knowledge, affect or practices of other organizational members'. Clearly, this can be provided by anybody at any level of the profession: it arises from someone's actions, not his or her position. Definitions of distributed leadership remain contested but Bennett *et al.* (2003) identify the following common characteristics:

- emerges within groups of interacting individuals

- exercised by the many not just the few

- openness to the situations and contexts in which leadership can be exercised.

Fairtlough (2005) asserts that hierarchical structures and relationships are often our default position for imagining how to get things done. However, there are alternative ways of getting things done that we can use to exercise distributed professional leadership. One approach that has been identified is 'heterarchy'. Heterarchy distributes decision-making amongst participants and allows power to be exercised in different directions, laterally and from the bottom up, not just through a pre-determined top-down hierarchy. Multiple forms of knowledge and experience are valued within this framework. Working through inter-professional forums, creating horizontal relationships between people within and across organisations to develop new practices, co-production with service users and carers, and various steering and 'task and finish' groups are all examples of heterarchical practices in social work and social work education. In order to exercise distributed leadership we also need to take – and be allowed to take – some degree of 'responsible autonomy'. Responsible autonomy delegates authority for aspects of decision-making and action-taking to individuals, groups or teams within a transparent framework for accountability. It is similar to the notion of self-leadership discussed above. In any organisation or practice system all three ways of getting things done (hierarchy, heterarchy and responsible autonomy) are likely to be needed, although their precise constellation will be dependent on context and situation.

Whole systems work brings an ecological dimension to thinking about how practice systems can respond to complex problems that are not amenable to simple single-agency fixes, such as child sexual exploitation (Pratt, Gordon and Plampling 1999). It provides a useful set of principles and practices for enabling distributed leadership, heterarchy and responsible autonomy. Attwood *et al.* (2003) identify five keys to this way of working: strategic leadership, public learning, the significance of difference and diversity, different meetings and follow-through actions. *Strategic leaders*, rather than being the sole initiators of responses to complex practice issues, provide 'holding frameworks' that enable others throughout the system to 'be free to make sense and take action' (p.61). *Public learning* signals the importance of genuine collaboration between professionals and service users, carers and the wider public in sense-making and action-taking. *Difference and diversity* are significant not only in promoting equitable socio-economic and cultural representation but also in terms of incorporating the ideas and perspectives of people from every part of the system. In contrast to traditional conferences or top-down led presentations, whole systems meetings actively engage all participants, taking them out of 'audience mode'. Pratt *et al.* (1999, pp.126–132) describe a range of tools that can be used for this purpose. 'System mapping' involves participants honestly exploring what would really happen in an archetypal situation. 'Future search' invites participants to imagine an aspirational but realistic future and to plan concrete steps together to achieve this. 'Real time strategic change' enables policies or practice frameworks to be shaped through conversations between people representing the whole system. People are encouraged to agree to take specific action steps following the meetings. In the turbulent environments in which we work, *follow-through actions* are often hard to sustain, but engaging people in creating change is the best way to foster their continuing support.

Learning to become a professional leader in relationship-based practice: Nana's story

These ideas are now explored further through the professional social work journey of Nana Bonsu. I first got to know Nana when she was newly in post as a lecturer in the university where Nana was training to be a social worker. I then met her again some 15 years later when Nana returned to the same university to facilitate reflective practice groups with students. Nana's expertise in relationship-based practice was immediately apparent to me and my colleagues and in feedback from students. The following is taken from an in-depth interview with Nana. It makes use of her actual words (in quotation marks) combined with my summaries, reflection and analysis. It covers the stages of Nana's career from being a student and a newly qualified social worker through to becoming an advanced practitioner who is also supporting the professional development of others. Although Nana has had supervisory responsibilities, her passion is practice and teaching others. The interview used an appreciative enquiry approach, which investigates the circumstances that allow things to work well (Bellinger and Elliott 2011), as Anna's intention was to find out what had helped Nana to develop her expertise in relationship-based practice and professional leadership. The case study is used to explore the internal and external conditions that best facilitate development of professional leadership for relationship-based practice by educators, practitioners and managers.

'Being pulled apart and put back together'
Nana's story begins with her experience of professional training and education.

> 'We had to do a lot of peer-directed group-based learning. We had to decide what we were going to do in our project and who would do it. Looking back, it was so clever because it enabled you to work in a multi-disciplinary way early on without realising it. You had to think about how to work with difference. Some people were challenging…and you had to find a way through and come up with a solution. We were there to learn from each other.
>
> Paying attention to issues around race and class and power was very important. There was a real strong sense of involving service users…I became aware of the experiences of marginalised communities. Whose needs get considered? Who gets the resources?
>
> The teaching staff were genuine…I felt we were able to challenge, to say no we don't want to do it like that. While there was a sense of being assessed there was also a sense of being able to influence things…That's what made it a safe space. A permission to challenge hierarchy and each other. Sometimes it was difficult

but I grew from it. I think of myself as having been pulled apart and put back together again. And I wasn't the same person when I was put back together.'

Nana's account identifies the following as crucial to this stage of her professional development:

- opportunities to make sense of her learning with peers in self-directed groups

- respect for the expertise of service users

- awakening to issues of power, diversity and justice

- non-hierarchical atmosphere where students' own experiences and knowledge are valued and students are able to challenge others and staff without fear

- relationships with teaching staff who were genuinely interested in understanding her.

Social work education requires both instrumental learning, which involves abilities to appraise the accuracy and logical coherency of information, and communicative learning, which necessitates participating freely and fully with others in continuing dialogue (Mezirow 2009). Learning involves cognitive, emotional and social dimensions (Illeris 2009). The 'enquiry and action learning group work model' (Burgess and Taylor 1996) adopted by the social work programme Nana was undertaking enables students to bring together these different dimensions of learning to actively construct joint learning. Although not all students experience this approach to learning so positively, from Nana's perspective it provided her with a foundation for lifelong self-directed learning, critical thinking and teamwork skills.

The learning conditions described allow students to make use of heterarchy and responsible autonomy. Learning takes place horizontally within the student group and between students and service users rather than only in a traditional hierarchical relationship with an educator. The students have autonomy to determine aspects of their own learning and choose topics for research. Nana identifies that her learning about how power and diversity operated within the learning groups formed a foundation for her subsequent practice with diverse professionals. Her description of being 'not being the same person when I was put back together' evokes the idea of transformational learning (Mezirow 2009, p.92), which is defined as 'the process by which we transform problematic frames of reference (mindsets, habits of mind, meaning perspectives) – sets of assumption and expectation – to make them more inclusive, discriminating, open, reflective and emotionally able to change'.

Nana identifies the role that supportive – genuine, individually attuned and accepting – relationships with teaching staff played in enabling her learning. The concept of epistemic trust is of value here. Fonagy and Allison (2014, p.373) define epistemic trust as 'trust in the authenticity and personal relevance of interpersonally transmitted knowledge'. They suggest that secure attachment is a key pathway for children to develop epistemic trust, which generates confidence in one's own judgements as well as trust in those from whom one is learning. Similar processes may well be at play when adults learn from each other in social work education and practice.

'You will go to court but not yet…'

Nana then moved into her first qualified social worker role. She saw other newly qualified colleagues taking on complex child protection court work right at the beginning of their careers. She thought that she too ought to be able to do this. Her manager, however, judged that she was not yet ready. Nana recalls:

> 'I felt that's not fair. She's holding me back. And I also remember being so nervous about going to someone's home and talking to them about their problems and then going to child protection conferences and having to explain my work to the conference chair. My manager was right. It was important that I incrementally developed my skills and exposure to more difficult work. I was also in a team with very experienced workers so I was blessed with a lot of knowledge around me. I was able to build my practice on solid ground, to feel contained and grow in confidence.'

The significance of the transition from student to a newly qualified social worker (NQSW) is widely recognised (Walker 2014). Social workers do not always experience the smooth transition that Nana describes. As one of the participants in Bates *et al.*'s (2010, p.162) research put it:

> I was supposed to have a slow, gentle introduction, but basically there were a number of crises, so it was a baptism of fire.

Healy, Meagher and Cullin (2009), in their study of novice child protection practitioners in England, Australia and Sweden, found a high proportion of newly qualified social workers were undertaking complex work and many felt they were not 'supported or protected in the emotionally challenging aspects of their work' (p.306). If Nana had been allowed – or required – to undertake more challenging professional tasks than she was ready for at that time it is unlikely she would have ever have gained that solid grounding she describes. She might have left within two years as around 50 per cent of child protection workers in Europe do (Frost *et al.* 2017). Or she might have adopted defensive strategies (Whittaker and Havard 2016) such as being overly risk-averse and reliant on her manager's judgement, prioritising completing paperwork over direct contact with families, or alternatively developing a superficial confidence to deal with anxiety and insecurity.

NQSWs particularly value managers who recognise the individual person within the professional (Jack and Donnellan 2010). The key professional leadership skills that her supervisor exercised were to accurately identify Nana's individual level of development, understand how this related to the professional tasks she was asking her to do, and put in place strategies to support her development and protect her case load while she was learning. Nana's experience, however, may not be typical: 72 per cent of NQSWs ($n = 116$) surveyed in a study by Manthorpe *et al.* (2015) reported that supervision helped them improve their professional practice only a little or less. Although this chapter argues that social workers should be enabled to exercise more professional leadership, this is of course not to say that people should be pushed, or push themselves, to act beyond their current level of expertise. Indeed accurate self-knowledge of one's own capabilities is an essential element of distributed leadership. The other key factor that Nana identifies is having experienced workers around her with whom she could consult, a point echoed in the literature (Grant, Sheridan and Webb 2017).

'I did an evening class in hairdressing…'

Nana did develop confidence and skills and started to work with more complex cases, including those that entailed court work, and she became a senior social worker in another local authority. This was not a good time in her career, however. She describes it like this:

> 'I started to lose my sense of good social work. It felt that I was just filling in statutory forms. Six years in and I was getting bored. It was soul destroying. I was knocking on people's doors, demanding that they follow through with a child protection plan. Reading the riot act. These were women who were being abused, and I was making them feel like they were the problem. So I went off and did an evening class in hairdressing. I was seriously thinking of leaving social work.'

Nana's experience of statutory social child care social work chimes with many studies published at the time. More generally, many practitioners in statutory social work (particularly child protection) settings felt caught up in an overly proceduralised system where direct work with families was increasingly being pushed to the margins. For instance, following an enquiry commissioned by the British government, Munro's reports into the child protection system (2010, 2011a, 2011b) concluded that it was over-bureaucratised and deterred social workers from using their professional judgment and skills effectively. Priorities had become skewed: there was too much emphasis on compliance with prescribed processes and completing paperwork rather than support for thoughtful, relationship-based practice with children and families.

It is clear that Nana seriously considered leaving social work at this point, reflecting a concerning trend across the profession which has significant implications for, amongst other things, the development of confident and experienced professional leadership. Turnover rates for experienced child care social workers are high not only in England but also in the USA, Canada and Australia (Baginsky 2013). Baginsky highlights the negative effect of poor retention rates on the quality and safety of practice and on the morale and expertise of those remaining in post.

'This bravery in me…'

Nana did not leave social work, however, but made a sideways move into a principal social worker role at a family centre. Her experience there was different.

> 'My manager there was my secure base who was consistent and reliable. I modelled myself on her. She would challenge me a lot. She would ask critical questions. "So why is that a risk? Who is saying that is a risk?" In the statutory setting it felt like it was "them and us" whereas in the family centre under her management, even though we were working with some of the most difficult court-mandated situations, it was different. She helped me get in contact with myself as a human being. She helped me transform who I was in terms of practice and leadership…to find this bravery in me, to go out and learn about other ways of doing things, to come back and change my organisation.'

Nana recalls some significant pieces of work that marked her growing professional satisfaction and expertise. Through these her manager was helping her to integrate authoritativeness with compassion. In one situation, Nana was enabled to acknowledge her fear of telling one father that they were recommending that his children should not be returned to him and think empathically about his experiences and feelings. The meeting that she had dreaded ended with him shaking her hand and apologising for having previously been abusive to staff.

In this environment Nana was able to rapidly expand both her expertise in relationship-based practice and her professional leadership capabilities. She was one of the first to bring the 'signs of safety model'[2] into the organisation. The signs of safety approach is a strength-based risk assessment model for child protection practitioners that emphasises collaboration with parents in designing safety-orientated plans. Although more widely known now, at that time this model was less used in the UK. Using this model, Nana helped a mother, whose previous four children had been removed from her care, to make changes in her life so that she could safely care for her new baby. Nana helped this woman understand better the impact of previous traumatic experiences, to identify her strengths and to recognise what was now

2   See www.signsofsafety.net

different in her life. A pivotal moment was when she broke down in tears with Nana for the first time and from then on their work together became more effective because of the trusting nature of the relationship they established. The assessment report that Nana and her colleagues produced was recognised by senior managers as an outstanding piece of work. After this Nana was allocated another complex assessment that might otherwise have been given to a (costly) outside expert. Instead, this expert was employed to give Nana consultation while Nana herself undertook the work.

Another important influence on Nana's practice at that time was undertaking a Masters level family therapy course. Intellectually, her learning about relationship-based practice and systemic work transformed her practice and helped her incorporate a growing belief in herself as a professional leader. As she gained a reputation on the programme as being the one who would enthuse others about new ideas she began to realise her capabilities as a teacher. Overcoming her fears about her practice being observed resulted in her valuing, as never before, feedback from a reflecting team. This became a cornerstone of her practice. Inspired by the work of Dr Ann York, a local child and adolescent psychiatrist, on promoting reflective practice,[3] Nana initiated a visit with her manager to Dr York's service to learn about how they were implementing multi-disciplinary peer group discussions. Senior managers encouraged and supported Nana and another practitioner to establish similar groups across their organisation. Later, these groups were particularly commended during a formal external inspection of the quality of practice in the organisation.

A number of factors seem to be significant in supporting Nana's growing capacity to take responsibility for providing leadership for relationship-based and reflective practice in her organisation. Foremost in her account is the relationship with her manager, which enabled Nana to recognise and work with the emotional impacts of the work and empowered her professionally. Nana's description of her manager as a 'secure base' echoes the discussion earlier of epistemic trust: clearly their relationship provided an environment for Nana to critically reflect on her practice and build confidence in her own judgements and expertise. Her manager here is both modelling relationship-based practice skills and demonstrating transformational leadership

---

3   See http://capa.co.uk/11-key-components/10-peer-group-discussion

attributes. Nana talks about being supported to find the emotional 'bravery', similar to the idea of 'moral courage' discussed above, that she needed in order to influence others and proactively introduce new practice methods and organisational innovations. This relationship also allowed Nana to reflect on the affordances and constraints that being an African woman of immigrant parents gave her. On the one hand her family experiences of immigration and of being a black parent in South London afforded her insights into the lives of many families she worked with. However, she also had to overcome the constraints of a self-narrative about not belonging and not being good enough.

Ruch's (2007a) research identifies the conditions that best enable holistic reflection – that is, reflection that integrates emotional and experiential knowledge and is concerned with sense-making as well as practical or procedural tasks. She proposes a notion of 'holistic containment' comprising emotional, epistemological and organisational elements, adapting Bion's (1968) original formulation. Containment has been defined as the process whereby 'one person receives and understands the emotional communication of another without being overwhelmed by it, processes it and communicates understanding and recognition back to the other person' (Douglas 2007, p.33). Emotional containment involves the presence of trusting relationships between practitioners, managers and other professionals, and spaces for emotions to be processed. Epistemological containment provides practitioners with practice frameworks that facilitate integration of multiple forms of knowledge with ethical decision-making. Organisational containment refers to the capacity of an organisation to provide clear and supportive managerial structures and processes. All three elements are present in Nana's description of the circumstances supporting her professional development at this time.

Nana was able to access significant continuing professional and career development opportunities. The family therapy programme supported her intellectual and professional growth. She describes the reading that she did on that programme about relationship-based and systemic practice as like a 'light bulb'. The family centre provided an environment that was receptive to her bringing back these ideas to improve their practice and model this for others. Nana's manager trusted her to act with responsible autonomy. Nana developed confidence in seeking mentoring and consultation from others outside the organisation. Senior managers recognised her growing expertise and through providing a 'holding framework' were willing to allow her to exercise distributed professional leadership and move beyond a narrow definition of her role. As a result, practice innovation was led not hierarchically by top-down management requirements but heterarchically by those with practice expertise.

'I want to be creative in my practice and not be stifled...'

Nana is now undertaking a senior family therapist role within children's services. She had this to say when asked about her next steps in social work:

> 'I like the idea of being a professional leader. I think I have the right attributes. I have something that people want, they come to me. I think social work is a kind of political thing. I question what is happening, if certain issues come up, if certain sections of the community are not being served. I have the confidence to say things are not good enough. To challenge and to find solutions. I want to be creative in my practice and not be stifled, to develop new projects. These are the things that excite me.'

One new professional leadership activity she is undertaking is the role of 'teaching consultant'. This role has been developed as part of a Teaching Partnership that provides formal links between the university and three local authority partners. As part of these arrangements, practitioners, recognised for their expertise in specific areas of practice, come into the university to teach social work students alongside academic staff, which has had the effect of bringing social work practitioners and academics closer together. Nana has been involved in 'intervision' groups, which offer students a space to reflect on practice experiences that they are finding challenging (Akhurst and Kelly 2006). As its name suggests, 'intervision' emphasises horizontal relationships between colleagues rather than the vertical, hierarchical relationship intrinsic to supervision. Like other structured reflection models, intervision aims to provide an emotionally containing space in which participants can critically examine conscious and unconscious assumptions and develop new insights into practice situations (Ruch 2007b; Fook 2010). The groups are informed by relationship-based, psychodynamic, systemic perspectives and by critical social theory. A particular feature of intervision groups is that they are peer-led; relationships are non-hierarchical, with the roles of presenter, facilitator, note-taker and group member being interchangeable. There are clear expectations for each of these roles and ground rules encouraging curiosity, respect for multiple perspectives and attention to processes of power and participation. The facilitator plays a key role in keeping time, managing the process and encouraging application of the ground rules. Groups use the following format:

- The presenter presents their dilemma and key question for the group.

- The presenter listens to, but does not actively participate in, the group members' reflection on their hunches, feelings and fantasies about and analysis of the situation.

- The presenter gives feedback on their responses.

- Group members, again without the presenter, consider potential solutions to the presenter's question.

- The presenter reflects on their learning and insights.

- The whole group reflects on key learning.

Nana thinks that what she can offer as a facilitator is to act as a role model so students can learn how to use the groups effectively. She had this to say about her contribution to intervision groups:

'I was trying to fuse what I have learned throughout my practice and my family therapy training. The idea that we can use peer supervision in a collaborative way to challenge ourselves. To help students think about how they position themselves in terms of their race, their class, their ability, and what that might mean about how they position the families they work with. With peers who are positioned differently...it can help us to take a different stance...I wanted to model how we can have conversations with each other, how to ask clarifying questions, how to hone down what the presenter wants. Everybody had the chance to act as the facilitator after watching me do it.'

Feedback on the experience of participating in one of these groups suggests that students found that the intervision groups helped them think about relationship-based practice issues and provided an emotionally containing environment in which to explore dilemmas they were experiencing during practice learning. The groups served as an important bridge between practice and academy. For some students, the groups provided a powerful experience of intimacy and trust not found elsewhere in the taught programme or in their placement agencies. Students identified that the involvement of teaching consultants, such as Nana, was particularly valuable. Nana was thus supporting the students to use holistic reflection through providing for them, in a parallel process, the holistic containment that she herself has experienced, and thereby enabling students to learn about and become professional leaders for relationship-based practice themselves.

In terms of her professional practice, Nana is interested in developing relationship-based practice interventions that go beyond work with individuals and families and extend into the wider community. She describes how she has worked with some young women who were vulnerable to child sexual exploitation (CSE).

'I had a spate of girls going missing. I was going into different homes and it was the same story in each of them. So I said to the mothers – I had a moment's hesitation about the ethics of this but I took the risk – "I know that your daughter is with so-and-so because they go missing together." I had a meeting with all these girls and they brought their friends. I asked a female colleague in my team to join the meeting. We had a massive group of girls in the room eating fried chicken. And we asked: "What is going on out there when you go missing? Do you guys know what CSE is?" There was this girl, she was a bit older and was almost taking on the role of a therapist but using their colloquial language. She was saying, "Do you want to know what others are calling you?" The girls were affronted that they were known as girls that gave "sexual favours" but it made them think. I had a meeting with the mothers too. They all shared numbers and agreed what they would do when the girls went missing. That was more sensible and useful than sitting in endless meetings with the police.'

The Teaching Partnership referred to earlier provides a vehicle by which 'whole systems working' could be deployed to develop this piece of work. The Teaching Partnership Board, which comprises senior staff from the partner agencies and provides governance for the partnership, is committed to supporting distributed leadership and is in the process of agreeing a common practice framework with relationship-based practice at its core. This provides the necessary 'holding framework'. The young woman who 'acted like a therapist' demonstrates the expertise already existing within local communities. This initiative incorporates the principle of 'public learning' discussed earlier as young people and parents are being empowered to make sense of what is happening in their communities and co-produce solutions (Social Care Institute for Excellence 2013, updated 2015). The relationships that Nana has built while undertaking this piece of work and those that have been developed between practitioners, experts by experience, academics and managers through the various activities of the Teaching Partnership would form a nucleus of people to develop new responses to child sexual exploitation in this locality. A whole system event could deploy a system-mapping exercise to bring together young people and families from communities affected by child sexual exploitation, social workers and their managers at all levels, social work academics, and other professionals such as police officers or teachers to honestly examine what is happening when young women go missing and use 'future search' to imagine alternative options. Once these options have been developed, 'real time strategic change' strategies could be used to shape new policies and practices. Academic partners could play a role in undertaking action research on this initiative or supporting others to do so.

Conclusion

This chapter has explored the place of professional leadership in promoting and sustaining relationship-based practice. Professional leadership has been understood as something that social workers undertake at all stages of their career, and as practitioners and educators, not only as managers. The idea of distributed leadership emphasises the actions that people take rather than the position they hold. The concepts of heterarchy and responsible autonomy have been proposed as mechanisms to understand how distributed leadership can be exercised. Whole systems working offers some useful principles and tools for organisations and practice systems seeking to promote distributed professional leadership. Teaching Partnerships provide an example of one organisational model for facilitating diverse groups of people from a practice system to come together to achieve these aims.

The chapter has traced a practitioner's journey from student social worker to expert professional leader. It demonstrates that in order to have strategic influence it is not necessary to become a senior manager, provided practitioners are supported to develop the necessary personal and professional qualities and, crucially, are given opportunities to exercise distributed leadership. Nana's account highlights the central role of relationships with peers, educators and managers in her continuing professional development. She describes the transformational effect of one manager who provided her with a secure base from which she could learn and try out new ways of working. Many social workers report that they feel ill-prepared for the transition from practitioner to front-line manager, which suggests that organisational attention to support for the continuing professional development for supervisors and managers is also vital (Patterson 2015). The concept of holistic containment, comprising emotional, epistemological and organisational components, provides a model for understanding how organisations can support the conditions needed for social workers, managers and educators to embed relationship-based practice.

Professional leadership for relationship-based practice requires personal and professional qualities of confidence, courage and self-awareness as well as expertise in the practice itself. Nana's story suggests that these qualities are best fostered when they are mirrored in the relationships between educators, practitioners and managers. Although Nana's rapid development occurred when she moved away from a child protection team into a family centre there is no reason why this is necessarily so. After all, she was working with the same families in the same complex situations. Although, as acknowledged earlier, 50 per cent of child protection workers leave within two years of practice, Frost et al.'s (2017) international research focuses on the factors that explain why 50 per cent of child protection workers stay. Their multi-layered findings resonate with much of what has been discussed in this chapter: while well-established factors such as workload management, good supervision and supportive colleagues featured highly in their participants' accounts they found that 'creativity, power, reflective spaces and interpersonal relationships' (p.1) were also important. All these factors have been important for Nana too and without opportunities to exercise and experience them she might well have left social work. Perhaps we could all agree that although Nana would undoubtedly have been a great hairdresser, hairdressing's gain would have been the social work profession's loss.

Chapter 14

What Future?

Organisational Forms, Relationship-Based Social Work Practice and the Changing World Order

ANDREW COOPER

Introduction

A children's service social worker who had worked for her organisation for 20 years returned to work after a period of sick leave and asked to hand in her resignation by the end of the month. Her request was accepted. She left without any event to mark her departure and without telling a number of her closest colleagues. No subsequent communication to staff about her departure was made by her managers. The colleagues with whom she had worked closely valued her hard work enormously, and among service users she was known as a very friendly, responsive and discreet professional. She had been a very creative and sound professional, committed to relationship-based practice and good at sustaining work in conflictual situations; but by her own admission she was not a fan of procedures, assessment deadlines, and the increasing requirement to generate 'throughput' in order to meet targets.

The backstory to this departure is that a year earlier a new head of service had embarked on a radical restructuring of the service, a 'transformation programme' in her words. New open-plan offices were created, administrative support to teams was reduced and resources redirected to other areas considered vital for organisational survival. Hot desking, home working and weekly statistical reporting became the order of the day. An offer of voluntary redundancy to staff was made, and some other long-standing workers accepted it. For those who stayed, a trial period of adjustment to the new system was allowed, as well as an offer of voluntary redundancy at its conclusion. However, this offer seemed to be subsequently withdrawn. Administrative loads in relation to the front-line teams were felt to be suddenly overwhelming; sickness rates among the administration group increased; more staff left and were quickly followed by some replacements who found the loads impossible. Many social workers and team leaders complained that they were no longer receiving an adequate administrative service.

A small group of the remaining social work staff took out grievance proceedings against their management. The process of hearing the grievance took many months; an adversarial atmosphere took hold and many social workers and their managers were drawn into this. The organisation had prided itself on its strong and resilient capacity for talking through internal difficulties in an open and dialogic manner, but suddenly this seemed to have been lost. Eventually, the grievances were heard, and largely not upheld. It was at this point that the staff member went sick and then left.

It took some months for the organisation to 'rebalance' itself, and find a way to reconcile the 'two cultures' which seemed to have entered an unnecessary 'clash of clans'. Front-line social work staff organised among themselves to press management for more dialogue, so that the sense of 'impasse' between them could be overcome. The better atmosphere and working relationships that eventually emerged felt hard won, and many thought that a different organisation might not have recovered as well.

How can we understand this story? Is it just a 'local difficulty' or does it have a wider significance? Is it a question of someone, or many people, 'finding change difficult', or something more? In 2017 is this kind of experience more common than before, and if so, what sense do we make of it?

The remainder of this chapter is an effort to explore answers to these questions.

The performative state: a new welfare settlement

The chapter explores some current macrosocial forces that produce organisational conditions which generate a climate of acute day-to-day and longer-term tension for relationship-based social work practice and practitioners. The argument of the chapter revolves around four elements:

- the 'performative' trend in modern public service politics, policy and organisations

- the associated trend towards the production of 'performative' citizens, professionals, children, service users and performative subjective states in all of us

- the ambivalent dynamics of caring processes and caring systems, in which tendencies towards fragmentation and emotional distancing are supported rather than discouraged by the first two trends

- recent tensions produced by the permeative influence of 'survival anxiety' in organisations which 'calls forth' or 'hails' a range of problematic behavioural and attitudinal tendencies in individuals, whether managers or front-line staff.

Managing and practising in the context of the new matrix of tensions produced by the interaction of these elements is a genuine challenge. What pathways, if any, lie between the extremes of rebelliousness against the overwhelming impact of the 'performance agenda' on everyday life in social care organisations and uncritical compliance with these regimes?

The organisational forms within which social work is now practised in Britain have been changing rapidly for the last two decades. These organisational changes reflect the transformed character of the entire welfare state project in this country, and to a significant degree the political transformation of our society from a nation state to something closely resembling a 'market state' (Bobbitt 2003). Thus, modern social work matured within one political and ideological epoch – that of the post-war welfare 'settlement' – but now finds itself significantly captured by broader currents of change that have ushered in a different one. Within the first settlement, relationship-based social work practice and theory occupied a recognised, congruent and publicly well-understood, even if contested, place. Is this true, or even potentially true, of the new sociopolitical order that social work now inhabits? This is one central question to which this chapter is addressed, although the answer turns out be a complex one.

This complexity is partly explained by the fact that although the new and emerging sociopolitical forces acting on organisations are extremely powerful, they are not fully determining of the nature of social work practice or the organisations within which it is carried out. The psychodynamics of the caring process are themselves complex and subtle, and to some degree operate independently of historically specific political or social 'formations', while also intersecting with these in identifiable ways. In his book *Managing Vulnerability* (2010), Tim Dartington argues that:

> Systems of care around vulnerable people are subject to pervasive dynamics of integration and fragmentation, as they address contradictory pressures for positive intervention in a context of dependency. They fit uneasily with conventional measures of productivity and their association with societal issues of morbidity and death leaves them exposed to ambivalent attitudes of respect and despair in their development and management. (p.3)

This is a well-rehearsed idea in some quarters of the therapeutic world, but a vitally important one nevertheless: the inherent pain and anxiety of the task of responding to vulnerability and need in others affects not just individuals but whole systems of care, whether they be designed to protect children, support people with mental health problems, facilitate personalised care for disabled people in the community or provide residential care for people with advanced dementia. The organisational and professional psychic effort required to pull together around these tasks is immense, and opposed by forces that dispose us to fly apart from one another, to fragment our systems.

The core emotional and relationship difficulties of the caring, safeguarding or socially controlling task vary considerably according to the nature of service-user populations. Thus, unthinkable anxieties about child torture and murder lie at the heart of the child safeguarding task, and fears about the slow, painful, irreversible decline towards death, in which there are usually few tangible rewards for caring effort, may be at the centre of the long-term care of people with chronic dementia. But, as Dartington also notes:

> The culture of targets and audit in the delivery of public services – a distortion of organisational theory developed in other sectors – has made the effective delivery of humane and responsive services more difficult to achieve and maintain. (Dartington 2010, p.xviii)

Targets and audit are not accidental features of the modern organisational landscape, but integral parts of the new welfare settlement which embodies a new social contract between government and citizens, in which the role of the former is to facilitate the provision of choice and opportunity (for education, child care, health, personal social services, residential provision in old age) and the role of citizens is to access these opportunities in an informed manner (Cooper 2008). Improved performance, offering demonstrated value for the taxpayers' money, in a dispersed organisational system that must meet auditable, transparent standards via processes of 'governance' (not quite 'government' but not quite 'not government') is the modern norm. A central feature of this new culture of welfare has become known as 'performativity'. Organisations, services, parents, children and professionals are all assessed on the basis of their behaviours, performances and success or failure in meeting defined performance standards. As Howe (1996, p.88) puts it, 'It is the client's performance which matters and not what causes it. "Performativity" becomes the dominant criterion for knowledge evaluation.' Performativity as a concept has been most fully elaborated within the field of cultural studies, often associated with intellectual stances that repudiate the idea of a human subject beyond or outside language and behaviour. Whether one agrees with this or not, similar assumptions seem to be in play in modern social policy's interest in the behavioural dimension of citizens' and professionals' functioning at the expense of any concern with their 'subjectivity'.

Under these conditions, what becomes of the whole spectrum of ideas and practices that are the traditional realm of the therapeutic or relationship-based professions – subjectivity, intersubjectivity, selfhood, human development, relationship, self-determination? How does, or can, the centrality of performance in modern health and social care square with a conviction that relationships are integral, as both means and ends, to this kind of work? This is the first question facing relationship-based social work in the early twenty-first century.

Professional identity: more than just a little misunderstood...

There is a pervasive tendency within the British social work profession to believe, and feel, that we are misunderstood by society and the political and policy processes. This disposition has some basis in reality since it is hard to think of another social grouping whose occasionally well-publicised mistakes and 'failures' repeatedly give rise to widespread attacks on the whole profession and its raison d'être. But over recent years it has become clear that governments have used moments of structural professional vulnerability – such as the Bristol children's heart surgery scandal – to acquire political leverage over all the key public health and social welfare professions. In the minds of some influential policymakers, once the power of protectionist professional associations has been breached, all our professional identities – as doctors, psychologists, nurses, social workers, therapists, teachers and so on – are to be refashioned within a single overarching 'modular' framework of transferable skills that will enable us to pursue portfolio careers but also be capable of maximum flexibility within an unpredictable market of labour needs. This is how the story unfolds.

More than 15 years ago a prescient sociological commentator on the changing nature of social work in Britain drew up a diagram of how he saw the future of this profession within the rapidly reconfiguring British public sector. The striking feature of this diagram, he noted, is that social work does not appear anywhere. Sure enough, the activity of social work and social care may continue, but no longer under the organisational rubric 'social work' or 'social services' (Clarke 1996). This imagined future is one in which:

> Nobody – and no organisation – does social work. No one is employed as a social worker. It represents a future in which social work has been fragmented into different types of service (child protection, family services and community care)... Not all of the services are organised through (much less provided by) local authorities – both child protection and community care have been moved to more independent positions within structures of multi-agency direction and control. (1996, p.56)

In 2010, if you were to ask any citizen, 'In which organisations do doctors, or teachers, work?' they would probably provide a confident and largely accurate answer – hospitals, general practice, schools and so on. There might be a less clear response to such a question about social workers, whose activities and primary organisational locations have been dispersed into a variety of new multiagency and multiprofessional service delivery networks – adult services, children's services, children's trusts, partnership trusts, to name but a few. What is the meaning of these developments and how do they relate to questions about social work practice methodology, which is, after all, the primary preoccupation of the present text?

The following diagram (Figure 14.1) is taken from a Department of Health (2009) workforce planning policy document in which all the familiar and traditional health care professions have disappeared in favour of a hierarchy of competencies (represented on the vertical axis by the levels 1–8) that range over a number of generic health care 'domains'. In principle, any individual might begin their career, in say, the bottom right-hand corner of the matrix and, across a working lifetime, make their way to the top left corner, having occupied various intermediate 'cells' through the years. In this model, professional identity is essentially uncoupled from the person or any sense that professional commitments and aspirations might have a basis in personal experience, biography or psychological processes such as identification or reparation (Cooper 2009a).

The notion of 'vocation' or professional 'calling' is alien to this concept of professionalism, for reasons that cohere with the central social anxieties driving this entire transformation of welfare. People who feel themselves to be deeply psychologically rooted in their professional identities are not likely to be casually flexible if called upon to transfer their practices in response to some new labour market demand. They are rather like 'dependent' welfare clients – unable and unwilling to adapt to the requirements of modern society, and a drag on the economy in consequence. In this new world order of portable skills and careers, it will not just be social workers who will have disappeared into the matrix of post-modern organisational forms, but everyone.

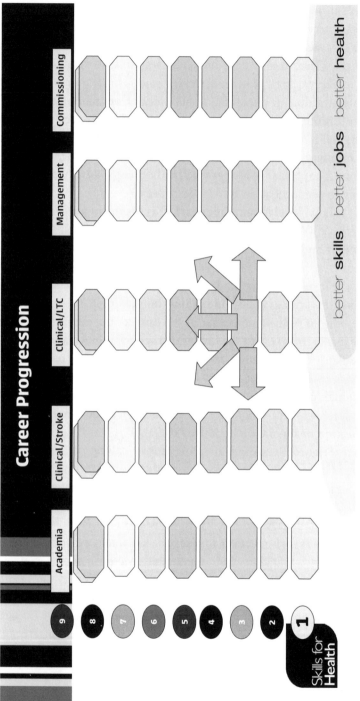

Figure 14.1 A representation of possible movement within a career framework
(Department of Health 2009)

This vision of 'new ways of working' goes far beyond familiar calls for better multiprofessional or interagency working practices, and entails a recasting of professional identities on lines that seem almost to invoke a revised concept of human nature. This new paradigm of professionalism challenges, or at best ignores, the roots of our deeper motivation to undertake social work; it is attempting to alter our relationship to ourselves as human beings each with, in Wendy Hollway's (2006) phrase, 'a unique life history of anxiety and desire provoking life events' that might constitute the ground of our sense of professional identity.

How to understand and respond to this challenge is the second big question facing relationship-based practice in our times.

Evidence-based practice or politics-based evidence?

So far, the argument of this chapter is that whereas debates about social work practice methodologies were once conducted in a context of wider public ideological contest about the nature of the welfare state and of society itself, this is no longer the case. The nature of human services – health, education, personal social services – including the organisations in which they work, as well as the principles shaping how professionals are trained for work in these services and how they are expected to develop across the span of a whole career, are all now heavily subordinated within a new and sometimes seemingly monolithic concept of social and political life. This is the ideological equivalent of a process of radical climate change. If the climate of a particular region alters dramatically, then so will the ecology of that region. Entire families or genera of flora and fauna will no longer flourish, not because they have declined in a context of competition, but because they are wholly unsustainable within the prevailing systemic conditions. There are no fish in the Mojave Desert.

Relationship-based social work practice, as well as many varieties of relationship-based psychotherapy, currently experience themselves as endangered species for just this reason – the political, policy and ideological climate seems to have swung decisively against them. On the surface, it seems the future of these methodologies is to be fought and decided in the court of 'evidence-based practice'; ostensibly this court offers a fair trial, with scientific method playing the part of judge and jury. Among those who accept this view, there is much angst concerning the failure of relationship-based practice or therapy to have entered this courtroom earlier and won some key precedent-setting cases that would have secured their place within the contemporary policy culture. There is some validity to this stance, if only because of the so-called 'Dodo bird' effect in which most varieties of relationship-based practice appear to perform equally well in well-conducted scientific trials so that 'all shall be winners and all shall have prizes' – as long as you enter yourself in the race. However, the argument has some important shortcomings.

First, the evidence-based practice movement is part of the new policy climate and is not neutral with respect to it. A 'trial', whether legal or scientific, may be scrupulously conducted, but its premises might still be called into question. Should there be a law against X at all? Can this question be decided by 'science' alone? Is the 'science' in question well adapted to the object of investigation or not? But second, and more important to the thesis advanced in this chapter, the new ideological climate is not primarily concerned with rational debate about the best way to run human services, but with a much more radical and far-reaching project of instigating a new and dominant set of assumptions about what it is to be human in the first place.

The role of new forms of service provision, and of the new training and career development instruments that underpin these, is simultaneously both to 'provide for' human populations on a set of revised premises about what it means to have needs and to proffer services with respect to these, and to advance the project of 'reconstructing' our view of ourselves and what it is to be human and to have needs. Not all of us are employed in the human service industries, but all of us who are so employed also use these services or have relatives and friends who do so – as patients, learners, dependants and so on. Thus, the scope of the new forms of relationship being ushered in under the guise of public sector modernisation, marketisation or transformation is vast and seems to entail nothing less than the nature of our citizenship.

In all this the role of formal organisations and organisational cultures is key because they are the most important intermediate social formations standing between the policy machine and citizens themselves; the emerging nature of relationships among the professionals and other staff groups who work in the new public sector, and between these people and those who use services, is a barometer of social and personal change. Thus, the third big question facing relationship-based social work is a political one. The struggle to find hope and meaning for relationship-based social work in contemporary political and cultural conditions is almost certainly not a passing difficulty. It is profoundly connected to processes of political transformation, and therefore calls upon us to consider whether, and how, to take a political stand in response. Can relationship-based social work find an effective political or cultural voice? This is the third big question it currently faces.

The contradictions of caring

In *Managing Vulnerability* (2010), Tim Dartington writes:

> I have worked as a researcher and consultant with different systems of care over a period of 40 years, and have observed the effects of these dynamics on the delivery of services to older people, to people with learning difficulties and physical disabilities, to children. In this time I have come to the view that an understanding of the underlying contradictions of what they are being asked to do is necessary to allow for the development and maintenance of good practice and the avoidance of abuse.

Some of these 'contradictions' are inherent to the task, and, we would argue, to human nature – tendencies towards organisational co-operation jostle permanently with trends towards fragmentation and a retreat into professionally narcissistic and self-protective states of mind (Cooper 2009a); our wish to care for the vulnerable may be directly opposed by a desire to turn a blind eye towards the violence, injustice or cruelty that powerful dependency needs arouse in us and in others. However, a key question is whether new and emerging organisational forms support adaptive or maladaptive defences against the difficulties of the task. Here a narrative developed by another organisational consultant, Tony McCaffrey, is particularly helpful.

The story begins with the familiar idea for which we are indebted to Isabel Menzies-Lyth (1988): the organisation as container of professional anxiety arising from the nature of the primary task. Strong systems for the provision of reflective supervision to front-line staff might be part of this picture. But at a certain juncture, in the 1980s perhaps, new forms of anxiety begin to bear down on institutions. 'Rationing anxiety' arises as we lose faith in the infinite capacity of the state to fund health and social welfare in this country – people are living longer, the proportionate tax base to fund pensions and the economically inactive is shrinking, medical technologies are proving expensive as well as effective – and in recognition of these developments, or perhaps emphasising them at the expense of seeking state-funded solutions to them, new ideologies of welfare and health provision make their appearance. The tension that begins to appear is well illustrated in a story told by Tony MCaffrey. He was consulting to a group of managers in a north London hospital, struggling with the impact of cost savings, so that acute bed spaces were full to overflowing. There was a serious road accident on a nearby busy highway, and a patient was flown into the hospital by air ambulance. The accident and emergency manager arrives late to the consultancy group as a result, related this story and adds, 'But, fortunately, the patient was dead on arrival.'

Markets or quasi-markets make their appearance, and in their wake comes the whole panoply of performance management systems, audit regimes and regulatory practices with which we are all familiar. New forms of survival anxiety appear – less directly associated with money, more with quality and the measurement of quality. For short, we call this 'performance anxiety'. As the imperative towards a mixed economy of care evolves in tandem with the new commissioner/ provider split, compulsory competitive tendering and 'contestability', traditional boundaries between different sectors of provision – public, private, independent – become blurred. Services are delivered via partnerships, networks and multiagency systems, and frequently no one seems to have single overall control or authority within these systems. The peculiarly named phenomenon of 'governance' referred to above appears in an effort to provide some form of order in the face of the potential chaos of these new systems, many of which operate at arm's length from the state. 'Partnership' or 'governance anxiety' is added to the gallery.

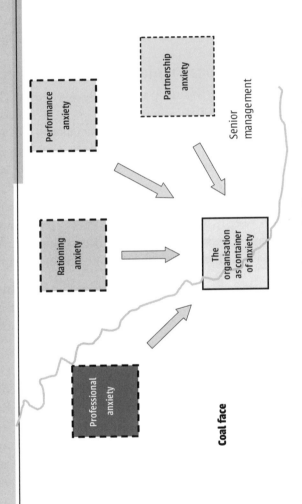

Anxiety in Organisations – a history

Performance anxiety

Partnership anxiety

Senior management

Rationing anxiety

The organisation as container of anxiety

Professional anxiety

Coal face

Figure 14.2 The evolution of public sector anxieties
(reproduced with kind permission of Tony McCaffrey)

Increasingly, a fracture appears within organisations (Figure 14.2): senior and middle managers face 'outwards' in their effort to manage the demands of cost, competition, performance and partnership, leaving front-line staff isolated in their struggle with the face-to-face task, which in truth may not have changed that much. Most first-line and middle managers to whom I have shown Figure 14.2 seem to recognise the picture; more than one has said something like 'I walk along that jagged line every day.'

At the organisational borderline

I have been narrating this story and writing about these predicaments for many years, but in 2017, after nearly a decade of 'austerity', it seems to me that the 'jagged line' metaphor is inadequate in various ways. The formulations now seem to me insufficiently dynamic, especially when I reflect on my experience of what is happening inside organisations labouring under the stress of contemporary survival anxieties. It's not that there is just a kind of stand-off at the boundary, the interface (or lack of it) between clinical or delivery systems and managerial ones; something more sinister and troubling occurs. In a recent interview the actress Maxine Peake, speaking of our contemporary politics, said:

> I cannot believe the callousness. Why are we not in the streets rioting? Why are we not in the streets going, 'You cannot treat people in this country like that'? It's absolutely distressing when you go to Manchester and see the homeless people on the street. Every time I go back, there's more. (Hattenstone 2017)

One might read this as a version of the age-old question about why the emmiserated masses do not conform or respond to the plans and exhortations of the revolutionary leadership. Whatever one's stance on this, or however you formulate the problem, it remains, I think, a pertinent and important question. Back in the 1970s I was never sure I understood Louis Althusser's theories of ideological state apparatuses and their relationship to the constitution of 'subjects', and so what follows is probably a travesty to any committed Althusserians here present; but it is my deep and distant recollection of these ideas that has given shape to my recent thinking about organisational experience. Althusser was among the first to propose that the symbolic structures and systems that bind individuals to the societies they inhabit are more subtle and complex than the original Marxist notion of ideology as 'false consciousness' suggests. Rational analysis of the 'true' state of affairs buried beneath the ideological overlay does not lead to inevitable emancipatory action. Why not? Well, because 'ideology' gets inside us in various ways, and so we misrecognise not just the external state of affairs, but ourselves too. In various ways, different thinkers took up the analogy between a psychoanalytic account of how we deceive ourselves, misrecognise our own afflictions or become alienated from our desires, and a political analysis that sought to understand a similar problematic at the level of social relations. Althusser's account of how this happens, how an individual becomes a subject within an ideological state apparatus, is as follows:

> I shall…suggest that ideology 'acts' or 'functions' in such a way that it 'recruits' subjects (it recruits them all) or 'transforms' the individuals into subjects (it transforms them all) by that very precise operation I have called interpellation or hailing, and which can be imagined along the lines of the most commonplace or everyday police (or other) hailing: 'Hey, you there!'
>
> Assuming the theoretical scene I have imagined takes place in the street, the hailed individual will turn round. By this mere one-hundred-and eighty-degree physical conversion he becomes a subject. Why? Because he has recognised that the hail was 'really' addressed to him and that 'it was really him who was hailed' (and not someone else). (Althusser 1971)

My own very 'local' experience is something like this — as the new commercial and business culture has taken hold I have a witnessed a number of decent, good people become fully signed-up recruits of the new organisational and managerial order, and unable any longer to openly or publicly articulate any sympathy with, or recognition of, those who 'carry' the continuing responsibility for delivering the organisation's 'primary task'. More precisely, what appears to have been 'hailed' in them are particular characterological dispositions which I recognise from the 'old selves' I knew, but which are now dominant in the service of the task to which they have become recruited. Sometimes this takes the form of a disposition towards rather brutal and insensitive treatment of subordinates in the system, or in other instances an extreme, cautious compliance with the dictates of the system and culture, a kind of 'follow orders at all costs' mentality.

In myself and among my own peers I observe different processes. People who once felt confident and free to speak out, question, interrogate organisational trends and decisions are publically silent. The moment I was 'hailed' into this subject position is clear to me. 'You have a bit of a reputation as a provocateur', said one of the new managerial class. Once, if someone in an equivalent position had made this remark to me, it would have been intended as, and received by me as a small badge of honour. This time I heard it, and internalised it, as a warning.

Thus has 'the organisational borderline' evolved in my experience. The capacity for internal 'relatedness' has dissolved, despite some genuine efforts on the part of the silenced majority to revive it. As I noted at the outset, it is not just a kind of stand-off, but a line across which fantasies and projections flow in abundance. Leaders and followers are sundered from one another, the latter continually fearful of attracting the label of dissenter, the former seemingly gripped by the belief that there is a constituency of provocateurs and saboteurs who must be controlled, suppressed or expelled if the 'project' is not to be derailed. Followers live in a state of some anxiety for themselves, some harbouring and containing rebellious impulses, but with little capacity to actually test the reality of their own fantasies of persecution. The constructive contribution of the followership to the total organisational effort is hampered, enacted through a more or less sullen compliance rather than a mature sense of co-operation.

So what actually is the 'project' now, and how can we explain or understand the state of affairs that has evolved? What is the relationship between 'material' or economic realities and fantasy structures in this set-up? I do believe that the forces and pressures bearing down on those at the top are immense, and I for one am grateful I do not have to directly contend with them. Organisational survival really is at stake in many circumstances and there really are predators out there waiting and watching for their chance to move in and asset strip organisations, while of course we are watching and waiting with the same aim in mind. Takeover of a failing outfit is one possible route to growth, and hence survival. Those 'at the top' feel themselves responsible for the project of 'survival' and I assume are haunted by the fear of failure. Cynically, we might believe that such a fear of failure is to be more explained by fear of reputational damage to career aspirations that 'failure' might engender, than anything else. But I don't want to buy this completely. In conclusion I want to explore the role of the superego and the ego ideal as important elements of the fantasy structure that shapes borderline functioning under conditions of survival anxiety.

There is a story about one of the great Kleinian psychoanalysts, who smoked well into her old age then managed to give up only to replace it with addiction to Nicotine chewing gum. The story goes that she was analysed by Klein herself, and when she first lay down on the couch, Klein said, 'You may smoke.' But the permissive communication was received as an instruction, with life-long consequences. Such is the power of the superego to shape our lives.

It is not an accident, I believe, that when Althusser evokes his scene of being 'hailed' by ideology, the persona of the one doing the hailing is a 'police' figure. Ideology typically hails us from a position of authority and power. But of course how we hear and internalise this communication is not determined. Rather it is received and taken on in accordance with the quality and character of our own superego and ego ideal functions. For reasons of my personal biography, I am still inclined, initially at least, to internalise demanding or aggressively charged communications from almost anyone as instructions or injunctions, rather than as propositions to be considered and thought about. So when I am informed by one of my bosses that I have a bit of a reputation as a provocateur, I am disposed to internalise this as an injunction – 'Stop that kind of behaviour, and behave yourself according to my rules in future!' Unthinking compliance or rebellion and delinquency are the ensuing binary possibilities, unless one can step back, find a 'third position' and mentalise the communication differently. Survival anxiety, and the associated fear of failure at the task of survival, seem to me often to generate a command and control culture in organisations that once had a capacity for more flexible and creative thought. This is the kind of 'new organisational borderline' I am proposing is now widespread, though not of course ubiquitous.

What is obscured in such a situation is the actual and potential continuing role of the ego ideal – the superego's friendlier counterpart that embodies the professional and ethical ideals and aspirations to do good work, that we all came into our sectors to pursue. Those who are subordinated in the command and control dynamic can no longer detect the ego ideal at work in their leaders and managers, because it ceases to be on show. Sometimes of course it is now genuinely absent, but frequently I believe it has actually gone into hiding, obscured by the anxious concern to ensure that deviance, dissent and disruption are eliminated from the followership. Such traits are felt to be dangerous. To show too much interest in the struggles, complexities and rewards of the front-line clinical or educational endeavour is felt to be risky, likely to encourage 'resistance to change' and so forth. The leadership is not experienced as valuing the ego-orientated nature of the primary task, and resenting this, those who labour at the front line are not inclined to want to understand or empathise with the struggles of the leadership. We become lost to one another, and this is both a tragedy and unlikely to assist with the very thing that ultimately unites everyone – survival – and beyond that finding maximum space to do creative work under very difficult circumstances.

Finding mental space: defending relationship-based practice in a cold climate

At worst, the organisational conditions outlined in this chapter will produce a parody of social work and professional care. One experienced practitioner, trained in another country where these processes are less advanced, described her experience of social work in an English children's service team as follows (Cooper 2009b):

> I am working in a factory. I have been working there for the last five years. When I started my job I did not think it was a factory. It didn't look like a factory, not from the outside and not from the inside.
>
> We produce initial and core assessments in our factory. Our management counts the assessments completed on a weekly basis and informs the workers of the results in team meetings and by emails. The workers don't seem to care about these numbers but they preoccupy the management.
>
> There have been many changes in our factory in the past five years, due to demands from above and competition from other factories. The management has been replaced, the teams were reconstructed, the machinery (workers, forms, IT systems) also saw great changes.
>
> I am quite confused about who is my master and who do I need to serve. Is it the customer or is it the government, and do they have conflicting interests? I am thinking of running away from this factory, to look for another job…in another factory.

Later she writes of how:

> The management measures (in percentages) the reports of initial and core assessments completed on time, and compare these to other teams. When the team manager reports these statistics in team meetings, I can recognise how my body becomes tense and my heart rate increases, and I get very angry. When we do not meet in team meetings, we often receive emails about the statistics, and I have the same bodily reaction. I have voiced my resentment to this ritual, but it was ignored by managers and other colleagues.

Speaking of her own organisation, she says:

> In order to adjust practice to inspection standards our organisation has become:
>
> - obsessive about records
>
> - obsessive about statistics
>
> - manipulative of the statistics.

The situation evoked here is just one of a range of outcomes in the new organisational world order that may be inimical to relationship-based work. We could summarise the most salient of them as follows:

- The commodification of care processes, and the deskilling of practitioners so that they become agents of a target culture, leading to experiences like those just described.

- A loss of authoritative leadership in organisations, and its replacement by excess 'managerialism', so that key tensions between, for example, business processes and professional value systems are obscured by the dominance of managerial imperatives.

- A loss of internal 'structures of thought and feeling' in organisations that have evolved out of the task performed, and their replacement by external structures that are experienced as alien, intrusive and demanding compliance. (See Hutten, Bazalgette and Armstrong (1994) for a discussion of how 'management' can be generated from within the organisation rather than be a vehicle of external imperatives.)

- In networked organisational forms, a difficulty in locating where responsibility or authority (as distinct from accountability) for complex tasks actually lies. Negotiation may be the only way to preserve an integrated focus on the work, but lack of clarity about lines of authority and responsibility will create 'fault lines' which facilitate fragmentation and splitting rather than integration. (See Conway (2009) for a discussion of these processes in work with looked-after children.)

- The replacement of familiar biographically rooted notions of professional identity with new skills-based, performative concepts of identity that require a kind of psychological deracination.

- And finally, a loss of 'relatedness' between the different layers of our organisations as they struggle with the forces acting on them, and start to fly apart. A degree of internal organisational tension is always healthy, but ultimately we need to be able to feel and believe in the idea that we are all on the same side in the human service endeavour.

In organisational circumstances where the anti-relational forces described in this chapter are in play, what can practitioners and managers do? I propose that the key question concerns the loss and/or recovery of a capacity to preserve organisational space for thinking and reflecting on working relationships and 'relatedness' among ourselves as the central tool of effective practice and organisational health.

On the one hand, many practitioners and managers acknowledge that the performance culture of modern social care organisations has resulted in some positive improvements: the development of a new sense of responsibility to ensure that interventions and decision-making are purposeful, needs-oriented and resource-efficient; and the importance of staff at all levels understanding the connections between local and particular decisions and processes and wider organisational purposes, constraints and possibilities. The new culture of 'accountability' for practice (if this extends beyond just ensuring that backs are covered to embrace an authentic sense of complex responsibility to different stakeholders) compares well with the unfocused but worthy, values-saturated culture of the 'old days'.

On the other hand, the extent to which organisational performance anxiety overtakes and defines, rather than supports and enhances, good practice and management frequently undermines and destroys any benefits that may accrue from this new culture. The state of mind of the practitioner who produced the factory narrative above is testament to the invasive and destructive power of these processes and the manner in which whole systems become dominated by them. Modern welfare organisations are businesses, and must needs go about their business in a businesslike manner. But it does not follow from this that every aspect of organisational functioning, including the subjectivities of staff, become saturated only with business principles. Yet it is precisely this category mistake that is perpetrated by the survivalist mentalities of so many managers in modern social work organisations. What are the alternatives?

I suggest that the first step is to develop a clear-sighted knowledge of the specific organisational conditions in which you operate. In particular:

1. an understanding of the particular emotional tensions inherent in the primary caring task of the team or organisation

2. an understanding of the particular character of the organisation within which the practice is located, arising from the sociopolitical forces acting on managers and leaders

3. an appreciation of the organisational culture produced by the interaction between 1 and 2 above.

Using these generic categories, one can evolve a more specific assessment of organisational culture. For example:

- How risk averse is the organisation? How inclined is it or not to support practice innovations that might entail 'risks'?

- How does the organisation manage its boundary conditions with respect to inspection, audit, regulation, performance, governance and so on? Does it easily project 'survival' and 'performance' anxieties downwards, or is it capable of engaging staff groups in thoughtful responses to these conditions?

- Can the management of the organisation tolerate the tension between the inherently uncertain and open-ended nature of direct practice and the requirement to meet the demands of the month-by-month performance agenda? And can it support its middle managers, in particular, in the complex task of walking the jagged line between competing outward- and inward-facing needs of practitioners and senior managers?

Knowledge of the above kind is power, or at least contains the potential for power. An understanding of the nature of the forces producing the conditions that shape our working experience is a variety of ideological work that contains the possibility of release from these same conditions. However, this is true if and only if we also engage with those aspects of ourselves that may be seduced into compliance with these same conditions or tempted to settle for blaming 'the system' in some way, rather than entering an active engagement with it. Few people relish the genuine risks that political struggles entail – and by now readers are likely to be in no doubt that this chapter is proposing that the threat to relationship-based social work is a political matter.

In the 1970s and 1980s, relationship-based social work in Britain found itself an unwilling participant in a pitched battle with the forces of 'radical social work' that attacked the former as reactionary, individualistic and un-political. Relationship-based practice was the decisive loser in this destructive civil war and lost confidence in itself thereafter. There are now signs of a recovery of confidence, but, as should be clear, the nature of the threat has altered dramatically; indeed, it has almost about-faced. So, the dark but, we hope, not completely dystopian message of this chapter is that relationship-based social workers and managers have a fight on their hands if good practice is to revive and flourish. This is nothing to do with any inherent weakness of relationship-based approaches but it is to do with the total political climate of modernised 'market state' Britain, which, by and large, does not offer a climate of warmth and nurture to the values and practices that are the central concern of this book.

Many of the trends discussed above are closely related to the dominance of market forces in the modern British public sector. However, particularly in the wake of the global financial crisis of 2008, many social and cultural commentators are now more actively questioning these trends (see, e.g., Sandel 2009) and calling for a renewed focus on values and social relationships as intrinsic social 'goods'. Likewise, there are signs of renewed vigour in some quarters of social work as efforts to reclaim social work and remodel it have become prominent. Relationship-based practices and 'bureaucracy busting' are aspects of these initiatives, and they are to be welcomed.

Conclusion

DANIELLE TURNEY, ADRIAN WARD AND GILLIAN RUCH

We started by acknowledging that the idea that the relationship is central to good practice in social work is not new, but argued that it still has that central role and, as such, deserves attention. We believe that the ways in which the different writers here have addressed the topic have shown that a commitment to relationship-based practice is still strong in social work, despite the many pressures and difficulties in maintaining this approach to practice, and that it is also as fundamental to the social work task as it has ever been. Social work has been and continues to go through enormous change. In many ways, it is a very different enterprise from that conducted during the 1950s and 1960s, in what might have been the heyday of psychoanalytically informed social work practice. But, as we conclude this book, it is not our intention to hark back to a presumed golden age of social work. If such a thing ever existed, it is now long gone and the task is to develop and promote a form of relationship-based practice that is fit for purpose in the twenty-first century.

As we have observed, questions about the nature of the professional relationship within current welfare configurations, how it has changed in recent years and the possibilities for its future development have pre-occupied many commentators on policy and practice, and the kinds of answers they come up with reflect their understandings of the broader context and 'direction of travel' of welfare practice. All agree, however, that the external environment plays a critical role in either facilitating or constraining the kind of thinking and practice that relationship-based work requires.

Working in and with relationships is emotionally demanding and frequently time-consuming. Even if the encounter itself is short-lived

279

it requires a level of engagement, openness and willingness to commit something of oneself. Maintaining relationships through time can be immensely satisfying and sustaining for the participants, but, again, this does not come without effort and, as the authors in Section 2 show, working with extremes of emotion can be extremely challenging.

If we are going to ask practitioners to take on this kind of emotional labour, we need to ensure that they are properly prepared for the task and properly supported by leaders and managers who value and promote relationship-based ways of working across the organisational structure. What this points to more generally is an acknowledgement right from the beginning of the process that social work education is about more than just technical competence. Clearly there is a range of basic skills and competences, and we would all opt for skilled and knowledgeable practitioners over the alternative! But perhaps one of the conclusions of this book is that this is a necessary but not sufficient condition for good practice, and without the interest in and ability to work with human relationships, the social work task is diminished. As part of their qualifying-level education and training, social workers need to have the opportunity to learn about the use of self and to apply their thinking in practice in a safe and supported way. Once in practice, the requirements to keep thinking and to develop further their understanding of the complex dynamics of inter- and intrapersonal relationships are integral to a broader programme of personal and professional development.

Having invited academics and practitioners to spend time thinking and writing about relationship-based practice, what has come through with increasing clarity is the view that this kind of work cannot be done in isolation or without support. The importance of thoughtful, process-aware supervision and the difficulties that arise in its absence are themes that recur frequently through the book. As different chapters make clear, there are some powerful – and potentially extremely informative – parallel processes that can be harnessed in the cause of relationship-based thinking and practice, or that otherwise may inhibit or reduce the possibility of working in this way. The relationship between service user and worker may be mirrored by that between worker and supervisor/manager. The conditions that support the development of empathic, empowering and effective relationships may be very similar in both cases, but each may therefore also be open to similar pressures and constraints.

Relationships take many different forms and work (or not) in a variety of ways. They are not in and of themselves either therapeutic or, necessarily, beneficial to the participants. It is the nature and quality of the relationship that matters, and these two aspects have been the focus of much of the discussion in this book. Good relationships take commitment, hard work and imagination; when they work, they can offer a vulnerable or emotionally damaged person the possibility of encountering themselves in a new and positive way, a chance to see themselves through different eyes – perhaps for the first time, as someone worthy of another's interest and respect.

This second edition has sought to address some of the gaps we identified in the conclusion to the first edition, attending more to the dynamics of power, prejudice and culture within relationships and specifically profiling relationship-based approaches to leadership and management within social care and social work settings, since we are arguing that these elements are so critical to the establishment of a truly relational approach to direct practice. There will always be more to write as relationships are themselves not static, constantly responding to the rapidly changing social and political context in which they are located. In that sense our job will never be done.

For now, though, we leave the last word to a social worker who is quoted by Lord Laming (2009, p.36) in *The Protection of Children in England: A Progress Report*. Said some while ago, it remains as pertinent as ever, and while the worker refers specifically to children, it is our view that the point being made has more universal application:

> Relationships are crucial; it's not about structures, it's about making it work out there for children.

Bibliography

Adams, R. (1998) 'Social Work Processes.' In R. Adams, L. Dominelli and M. Payne (eds) *Social Work: Themes, Issues and Critical Debates.* Basingstoke: Macmillan.

Advisory Council on the Misuse of Drugs (ACDM) (2003) *Hidden Harm: Responding to the Needs of the Children of Problem Drug Users.* London: Home Office.

Ainsworth, M. (1991) 'Attachment and Other Affectional Bonds Across the Life Cycle.' In C.M. Parkes, J. Stevenson-Hinde and P. Marris (eds) *Attachment Across the Life Cycle.* London: Tavistock/Routledge.

Akhurst, J. and Kelly, K. (2006) 'Peer group supervision as an adjunct to individual supervision: Optimising learning processes during psychologists' training.' *Psychology Teaching Review 12*, 1, 3–15.

Aldgate, J. (2009) 'The Place of Attachment Theory in Social Work with Children and Families.' In J. Lishman (ed.) *Handbook for Practice Learning in Social Work and Social Care: Knowledge and Theory.* London: Jessica Kingsley Publishers.

Althusser, L. (1971) 'Ideology and Ideological State Apparatuses (Notes Towards an Investigation).' In *Lenin, Philosophy and Other Essays.* London: New Left Books.

American Psychiatric Association (2000) 'Mood Disorders.' In *Diagnostic and Statistical Manual of Mental Disorders.* Fourth Edition Text Revision. Washington, DC: American Psychiatric Association.

American Psychiatric Association (2015, Fifth Edition) *Diagnostic and Statistical Manual of Mental Disorders.* Arlington, Vancouver: APA Publishing.

Anderson, T. (1987) 'Reflecting teams: Dialogue and meta-dialogue in clinical work.' *Family Process 26*, 4, 415–428.

Archer, C. (2004) 'Substance Misuse, Attachment Organisation and Adoptive Families.' In R. Phillips (ed.) *Children Exposed to Parental Substance Misuse: Implications for Family Placement.* London: British Association for Adoption and Fostering.

Aristotle (1981) *Ethics.* Harmondsworth: Penguin.

Arman, M. and Rehnsfeldt, A. (2006) 'The presence of love in ethical caring.' *Nursing Forum 41*, 1, 4–12.

Armstrong, D. and Rustin, M. (2015) *Social Systems as Defences against Anxiety.* London: Karnac Books.

Attwood, M., Pedler, P., Pritchard, S. and Wilkinson, D. (2003) *Leading Change – A Guide to Whole Systems Working.* Bristol: Policy Press.

Audit Commission. (1994) *Seen but not Heard: Co-ordinating Community Health and Social Services to Children in Need: Detailed Evidence.* London: HMSO.

Aymer, C. and Okitikpi, T. (2000) 'Epistemology, ontology and methodology: What's that got to do with social work?' *Social Work Education 19*, 1, 67–75.

Bachelard, G. (1969) *The Poetics of Space.* Boston, MA: Beacon Press.

Baginsky, M. (2013) *Retaining Experienced Social Workers in Children's Services: The Challenge Facing Local Authorities In England – Report to Department for Education.* London: Kings College. Accessed on 29/06/2017 at www.kcl.ac.uk/sspp/policy-institute/scwru/pubs/2013/reports/baginsky13retaining.pdf.

Bancroft, A., Wilson, S., Cunningham-Burley, S., Backett-Milburn, K. and Masters, H. (2004) *Parental Drug and Alcohol Misuse: Resilience and Transition Among Young People.* York: Joseph Rowntree Foundation.

Barker, C. (1986) *Flower Fairies of the Summer.* London: Blackie.

Barnard, M. (2005) 'Discomforting research: Colliding moralities and looking for "truth" in a study of parental drug problems.' *Sociology of Health and Illness 27*, 1, 1–19.

Barnard, M. (2007) *Drug Addiction and Families.* London: Jessica Kingsley Publishers.

Barnes, M (1997) *Care, Communities and Citizens.* Harlow: Addison Wesley Longman.

Bass, B.M. (1985) *Leadership and Performance Beyond Expectations.* New York: Free Press.

Bateman, A. and Fonagy, P. (2004) *Psychotherapy for Borderline Personality Disorder: Mentalization-Based Treatment.* Oxford: Oxford University Press.

Bates, N., Immins, T., Parker, J., Keen, S., Rutter, L., Brown, K. and Zsigo, S. (2010) '"Baptism of fire": The first year in the life of a newly qualified social worker.' *Social Work Education: The International Journal 29*, 2, 152–170.

Batmanghelidjh, C. (2006) *Shattered Lives: Children Who Live with Courage and Dignity.* London: Jessica Kingsley Publishers.

Bauman, Z. (2007) *Liquid Times: Living in an Age of Uncertainty.* Cambridge: Polity Press.

Bell, M., Shaw, I., Sinclair, I., Sloper, P., Mitchell, W. and Clayden, J. (2008) 'Put on ICS: Research finds disquiet with ICS.' Accessed on 05/06/2008 at www.communitycare.co.uk/Articles/2008/06/03/108421/analysis-of-the-integrated-childrens-system-pilots.htm.

Bellinger, A. and Elliott, T. (2011) 'What are you looking at? The potential of appreciative inquiry as a research approach for social work.' *British Journal of Social Work 41*, 4, 708–725.

Bennett, N., Wise, C., Woods, P.A. and Harvey, J.A. (2003) *Distributed Leadership.* Nottingham: National College of School Leadership.

Beresford, P., Croft, S. and Adshead, L. (2008) '"We don't see her as a social worker": A service user case study of the importance of the social worker's relationship and humanity.' *British Journal of Social Work 38*, 1388–1407.

Bertrand, D. (2000) 'The Autobiographical Method of Investigating the Psychosocial Wellness of Refugees.' In F.L. Ahern (ed.) *Psychosocial Wellness of Refugees. Issues of Qualitative and Quantitative Research.* New York: Berghahn Books.

Bettelheim, B. (1987) *A Good Enough Parent: Guide to Bringing Up Your Child.* London: Thames and Hudson.

Biehal, N. (2012) 'A sense of belonging: Meanings of family and home in long-term foster care.' *British Journal of Social Work 44*, 4, 955–971.

Biehal, N., Cusworth, L., Wade, J. and Clarke, S. (2014) *Keeping Children Safe: Allegations Concerning the Abuse or Neglect of Children in Care.* London: University of York, NSPCC.

Biestek, F. (1957) *The Casework Relationship.* Chicago: Loyola Press.

Bilson, A. (2007) 'Promoting compassionate concern in social work: Reflections on ethics, biology and love.' *British Journal of Social Work 37*, 1371–1386.

Bion, W. (1962) *Learning from Experience.* London: Heinemann.

Bion, W. (1968) *Experiences in Groups and Other Papers.* London: Tavistock Publications.

Bion, W. (1990) *Brazilian Lectures.* London: Karnac Books.

Bland, R., Laragy, C., Giles, R. and Scott, V. (2006) 'Asking the consumer: Exploring consumers' views in the generation of social work practice standards.' *Australian Social Work 59*, 1, 35–46.

Blaug, R. (1995) 'Distortion of the face-to-face: Communication, reason and social work practice.' *British Journal of Social Work 25*, 424–439.

Blos, P. (1962) *On Adolescence: A Psychoanalytic Interpretation.* New York: Free Press.

Bobbitt P. (2003) *The Shield of Achilles: War, Peace and the Course of History.* London: Penguin.

Bögner, D., Herlihy, J. and Brewin, C.R. (2007) 'Impact of sexual violence on disclosure during Home Office interviews.' *British Journal of Psychiatry 191*, 75–81.

Bolden, R. (2011) 'Distributed leadership in organizations: A review of theory and research.' *International Journal of Management Reviews, 13*, 3, 251–269.

Bower, M. (2005) 'Psychoanalytic Theories for Social Work Practice.' In M. Bower (ed.) *Psychoanalytic Theory for Social Work Practice: Thinking under Fire.* London: Routledge.

Bowlby, J. (1969) *Attachment. Attachment and Loss Volume One.* London: Hogarth Press.

Bowlby, J. (1979) *The Making and Breaking of Affectional Bonds.* London: Tavistock.

Bowlby, J. (1980) *Separation: Anxiety and Anger.* London: Hogarth Press.

Bowlby, J. (1988) *A Secure Base: Clinical Applications of Attachment Theory.* London: Routledge.

Boyd, E. (2007) 'Commentary – containing the container.' *Journal of Social Work Practice 21*, 2, 203–206.

Brandon, D. (1998) 'Zen healing.' *Journal of Interprofessional Care 12*, 4, 407–410.

Brearley, J. (2007) 'A Psychodynamic Approach to Social Work.' In J. Lishman (ed.) *Handbook for Practice Learning in Social Work and Social Care: Knowledge and Theory.* London: Jessica Kingsley Publishers.

British Association of Social Workers (n.d.) *Professional Capabilities Framework.* Accessed on 23/10/2017 at www.basw.co.uk/pcf.

Britton, R.S. (1989) 'The Oedipus Situation and the Depressive Position.' In R. Anderson (1992) *Clinical Lectures on Klein and Bion.* Robin Anderson (1992 reprinted 2009) (ed.) London: The New Library of Psychoanalysis, Routledge.

Broadhurst, K., Wastell, D., White, S., Hall, C., Peckover, S., Thompson, K., Pithouse A. and Davey, D. (2009) 'Performing "Initial Assessments": Identifying the latent conditions for error at the front door of local authority children's services.' *British Journal of Social Work*, doi:10.1093/bjsw/bcn162.

Browne, J. and Russell, S. (2005) 'My home, your workplace: People with physical disability negotiate their sexual health without crossing professional boundaries.' *Disability & Society 20*, 4, 375–388.

Burgess H. and Taylor, I. (1996) 'Facilitating enquiry and action learning groups for social work education.' *Groupwork 8*, 2, 117–133.

Burke, C. and Cooper, A. (2007) 'Dialogues and developments in social work practice: Applying systemic and psychoanalytic ideas in real world contexts.' *Journal of Social Work Practice 21*, 2, 193–196.

Burnham, J. (2005) 'Relational reflexivity: A Tool for socially constructing therapeutic relationships.' In C. Flaskas, A. Mason and T. Perlesz (eds) *The Space Between: Experience, Context and Process in the Therapeutic Relationship.* London: Karnac Books.

Burns, J.M. (1978) *Leadership.* New York: Harper and Row.

Burns, K. (2009) 'Job retention and turnover: a study of child protection and welfare social workers in Ireland.' Unpublished thesis, Cork: UCC.

Campbell, J. (1993) *The Hero with a Thousand Faces.* London: Fontana.

Care Inquiry (2013) *Making not Breaking: Building Relationships for our Most Vulnerable Children.* London: House of Commons.

Carers Trust and National Mental Health Development Unit (2010) *The Triangle of Care.* London: Carers Trust.

Carpenter, J., Schneider, J., Brandon, T. and Wooff, D. (2003) 'Working in multidisciplinary community mental health teams: The impact on social workers and health professionals of integrated mental health care.' *British Journal of Social Work 33*, 1081–1103.

Casement, P. (1991) *On Learning from the Patient.* London: Routledge.

Cecchin, G. (1987) 'Hypothesising, circularity and neutrality revisited: An invitation to curiosity.' *Family Process 26*, 4, 405–413.

Cheetham, J., Fuller, R., McIvor, G., and Petch, A. (1992) *Evaluating Social Work Effectiveness.* Buckingham: Open University Press.

Clare, B. (2007) 'Promoting deep learning: A teaching, learning and assessment endeavour.' *Journal of Social Work Practice 26*, 5, 433–446.

Clark, C. (2006a) 'Against confidentiality? Privacy, safety and the public good in professional communications.' *Journal of Social Work 6*, 2, 117–136.

Clark, C. (2006b) 'Children's voices: The views of vulnerable children on their service providers and the relevance of services they receive.' *British Journal of Social Work 36*, 21–39.

Clarke J. (1996) 'After Social Work?' In N. Parton (ed.) *Social Theory, Social Change and Social Work*. London: Routledge.

Clarke, J., Lovelock, R. and Crichton, N. (2016) 'Liberal arts and the development of emotional intelligence in social work education.' *British Journal of Social Work 46*, 3, 635–651.

Cohen, M.B. (1998) 'Perceptions of power in client/worker relationships.' *Families in Society 79*, 4, 433–441.

Cohen, M.B. (1999) 'On the receiving end of social work services.' *Reflections Winter 1999*, 45–50.

College of Social Work (2015) *Review of the Professional Capability Framework: Final Report*. Accessed on 28/06/2017 at www.basw.co.uk/pcf/pcfreview2015.pdf.

Collie, A. (2008) 'Consciously working at the unconscious level: Psychodynamic theory in action in a training environment.' *Journal of Social Work Practice 22*, 3, 345–358.

Conway P. (2009) 'Falling between minds: The effects of unbearable experiences on multiagency communication in the care system.' *Fostering and Adoption 33*, 1, 18–29.

Cooper, A. (2005) 'Surface and depth in the Victoria Climbié inquiry report.' *Child and Family Social Work 10*, 1, 1–11.

Cooper, A. (2008) Welfare: Dead, dying or just transubstantiated?' *Soundings 38*, 29–41.

Cooper A. (2009a) 'Interprofessional working: Choice or destiny?' *Clinical Child Psychology and Psychiatry 14*, 4, 531–536.

Cooper A. (2009b) 'Be Quiet and Listen: Emotion, Public Policy and Social Totality'. In S. Day Sclater, D. Jones, H. Price, C. Yates (eds) *Emotion: New Psychosocial Perspectives*. London Basingstoke: Palgrave.

Cooper, A. and Lousada, J. (2005) *Borderline Welfare: Feelings and Fear of Feeling in Modern Welfare*. London: Tavistock Clinic Series.

Cree, V. (2003) 'Introduction.' In V. Cree (ed.) *Becoming a Social Worker*. Abingdon: Routledge.

Danbury, H. and Wallbridge, D. (1989) 'Directive teaching and gut learning: The seminar technique and its use on video-based role play.' *Journal of Social Work Practice* May, 53–67.

Dartington T. (2010) *Managing Vulnerability*. London: Karnac Books.

Daws, D. (1989) *Through the Night: Helping Parents and Sleepless Infants*. London: Free Association Books.

de Becker, G. (1997) *The Gift of Fear: Survival Signals that Protect Us From Violence*. London: Bloomsbury.

de Boer, C. and Coady, N. (2007) 'Good helping relationships in child welfare: Learning from stories of success.' *Child and Family Social Work 12*, 32–42.

Department for Education (2012) *Care Planning Placement and Case Review Regulations.* London: Department for Education.

Department for Education (2013) *Working Together to Safeguard Children.* London: Department for Education. Accessed on 5/10/2017 at www.gov.uk/government/publications/working-together-to-safeguard-children--2.

Department for Education (2014) *Consultation on Knowledge and Skills for Child and Family Social Work: Government Response.* London: Department for Education.

Department for Education (2015) *Consultation on Knowledge and Skills for Practice Leaders and Practice Supervisors: Government Response.* Accessed on 6/11/2017 at www.gov.uk/government/uploads/system/uploads/attachment_data/file/478277/Government_response_to_consultation_on_knowledge_and_skills_statements.pdf.

Department of Health (1999) *The Government's Objectives for Children's Social Services.* London: DoH.

Department of Health (2000) *Framework for the Assessment of Children in Need and their Families.* London: The Stationery Office.

Department of Health (2004) *Social Work Careers.* London: DOH.

Department of Health (2009) *Career Framework Briefing.* www.skillsforhealth.org.uk/careers-individual-development/career-pathways.aspx.

Department of Health (2014) *The Care Act.* London: HMSO.

Department of Health (2015) *The Care Act Fact Sheets 1–9.* London: Department of Health. Accessed on 5/10/2017 at www.careact2016.dh.gov.uk.

Department of Health and Department of Children, Schools and Families (2009) *Facing Up to the Task: The Interim Report of the Social Work Task Force.* London: DH/DCSF.

Dietz, C. and Thompson, J. (2004) 'Rethinking boundaries: Ethical dilemmas in the social worker-client relationship.' *Journal of Progressive Human Services 15,* 2, 1–24.

Dingwall, R., Eekelaar, J. and Murray, T. (1983) *The Protection of Children: State Intervention and Family Life.* Blackwell: Oxford.

Doel, M. (2010) 'Service-User Perspectives on Relationships.' In G. Ruch, D. Turney and A. Ward (eds) *Relationship-Based Social Work.* London: Jessica Kingsley Publishers.

Doel, M., Allmark, P., Conway, P., Cowburn, M., Flynn, M., Nelson, P. and Tod, A. (2009) 'Professional boundaries: Crossing a line or entering the shadows?' *British Journal of Social Work,* doi: 10.1093/bjsw/bcp106.

Doel, M. and Best, L. (2008) *Experiencing Social Work: Learning from Service Users.* London: Sage.

Doel, M. and Marsh, P. (1992) *Task-Centred Social Work.* Aldershot: Ashgate.

Dominelli, L. (1996) 'Deprofessionalising social work: Anti-oppressive practice, competencies and post-modernism.' *British Journal of Social Work 16,* 4, 407–430.

Douglas, H. (2007) *Containment and Reciprocity: Integrating Psychoanalytic Theory and Child Development Research for Work with Children.* London: Routledge.

Egan, G. (1975) *The Skilled Helper: A Systematic Approach to Effective Helping.* Fourth Edition. Pacific Grove, CA: Brooks/Cole.

Ernst, S. and Maguire, M. (eds) (1987) *Living with the Sphinx: Papers from the Women's Therapy Centre.* London: The Women's Press.

Etherington, K. (2008) *Trauma, Drug Misuse and Transforming Identities: A Life Story Approach.* London: Jessica Kingsley Publishers.

Fairtlough, A. (2017) *Professional Leadership for Social Work Practitioners and Educators.* London and New York: Routledge.

Fairtlough, G. (2005) *The Three Ways of Getting Things Done: Hierarchy, Heterarchy and Responsible Autonomy in Organisations.* Axminster: Triarchy Press.

Farnfield, S. and Kaszap, M. (1998) '"What makes a helpful grown-up?" Children's views of professionals in the mental health services.' *Health Informatics Journal 4*, 3–11.

Featherstone, B. *et al.* (2014) *Re-imagining Child Protection: Towards Humane Social Work with Families.* Bristol: Policy Press.

Featherstone, B., Gupta, A., Morris, K.M. and Warner, J. (2016) 'Let's stop feeding the risk monster: Towards a social model of "child protection".' *Families, Relationships and Societies.* Accessed on 07/11/2017 at http://eprints.whiterose.ac.uk/94959/9/Morris%252C%20K%20-%20Let%E2%80%99s%20stop%20feeding%20the%20risk%20monster%20-%20AFC%202015-12-07.pdf.

Ferard, M. and Hunnybun, N. (1962) *The Caseworker's Use of Relationships.* London: Tavistock.

Ferguson, H. (2005) 'Working with violence, the emotions and the psycho-social dynamics of child protection: Reflections on the Victoria Climbié case.' *Social Work Education 24*, 7, 781–795.

Ferguson, H. (2008) 'Liquid social work: Welfare interventions as mobile practices.' *British Journal of Social Work 38*, 561–579.

Fisher, M. (1983) *Speaking of Clients.* Sheffield: Joint Unit for Social Services Research.

Fisher, M., Marsh, P. and Phillips, D. with Sainsbury, E. (1986) *In and Out of Care.* London: Batsford.

Flaskas, C., Mason, B. and Perlesz, A. (2005) *The Space Between: Experience, Context and Process in the Therapeutic Relationship.* London: Karnac Books.

Flores, P.J. (2001) 'Addiction as an attachment disorder: Implications for group therapy.' *International Journal of Group Psychotherapy 51*, 1, 63–81.

Fonagy, P. and Allison, E. (2014) 'The role of mentalizing and epistemic trust in the therapeutic relationship.' *Psychotherapy 51*, 3, 372–380.

Fonagy, P., Gergely, G., Jurist, E. and Target, M. (2002) *Affect Regulation, Mentalization, and the Development of the Self.* New York: Other Press.

Fonagy, P., Rost, F., Carlyle, J.-A., McPherson, S., Thomas, R., Pasco Fearon, R.M., Goldberg, D. and Taylor, D. (2015) 'Pragmatic randomized controlled trial of long-term psychoanalytic psychotherapy for treatment-resistant depression: The Tavistock Adult Depression Study (TADS).' *World Psychiatry 14*, 312–321. doi:10.1002/wps.20267. Accessed on 25/07/2017.

Fonagy, P., Steele, M., Moran, G., Steele, H. and Higgitt, A. (1993) 'Measuring the ghost in the nursery: An empirical study of the relation between parents' mental representations of childhood experiences and their infants' security of attachment.' *Journal of the American Psychoanalytic Association 41*, 957–989.

Fook, J. (2007) 'Reflective Practice and Critical Reflection.' In J. Lishman (ed.) *Handbook for Practice Learning in Social Work and Social Care: Knowledge and Theory.* London: Jessica Kingsley Publishers.

Fook, J. (2010) 'Beyond Reflective Practice: Reworking the "Critical" in Critical Reflection.' In H. Bradbury, N. Frost, S. Kilminster and M. Zukas (eds) *Beyond Reflective Practice.* London: Routledge.

Foster, A. (2001) 'The duty to care and the need to split.' *Journal of Social Work Practice 15*, 1, 81–90.

Fraiberg S., Adelson, E. and Shapiro V. (1975) 'Ghosts in the nursery: A psychoanalytic approach to the problems of impaired infant–mother relationships.' *Journal of American Academic Child Psychiatry 14*, 3, 387–421.

Fredman, G. (2004) *Transforming Emotion: Conversations in Counselling and Psychotherapy.* London and Philadelphia PA: Whurr Publishers.

Freedman, J. and Combs, G. (1996) *Narrative Therapy: The Social Construction of Preferred Realities.* New York: W.W. Norton.

Freud, S. (1914) *On Narcissism: An Introduction.* Standard Edition X1V. London: The Hogarth Press.

Freud, S. (1917) *Mourning and Melancholia.* Standard Edition XIV. London: The Hogarth Press.

Freud, S. (1991) *Civilization and its Discontents (1930).* Penguin Freud Library Volume 12: Civilization, Society and Religion. London: Penguin.

Frost, L., Hojer, S., Campanini, A., Sicora, A. and Kulberg, K. (2017) 'Why do they stay? A study of resilient child protection workers in three European countries.' *European Journal of Social Work*, published online 20 February 2017. Accessed on 28/06/2017 at http://dx.doi.org/10.1080/136914 57.2017.1291493.

Galinsky, M., Terzian, M.A., and Fraser, M.W. (2007) 'The art of groupwork practice with manualized curricula.' *Groupwork 17*, 2, 74–92.

Garrett, P. (2005) 'Social Work's "electronic turn": Notes on the deployment of information and communication technologies in social work with children and families.' *Critical Social Policy 24*, 4, 529–553.

General Social Care Council (2007) *Specialist Standards and Requirements for Post-Qualifying Social Work Education and Training: Social Work in Mental Health Services.* London: General Social Care Council.

Gibson, M. (2016) 'Constructing pride, shame, and humiliation as a mechanism of control: A case study of an English local authority child protection service.' *Children and Youth Services Review 70*, 120–128.

Gladwell, M. (2005) *Blink: The Power of Thinking Without Thinking.* London: Penguin.

Goldstein, H. (1983) 'Starting where the client is.' *Social Casework: The Journal of Contemporary Social Work 64*, 267–275.

Goodman, J.H. (2004) 'Coping with trauma and hardship among unaccompanied refugee youths from Sudan'. *Qualitative Health Research 14*, 9, 1177–1196.

Gorin, S. (2004*) Understanding What Children Say: Children's Experiences of Domestic Violence, Parental Substance Misuse and Parental Health Problems.* London: National Children's Bureau for The Joseph Rowntree Foundation.

Grant, L. and Kinman, G. (eds) (2014) *Developing Resilience for Social Work Practice.* London: Palgrave.

Grant, L., Kinman, G. and Baker, S. (2015) 'Put on your own oxygen mask before assisting others. Social work educators' perspectives on an Emotional Cirriculum.' *British Journal of Social Work 45*, 8, 2351–2367.

Grant, S., Sheridan, L. and Webb, S.A. (2017) 'Newly Qualified Social Workers' Readiness for Practice in Scotland.' *British Journal of Social Work 47*, 2, 487–506.

Gray, I., Field, R. and Brown, K. (2010) *Effective Leadership and Management in Health and Social Care.* Exeter: Learning Matters.

Green, B.L., Furrer, C. and McAllister, C. (2007) 'How do relationships support parenting? Effects of attachment style and social support on parenting behaviour in an at risk population.' *American Journal of Community Psychology 40*, 96–108.

Hafford-Letchfield, T., Leonard, K., Begum, N. and Chick, N.F. (2008) *Leadership and Management in Social Care.* London: Sage.

Hafford-Letchfield, T., Lumbley, S., Spolander, G. and Cocker, C. (2014) *Inclusive Leadership in Social Work and Social Care.* Bristol: The Policy Press.

Haringey Local Safeguarding Children Board (2009) Serious Case Review Executive Summary Report on Case of Baby Peter.

Harrison, K. and Ruch, G. (2007) 'Social Work and the Use of Self: On Becoming and Being a Social Worker.' In M. Lymbery and K. Postle (eds) *Social Work: A Companion to Learning.* London: Sage.

Hattenstone, S. (2017) 'Maxine Peake: I'm a Corbyn Supporter. We need a coup.' *The Guardian*, 29 April, 2017. Available at www.theguardian.com/culture/2017/apr/29/maxine-peake-corbyn-supporter-need-coup#img-1.

Hawkins, P. and Shohet, R. (2006) *Supervision in the Helping Professions.* Second Edition. Maidenhead: Open University Press.

Healy, K., Meagher, G. and Cullin, J. (2009) 'Retaining novices to become expert child protection practitioners: Creating career pathways in direct practice.' *British Journal of Social Work 39*, 2, 299–317.

Heard, D. and Lake, B. (1997) *The Challenge of Attachment for Caregiving.* London: Routledge.

Hedges, F. (2005) *An Introduction to Systemic Therapy with Families.* Basingstoke: Palgrave Macmillan.

Held, V. (2006) *The Ethics of Care: Personal, Political, and Global.* Oxford: Oxford University Press.

Hem, M.H. and Heggen, K. (2003) 'Being professional and being human: One nurse's relationship with a psychiatric patient.' *Journal of Advanced Nursing 43*, 1, 101–108.

Herlihy, J., Scragg, P. and Turner, S. (2002) 'Discrepancies in autobiographical memories – implications for the assessment of asylum seekers: Repeated interviews study.' *British Medical Journal 324*, 324–327.

Hey, J., Leheup, R. and Almudevar, M. (1995) 'Family therapy with "invisible" families.' *British Journal of Medical Psychology 68*, 125–133.

Hingley-Jones, H. and Ruch, G. (2016) 'Stumbling through? Relationship-based social work practice in austere times.' *Journal of Social Work Practice 30*, 3, 235–248.

Hinshelwood, R.D (2004) *Suffering Insanity*. Hove: Brunner-Routledge.

Hinshelwood, R.D and Skogstad, W. (2002) *Observing Organisations: Anxiety, Defence and Culture in Health Care*. London: Routledge.

Hochschild, A.R. (1979) 'Emotion work, feeling rules, and social structure.' *American Journal of Sociology 85*, 3, 551.

Hoggett, P (2015) 'A Psycho-social Perspective on Social Defences.' In D. Armstrong and M. Rustin (eds) *Social Defences Against Anxiety*. London: Karnac Books.

Hollis, F. (1964) *Casework: A Psychosocial Therapy*. New York: Random House.

Hollis, F. (1990) 'Termination.' In F. Hollis and M. Woods (Eds) *Casework: A Psychosocial Therapy*. New York: McGraw Hill.

Hollway, W. (2006) 'Paradox in the pursuit of a critical theorization of the development of self in family relationships.' *Theory and Psychology 16*, 465–482.

Howe, D. (1986) *Social Workers and their Practice*. Aldershot: Gower.

Howe, D. (1994) 'Modernity, postmodernity and social work.' *British Journal of Social Work 25*, 5, 513–532.

Howe, D. (1995) *Attachment Theory for Social Work Practice*. London: Macmillan.

Howe, D. (1996) 'Surface and Depth in Social Work Practice.' In N. Parton (ed.) *Social Theory, Social Work and Social Change*. London: Routledge.

Howe, D. (1998) 'Relationship-based thinking and practice in social work.' *Journal of Social Work Practice 12*, 1, 45–56.

Howe, D. (2005) *Child Abuse and Neglect: Attachment, Development and Intervention*. Basingstoke: Palgrave Macmillan.

Howe, D. (2008) *The Emotionally Intelligent Social Worker*. Basingstoke: Palgrave Macmillan.

Howe, D. (2009) *A Brief Introduction to Social Work Theory*. Basingstoke: Palgrave Macmillan.

Howe, D., Brandon, M., Hinings, D. and Schofield, G. (1999) *Attachment Theory, Child Maltreatment and Family Support: A Practice and Assessment Model*. Basingstoke: Macmillan.

Hunter, M. (2009) 'Whatever happened to supervision?' *Community Care 1767*, 18–19.

Hutten, J. (1977) *Short-Term Contracts in Social Work*. London: Routledge and Kegan Paul.

Hutten, J., Bazalgette, J. and Armstrong, D. (1994) 'What Does Management Really Mean?' In R. Casemore *et al.* (eds) *What Makes Consultancy Work: Understanding the Dynamics.* London: South Bank University Press.

Illeris, K. (2009) 'A Comprehensive Understanding of Human Learning.' In K. Illeris (ed.) *Contemporary Theories of Learning: Learning Theorists…in their Own Words.* London and New York: Routledge.

Jack, G. and Donnellan, H. (2010) 'Recognising the person within the developing professional: Tracking the early careers of newly qualified child care social workers in three local authorities in England.' *Social Work Education 29*, 3, 305–318.

Jack, G. and Gill, O. (2003) *The Missing Side of the Triangle. Assessing the Importance of Family and Environmental Factors in the Lives of Children.* Ilford: Barnardo.

Jaques, E. (1965) 'Death and the mid-life crisis.' *International Journal of Psychoanalysis 46*, 502–514.

Jewitt, C. (1984) *Helping Children Cope with Separation and Loss.* London: British Association of Adoption and Fostering.

Jones, R. (2015) 'The end game: The marketisation and privatisation of children's social work and child protection.' *Critical Social Policy 35* ,4, 447–469.

Jones, W.D. (2002) *Myths, Madness and the Family.* Basingstoke: Palgrave.

Jordan, B. and Drakeford, M. (2012) *Social Work and Social Policy under Austerity.* Basingstoke: Palgrave Macmillan.

Karpman, S. (1968) 'Fairy tales and script drama analysis.' *Transactional Analysis Bulletin 7*, 26, 39–44.

Kearns, A. (ed.) (2007) *The Mirror Crack'd: When Good Enough Therapy goes Wrong and Other Cautionary Tales for Humanistic Practitioners.* London: Karnac Books.

Keinemans, S. (2015) 'Be sensible: Emotions in social work ethics and education.' *British Journal of Social Work 45*, 7, 2176–2191.

Kendrick, A. and Smith, M. (2002) 'Close enough? Professional closeness and safe caring.' *Scottish Journal of Residential Child Care 1*, 46–54.

Keval, N. (2005) 'Racist States of Mind: An Attack on Thinking and Curiosity.' In M. Bower (ed.) *Psychoanalytic Theory for Social Work Practice: Thinking Under Fire.* Abingdon and New York: Routledge.

Kierkegaard, S. (1944) *The Concept of Dread.* Oxford: Oxford University Press.

Klein, M. (1935) 'A Contribution to the Psychogenesis of Manic Depressive States.' In M. Klein (1975) *Love, Guilt and Reparation and Other Works 1921–1945.* London: Hogarth Press.

Klein, M. (1940) 'Mourning: Its Relation to Manic Depressive States.' In J. Mitchell (ed.) *The Selected Melanie Klein (1986).* Harmondsworth: Penguin.

Klein, M. (1952) 'The origins of transference.' *The International Journal of Psychoanalysis 33*, 433.

Klein, M. (1975) *The Writings of Melanie Klein, Volume 3.* London: Hogarth Press.

Kohli, R.K.S (2006) 'The sound of silence: Listening to what unaccompanied children say and do not say.' *British Journal of Social Work 36*, 707–721.

Kohli, R.K.S (2007) *Social Work with Unaccompanied Asylum Seeking Children.* Basingstoke: Palgrave MacMillan.

Kohli, R.K.S. and Mitchell, F. (2007) *Working with Unaccompanied Asylum Seeking Children: Issues for Policy and Practice.* Basingstoke: Palgrave Macmillan.

Kolb, D.A. (1984) *Experiential Learning: Experience as the Source of Learning and Development* (Vol. 1). Englewood Cliffs, NJ: Prentice-Hall.

Kroll, B. (1994) *Chasing Rainbows: Children, Divorce and Loss.* Lyme Regis: Russell House Publishing.

Kroll, B. (2002) 'Children and Divorce.' In N. Thompson (ed.) *Loss and Grief: A Guide for Human Services Practitioners.* Basingstoke: Palgrave Macmillan.

Kroll, B. (2004a) 'Living with an elephant: Growing up with parental substance misuse.' *Child and Family Social Work 9,* 129–140.

Kroll, B. (2004b) 'The challenge of post qualifying child care award teaching: Reflexivity and the role of books and biscuits.' *Social Work Education 23,* 6, 653–666.

Kroll, B. and Taylor, A. (2003) *Parental Substance Misuse and Child Welfare.* London: Jessica Kingsley Publishers.

Kroll, B. and Taylor, A. (2008) *Interventions for Children and Families Where There is Parental Drug Misuse: Executive Summary.* London: Department of Health.

Kumsa, M.K. (2007) 'Encounters in social work practice.' In D. Mandell (ed.) *Revisiting the Use of Self: Questioning Professional Identities.* Toronto: Canadian Scholars' Press.

Laming, H. (2003) *The Victoria Climbié Inquiry: Report of an Inquiry by Lord Laming.* London: The Stationery Office.

Lawler, J. (2007) 'Leadership in social work: a case of caveat emptor?' *British Journal of Social Work 37,* 1, 123–141.

Lee, C.D. and Ayon, C. (2004) 'Is the client-worker relationship associated with better outcomes in mandated child abuse cases?' *Research on Social Work Practice 14,* 5, 351–357.

Lees, A., Meyer, E., and Rafferty, J. (2013) 'From Menzies-Lyth to Munro: The problem of managerialism.' *British Journal of Social Work 43,* 542–558.

Le Grand, J. (2007) Consistent Care Matters: Exploring the Potential of Social Work Practice. DFES-00526-2007. Department for Education and Skills.

Leary, M. (2004) *The Curse of the Self: Self-Awareness, Egotism, and the Quality of Human Life.* Oxford: Oxford University Press.

Lieberman, F. (1979) *Social Work with Children.* New York: Human Sciences Press.

London Borough of Brent (1985) A Child in Trust: The Report of the Panel of Inquiry into the Circumstances Surrounding the Death of Jasmine Beckford.

London Borough of Greenwich (1987) A Child in Mind: Protection of Children in a Responsible Society. The Report of the Commission of Inquiry into the Circumstances Surrounding the Death of Kimberley Carlile.

Lonne, B., Harries, M., Featherstone, B. and Gray, M. (2015) *Working Ethically in Child Protection.* London: Routledge.

Lord Laming (2009) *The Protection of Children in England: A Progress Report.* London: HMSO.

Lord Nelson, L.G., Summers, J.A. and Turnbull, A.P. (2004) 'Boundaries in Family-Professional Relationships: Implications for Special Education'. *Remedial and Special Education 25*, 3, 153–165.

Lorenz, K. (1967) *On Aggression.* London: Methuen.

Loshak, R. (2013) *Out of the Mainstream: Helping Children of Parents with Mental Illness.* London: Routledge.

LSCB (2017) *London Child Protection Procedures and Practice Guidance (5th Edition).* London: LSCB. Accessed on 5/10/2017 at www.londoncp.co.uk.

Luft, J. (1984) *Group Processes: An Introduction to Group Dynamics.* Mountain View, CA: Mayfield.

McCluskey, U. and Hooper, C.A. (2000) *Psychodynamic Perspectives on Abuse: The Cost of Fear.* London: Jessica Kingsley Publishers.

McKitterick, B. (2015) *Self-Leadership in Social Work: Reflections from Practice.* Bristol: Policy Press.

McLeod, A. (2007) 'Whose agenda? Issues of power and relationship when listening to looked after young people.' *Child and Family Social Work 12*, 278–286.

McLeod, A. (2008) '"A friend and an equal": Do young people in care seek the impossible from their social workers?' *British Journal of Social Work.* Advance Access published 24 November, 2008 doi:10.1093/bjsw/bcn143.

Mack, B. (2002) 'Psycho-analytic insight and relationships.' *Journal of Social Work Practice 16*, 2, 191–201.

Main, M. (1991) 'Metacognitive Knowledge, Metacognitive Monitoring and Singular (Coherent) vs Multiple (Incoherent) Model of Attachment.' In C.M. Parkes, J. Stevenson-Hinde and P. Marris (eds) *Attachment Across the Life Cycle.* London: Tavistock/Routledge.

Main, M. and Goldwyn, R. (1998) Adult Attachment Scoring and Classification System (manuscript). Berkeley, CA: Department of Psychology, University of California; 1985–1994.

Mandell, D. (2007) *Revisiting the Use of Self: Questioning Professional Identities.* Toronto: Canadian Scholars' Press.

Mandell, D. (2008) 'Power, care and vulnerability: Considering the use of self in child welfare work.' *Journal of Social Work Practice 22*, 2, 235–248.

Manthorpe, J., Moriarty, J., Hussein, S., Stevens, S., and Sharpe, E. (2015) 'Content and purpose of supervision in social work practice in England: Views of newly qualified social workers, managers and directors.' *British Journal of Social Work 45*, 52–68. doi:10.1093/bjsw/bct102.

Marquis, R. and Jackson, R. (2000) 'Quality of life and quality of services relationships: Experiences of people with disabilities.' *Disability and Society 15*, 3, 411–425.

Marris, P. (1974) *Loss and Change.* London: Routledge and Kegan Paul.

Marsh, P. and Doel, M. (2006) *The Task-Centred Book.* London: Routledge/Community Care.

Mattinson, J. (1970) *The Reflection Process in Casework Supervision.* London: Tavistock Institute of Marital Studies.

Mattison, D., Jayaratne, S. and Croxton, T. (2002) 'Client or former client? Implications of ex-client definition on social work practice.' *Social Work 47*, 1, 55–64.

Mattison, V. and Pistrang, N. (2000) *Saying Goodbye: Stories of Separation Between Care Staff and People With Learning Disabilities.* London: Free Association Books.

Mayer, N. and Timms, N. (1970) *The Client Speaks: Working Class Impressions of Casework.* London: Routledge.

Meakings, S. and Selwyn, J. (2016) '"She was a foster mother who said she didn't give cuddles": The adverse early foster care experiences of children who later struggle with adoptive family life.' *Clinical Child Psychology and Psychiatry 21*, 4, 509–519.

Meier, P., Donmall, M., Burrowclough, C., Elduff, P. and Heller, R. (2005) 'Predicting the early therapeutic alliance in the treatment of drug misuse.' *Addiction, 100*, 500–511.

Menzies-Lyth, I. (1988) *Containing Anxiety in Institutions: Selected Essays Volume One.* London: Free Association Books.

Mezirow, J. (2009) 'An Overview on Transformative Learning.' In K. Illeris (ed.) *Contemporary Theories of Learning: Learning Theorists…in their Own Words.* London and New York: Routledge.

Mikulincer, M. and Shaver, P. (2014) *Mechanisms of Social Connection: From Brain to Group.* London: American Psychological Association.

Miller, E. and Gwynne, G. (1972) *A Life Apart: a Pilot Study of Residential Institutions for the Physically Handicapped and the Young Chronic Sick.* London: Tavistock.

Mor Barak, M.E., Levin, A., Nissly, J.A. and Lane, C.J. (2006) 'Why do they leave? Modelling child welfare workers' turnover intentions.' *Children and Youth Services Review 28*, 548–577.

Morrison, T. (2007) 'Emotional intelligence, emotion and social work: Context, characteristics, complications and contribution.' *British Journal of Social Work 37*, 2, 245–263.

Morriss, L. (2016) 'AMHP work: Dirty or prestigious? Dirty work designations and the Approved Mental Health Professional.' *British Journal of Social Work 46*, 3, 703–718.

Mudaly, N. and Goddard, C. (2006) *The Truth is Longer Than a Lie: Children's Experiences of Abuse and Professional Intervention.* London: Jessica Kingsley Publishers.

Munro, E. (1999) 'Common errors of reasoning in child protection work.' *Child Abuse and Neglect 23*, 745–758.

Munro, E. (2000) 'Defending Professional Social Work Practice.' In J. Harris, L. Froggett and I. Paylor (eds) *Reclaiming Social Work: The Southport Papers Volume One.* Birmingham: Venture Press.

Munro, E. (2004) 'The impact of audit on social work practice.' *British Journal of Social Work 34*, 1075–1095.

Munro, E. (2010) *The Munro Review of Child Protection: Part 1 – A Systems Analysis.* London: The Stationery Office. Accessed on 30/06/2017 at www.gov. uk/government/publications/munro-review-of-child-protection-part-1-a-systems-analysis.

Munro, E. (2011a) *The Munro Review of Child Protection: Interim Report – The Child's Journey.* London: The Stationery Office. Accessed on 30/06/2017 at www.gov.uk/government/uploads/system/uploads/attachment_data/file/206993/DFE-00010-2011.pdf.

Munro, E. (2011b) *The Munro Review of Child Protection: Final Report, A Child-Centred System (Vol. 8062).* London: The Stationery Office. Accessed on 30/06/2017 at www.gov.uk/government/uploads/system/uploads/attachment_data/file/175391/Munro-Review.pdf.

National Institute for Health and Care Excellence (NICE) (2013) *Looked-After Children and Young People: Quality Standard (QS31).* Accessed on 5/10/2017 at www.nice.org.uk/guidance/qs31.

Newman, L. and Stevenson, C. (2005) 'Parenting and borderline personality disorder: Ghosts in the nursery.' *Clinical Child Psychology and Psychiatry 10,* 385–394.

NICE Guidelines (2017) Depression in Adults: Treatment and Management. NICE Guidelines, short version, draft for consultation.

Northouse, P. (2013) *Leadership: Theory and Practice.* Sixth Edition. London: Sage.

Obholzer, A. and Roberts, V. (eds) (1994) *The Unconscious at Work: Individual and Organizational Stress in the Human Services.* London: Routledge.

O'Donoghue, K. and Tsui, M. (2015) 'Social work supervision research (1970–2010): The way we were and the way ahead.' *British Journal of Social Work 45,* 2, 616–633. doi:10.1093/bjsw/bct115.

Ogden, T.H. (2005) *This Art of Psychoanalysis: Dreaming Undreamt Dreams and Interrupted Cries.* London: Routledge.

Oswin, M. (1991) *Am I Allowed to Cry? A Study of Bereavement Amongst People with Learning Difficulties.* London: Souvenir Press.

Papadopoulos, R.K. (ed.) (2002) *Therapeutic Care for Refugees: No Place like Home.* London: Karnac Books.

Parker, J. and Bradley, G. (2007) *Social Work Practice: Assessment, Planning, Intervention and Review.* Exeter: Learning Matters.

Parton, N. (1994) 'Problematics of government, (post)modernity and social work.' *British Journal of Social Work 24,* 9–32.

Parton, N. (1998a) Child Protection and Family Support: Possible Future Directions for Social Work. Eighteenth Annual Lecture, Department of Social Work Studies, University of Southampton.

Parton, N. (1998b) 'Risk, advanced liberalism and child welfare: The need to rediscover uncertainty and ambiguity.' *British Journal of Social Work,* 28, 5–27.

Parton, N. (2008) 'Changes in the form of knowledge in social work: From the "social" to the "informational".' *British Journal of Social Work,* 38, 253–268.

Parton, N. (2014) 'Social work, child protection and politics: Some critical and constructive reflections.' *British Journal of Social Work 44,* 7, 2042–2056.

Patterson, F. (2015) 'Transition and metaphor: Crossing a bridge from direct practice to first line management in social services.' *British Journal of Social Work 45*, 7, 2072–2088.

Pithouse, A., Hall, C., Peckover, S. and White, S. (2009) 'A tale of two CAFs: The impact of the electronic common assessment framework.' *British Journal of Social Work 39*, 599–612.

Platt, D. (2007) 'Congruence and co-operation in social workers' assessments of children in need.' *Child and Family Social Work 12*, 4, 326–335.

Power, M. (1996) *The Audit Explosion.* London: Demos.

Pratt, J., Gordon, P. and Plampling, D. (1999) *Working Whole Systems: Putting Theory into Practice into Organisations.* London: Kings Fund.

Preston-Shoot, M. (1996) 'W(h)ither social work? Social work, social policy and law at an interface: Confronting the challenges and realising the potential in work with people needing care of services.' *The Liverpool Law Review XVIII*, 1, 19–39.

Preston-Shoot, M. and Agass, D. (1990) *Making Sense of Social Work: Psychodynamics, Systems and Practice.* London: Macmillan.

Reder, P. and Duncan, S. (1995) 'Closure, covert warnings and escalating child abuse.' *Child Abuse and Neglect 19*, 1517–1521.

Reed, G.M., McLaughlin, C.J. and Newman, R.R. (2002) 'The development and evaluation of guidelines for professional practice.' *American Psychologist 57*, 12, 1041–1047.

Rees, S. and Wallace, A. (1982) *Verdicts on Social Work.* London: Edward Arnold.

Rogers, C. (1967) *On Becoming a Person: A Therapist's View of Psychotherapy.* London: Constable.

Rogowski, S. (2016) *Social Work with Children and Families: Reflections of a Critical Practitioner.* London: Routledge.

Roth, A. and Fonagy, P. (eds) (2005) *What Works for Whom? A Critical Review of Psychotherapy Research. Second Edition.* London: Guilford Press.

Ruch, G. (2002) 'From triangle to spiral: Reflective practice in social work education, practice and research.' *Social Work Education 21*, 2, 199–216.

Ruch, G. (2005) 'Relationship-based practice and reflective practice: Holistic approaches to contemporary child care social work.' *Child and Family Social Work 10*, 2, 111–125.

Ruch, G. (2007a) 'Reflective practice in contemporary child-care social work: The role of containment.' *British Journal of Social Work 37*, 4, 659–680.

Ruch, G. (2007b) '"Thoughtful" practice: Child care social work and the role of case discussion.' *Child and Family Social Work 12*, 370–379.

Rustin, M. (2005) 'Conceptual analysis of critical moments in Victoria Climbié's life.' *Child and Family Social Work 10*, 11–19.

Rustin, M. and Bradley, J. (eds) (2008) *Work Discussion: Learning from Reflective Practice in Work with Children and Families.* London: Karnac Books.

Saarnio, P. (2000) 'Does it matter who treats you?' *European Journal of Social Work 3*, 3, 261–268.

Sachrajda, A. and Griffith, P. (2014) *Shared ground: Strategies for living well together in an era of high immigration.* IPPR. Accessed on 5/10/2017 at www.ippr. org/publications/shared-ground

Sainsbury, E. (1987) 'Client studies: Their contribution and limitations in influencing social work practice.' *British Journal of Social Work 17*, 6, 635–644.

Sainsbury, E. (1989) 'What clients value.' Unpublished paper, BASW Study Day, Task-Centred Special Interest Group, April 1989.

Salzberger-Wittenberg, I. (1970) *Psycho-Analytic Insight and Relationships: A Kleinian Approach.* London: Routledge.

Sandel, M. (2009) The Reith Lectures. Broadcast on BBC Radio 4.

Schon, D. (1987) *Educating the Reflective Practitioner: Towards a New Design for Teaching and Learning in the Professions.* San Francisco, CA: Jossey Bass.

Schon, D. (2000) *The Reflective Practitioner: How Professionals Think in Action.* Aldershot: Ashgate.

Sevenhuijsen, S. (1998) *Citizenship and the Ethics of Care: Feminist Considerations on Justice, Morality and Politics.* London: Routledge.

Shardlow, S.M. and Doel, M. (1996) *Practice Teaching and Learning.* Basingstoke: Macmillan.

Shaw, I., Bell, M., Sinclair, I., Sloper, P., Mitchell, W., Dyson, P., Clayden, J. and Rafferty, J. (2009) 'An exemplary scheme? An evaluation of the Integrated Children's System.' *British Journal of Social Work 39*, 4, 613–626.

Sheldon, B. and Macdonald, G. (2008) *A Textbook of Social Work.* London: Routledge.

Sheppard, M. (2007) 'Assessment: From reflexivity to Process Knowledge.' In J. Lishman (ed.) *Handbook for Practice Learning in Social Work and Social Care: Knowledge and Theory.* London: Jessica Kingsley Publishers.

Sheppard, M. and Charles, M. (2015) 'Head and heart. An examination of the relationship between the intellectual and interpersonal in social work'. *British Journal of Social Work 45*, 6, 1837–1854.

Shoesmith, S. (2016) *Learning from Baby P: The Politics of Blame, Fear and Denial.* London: Jessica Kingsley Publishers.

Shohet, R. (1999) 'Whose Feelings Am I Feeling? Using the Concept of Projective Identification.' In A. Hardwick and J. Woodhead (eds) *Loving, Hating and Survival: A Handbook for All Who Work with Troubled Children and Young People.* Aldershot: Ashgate.

Shulman, L. (1999) *The Skills of Helping Individuals, Families, Groups and Communities. Fourth Edition.* Itasca, IL: Peacock.

Sinason, V. (1992) *Mental Handicap and the Human Condition.* London: Free Association Press.

Sinason, V. and Hollins, S. (2004) 'The Ideal Home and Community for People with Learning Disabilities.' In P. Campling, S. Davies and G. Farquharson (eds) *From Toxic Institutions to Therapeutic Environments: Residential Settings in Mental Health Services.* London: Gaskell.

Skivenes, M. and Skramstad, H. (2015) 'The emotional dimension in risk assessment. A cross-country study of the perceptions of child welfare workers in England, Norway and California (United States).' *British Journal of Social Work 45*, 3, 809–824.

Skynner, R. (1989) 'Make Sure to Feed the Goose That Lays the Golden Eggs: A Discussion on the Myth of Altruism.' In R. Skynner (ed.) *Institutes and How to Survive Them: Mental Health Training and Consultation.* London: Routledge.

Smith, C. and White, S. (1997) 'Parton, Howe and postmodernity: A critical comment on mistaken identity.' *British Journal of Social Work 27*, 275–295.

Smith, D. (1996) 'An Injudicious Approach.' In D. Batty and D. Cullen (eds) *Child Protection: The Therapeutic Option.* London: British Association for Adoption and Fostering.

Smith, M. (2005) *Surviving Fears in Health and Social Care: The Terrors of Night and the Arrows of Day.* London: Jessica Kingsley Publishers.

Smith, M. (2009a) *Rethinking Residential Child Care: Positive Perspectives.* Bristol: Policy Press.

Smith, M. (2009b) 'Smoke Without Fire? Social Workers' Fears of Threats and Accusations.' In P. Chamberlayne and M. Smith (eds) *Art, Creativity and Imagination in Social Work Practice.* Oxford: Routledge.

Smith, M. (2016) Editorial. [Joint Special Issue, Love in Professional Practice] *Scottish Journal of Residential Child Care*, 15, 3, and *International Journal of Social Pedagogy*, 5, 1, 2–5. doi: https://doi.org/10.14324/111.444. ijsp.2017.01 Accessed on 6/11/2017 at www.celcis.org/journal and www.ingentaconnect.com/content/uclpress/ijsp.

Social Care Institute for Excellence (2013, updated 2015) guide 51 *Co-Production in Social Care. What it is and how to do it.* Accessed on 30/06/2017 at www.scie.org.uk/publications/guides/guide51/files/guide51.pdf.

Solomon, R. (in press) 'No Shit!: A Psycho-Educational Group for Foster Carers.' In M. Bower and R. Solomon (eds) *What Social Workers Need to Know: A Psychoanalytic Approach.* London: Routledge.

Spillane, J.P. (2006) *Distributed Leadership (First Edition).* San Francisco: Jossey-Bass.

Spratt, T. and Houston, S. (1999) 'Developing critical social work in theory and practice: Child protection and communicative reasoning.' *Child and Family Social Work 4*, 315–324.

Steiner, J. (1993) *Psychic Retreats.* London: Routledge.

Stern, D. (1977) *The First Relationship: Mother and Infant.* Cambridge, MA: Harvard University Press.

Stevenson, O. (2005) 'Foreword.' In M. Bower (ed.) *Psychoanalytic Theory for Social Work Practice: Thinking under Fire.* London: Routledge.

Stickley, T. and Freshwater, D. (2002) 'The art of loving and the therapeutic relationship.' *Nursing Inquiry 9*, 4, 250–256.

Sudbery, J. (2002) 'Key features of therapeutic social work: The use of relationship.' *Journal of Social Work Practice 16*, 2, 149–162.

Taylor, A. (2009) A Study into the Difficulties of Engaging Children and Parents in Treatment When Parents Use Alcohol Problematically. Unpublished PhD Thesis. Bath: University of Bath.

Taylor, A. and Kroll, B. (2004) 'Working with parental substance misuse: Dilemmas for practice.' *British Journal of Social Work 34*, 1115–1132.

Taylor, A., Toner, P., Templeton, L. and Velleman, R. (2006) 'Parental alcohol misuse in complex families: The implications for engagement.' *British Journal of Social Work 38*, 5, 843–864.

Taylor, H., Beckett, C. and McKeigue, B. (2008) 'Judgements of Solomon: Anxieties and defences of social workers involved in care proceedings.' *Child and Family Social Work 13*, 23–31.

Trevithick, P. (2003) 'Effective relationship-based practice: A theoretical exploration.' *Journal of Social Work Practice 17*, 2, 163–176.

Trevithick, P. (2005) *Social Work Skills: A Practice Handbook. Second Edition.* Maidenhead: Open University Press.

Treweek, G.L. (1996) 'Emotion Work, Order and Emotional Power in Care Assistant Work.' In V. James and J. Gabe (eds) *Health and the Sociology of the Emotions.* Oxford: Blackwell.

Trowell, J. (1995) 'Key Psychoanalytic Concepts.' In J. Trowell and M. Bower (eds) *The Emotional Needs of Young Children and their Families: Using Psychoanalytic Ideas in the Community.* London: Routledge.

Turney, D. (2012) 'A relationship-based approach to engaging involuntary clients: The contribution of recognition theory.' *Child & Family Social Work 17*, 2, 149–159.

Turton, D. (2004) The Meaning of Place in a World of Movement: Lessons from Long-term Field Research in Southern Ethiopia. RSC Working Paper 18. University of Oxford: International Development Centre.

UNISON (2009) Still Slipping Through the Net? Front-line Staff Assess Children's Safeguarding Progress. UNISON.

United Nations High Commission for Refugees (2007) Convention and Protocol Relating to the Status of Refugees. Accessed on 7/4/2009 at www.unhcr.org/protect/PROTECTION/3b66c2aa10.pdf.

Urry, J. (2005) 'The Place of Emotions Within Place.' In J. Davidson, L. Bondi and M. Smith (eds) *Emotional Geographies.* Aldershot: Ashgate.

Van der Kolk, B., McFarlane, A. and Weisaeth, L. (eds) (1996) *Traumatic Stress: The Effects of Overwhelming Experience on Mind, Body and Society.* London: The Guildford Press.

Waddell, M. (1989) 'Living in two worlds: Psychodynamic theory and social work practice.' *Free Association 15*, 11–35.

Walker, C. (2014) *Reflections on the Newly Qualified Social Worker's Journey: From University Training to Qualified Practice.* (Unpublished doctoral thesis) Cambridge: Anglia Ruskin University. Accessed on 30/06/2017 at http://arro.anglia.ac.uk/347147.

Ward, A. (1998) 'The Matching Principle: Connections Between Training and Practice.' In A. Ward and L. McMahon (eds) *Intuition is Not Enough: Matching Learning with Practice in Therapeutic Child Care.* London: Routledge.

Ward, A. (2006) *Working in Group Care Social Work and Social Care in Residential and Day Care Settings.* Bristol: Policy Press.

Ward, A. (2008) 'Beyond the instructional mode: Creating a holding environment for learning about the use of self.' *Journal of Social Work Practice 22,* 1, 67–83.

Ward, A. (2014) *Leadership in Residential Child Care: A Relationship-Based Approach.* Norwich: Smokehouse Press.

Ward, A., Kasinski, K., Pooley, J. and Worthington, A. (2003) *Therapeutic Communities for Children and Young People.* London: Jessica Kingsley Publishers.

Ward, A. and McMahon, L. (eds) (1998) *Intuition is Not Enough: Matching Learning with Practice in Therapeutic Child Care.* London: Routledge.

Webb, S. (2001) 'Some considerations on the validity of evidence-based practice in social work.' *British Journal of Social Work 31,* 1, 57–79.

White, S., Fook, J. and Gardner, F. (2006) *Critical Reflection in Health and Social Care.* Maidenhead: Open University Press.

White, S., Hall, C. and Peckover, S. (2008) 'The descriptive tyranny of the common assessment Framework: technologies of categorization and professional practice in child welfare. *British Journal of Social Work* doi:10.1093/bjsw/bcn053.

White, S., Hall, C. and Peckover, S. (2009) 'The descriptive tyranny of the Common Assessment Framework: Technologies of categorization and professional practice in child welfare.' *British Journal of Social Work 39,* 1193–1196.

Whittaker, A. (2011) 'Social defences and organisational culture in a local authority child protection setting: Challenges for the Munro Review?' *Journal of Social Work Practice 25,* 4, 481–495.

Whittaker, A. and Havard, T. (2016) 'Defensive practice as 'fear-based' practice: Social work's open secret?' *British Journal of Social Work 46,* 5, 1158–1174.

Whitwell, J. (2002) 'Therapeutic child care.' In K. White (ed.) *Re-framing Children's Services. NCVCCO Annual Review Journal 3.*

Whyte, C. (2003) 'Struggling to separate: Observation of a young child in a playgroup' *Infant Observation 6,* 2 128–142.

Winnicott, D.W. (1947) 'Hate in the Countertransference.' Through Paediatrics to Psychoanalysis: Collected Papers (pp.194–203).

Winnicott, D. (1953) 'Transitional objects and transitional phenomena.' *International Journal of Psychoanalysis,* 34, 89–97.

Winnicott, D.W. (1960) 'The Theory of the Parent–Infant Relationship.' In D.W. Winnicott (1965) *The Maturational Processes and the Facilitating Environment.* London: Karnac Books.

Winnicott, D.W. (1963) 'Fear of Breakdown.' In C. Winnicott, R. Shepherd and M. Davis (eds) *Psychoanalytic Explorations.* Cambridge, MA: Harvard University Press.

Winnicott, D.W. (1971) *Playing and Reality.* London: Tavistock.

Winnicott, D.W. (1986) *Home is Where We Start From. Essays by a Psychoanalyst.* Harmondsworth: Penguin.

Winnicott, D.W. (1989) 'The Fate of the Transitional Object.' In *Psycho-Analytic Explorations.* London: Karnac Books.

Winnicott, D.W. (1992) 'Hate in the Countertransference.' In D. Winnicott (ed.) *Through Paediatrics to Psychoanalysis.* London: Karnac Books.

Wittenberg, I. (1999) 'Ending therapy.' *Journal of Child Psychotherapy 25*, 3, 339–356.

Woodcock, J. (1995) 'Healing rituals with families in exile.' *Journal of Family Therapy 17*, 4, 397–409.

Yelloly, M. and Henkel, M. (1995) 'Introduction' in Yelloly, M. and Henkel, M. *Learning and Teaching in Social Work: Towards Reflective Practice.* London: Jessica Kingsley Publishers.

Young, R.M (1994) *Mental Space.* London: Process Press.

Youll, P. (1996) 'Organisational or Professional Leadership? Managerialism and Social Work Education.' In M. Preston-Shoot and S. Braye (eds) *Educating Social Workers in a Changing Policy Context.* London: Whiting and Birch.

The Contributors

Andrew Cooper is Professor of Social Work at the Tavistock Centre and University of East London. He is also a founder and Trustee of the Centre for Social Work Practice, a national network that promotes the importance of relationship-based approaches to social work practice, teaching and management. He has a long-standing interest in the evolution of the British welfare state, and among other publications in this area co-authored *Borderline Welfare: Feeling and Fear of Feeling in Modern Welfare* (Karnac Books, 2005) with Julian Lousada.

Jane Dutton is a social work qualified Consultant Systemic Psychotherapist and a mentalisation-based therapist and trainer at the Anna Freud National Centre for Children and Families, London. She has extensive experience of working in child protection in social care contexts. She has worked as a family therapist within a Child and Adolescent Mental Health Service in the NHS. She is focused on services for people who have experienced traumatic events in their lives. Her clinical practice uses systemic and mentalisation-based approaches.

Anna Fairtlough is a research and development officer and visiting Lecturer at Goldsmiths, University of London. Her interests are in social work with parents, professional leadership, and equalities in social work practice, education and organisations. She has published widely in these fields and her latest book is *Professional Leadership for Social Work Practitioners and Educators* (Routledge, 2017).

Ravi KS Kohli is Professor of Child Welfare at the University of Bedfordshire. His research explores the ways people who seek asylum re-make a sense of 'home' in practical and psychologically sustaining ways. He has contributed internationally to legal, policy and practice

305

306 • Relationship-Based Social Work

developments on the subject of forced migration. He is keen to ensure that people who seek asylum and become refugees are seen in terms of their capacities and talents to do good and make good in ways that enrich the countries where they live new lives.

Linnet McMahon is a retired Lecturer in Social Work at the University of Reading, where she tutored and for some years led the MA in Therapeutic Child Care course and has provided training and consultancy in therapeutic work with children. She is author of *The Handbook of Play Therapy and Therapeutic Play* (second edition Routledge, 2009) and with Adrian Ward co-editor of *Helping Families in Family Centres* (Jessica Kingsley Publishers, 2003) and of *Intuition is not Enough: Matching Learning with Practice in Therapeutic Child Care* (Routledge, 1998).

Clare Parkinson is a senior social worker, clinical lecturer and MA Social Work course lead at the Tavistock. Her interests are in human growth and development; baby and organisational observation; and reflective supervision in health and social care. Clare has co-edited with Helen Hingley-Jones and Lucille Allain *Observation in Health and Social Care: Applications for Learning, Research and Practice with Children and Adults* (Jessica Kingsley Publishers, 2017).

Gillian Ruch is Professor of Social Work at the University of Sussex where she teaches and researches in the areas of child care social work, relationship-based and reflective practice. She is committed to enhancing the well-being of practitioners and interested in promoting reflective forums for effective practice. *Relationship-Based Research: Getting to the Heart of Research in Social Work* (Jessica Kingsley Publishers, 2016), which is co-edited with her Finnish colleague, Ilse Julkenen, is a companion publication to this book.

John Simmonds is Director of Policy, Research and Development at CoramBAAF, previously the British Association for Adoption and Fostering (BAAF). Before coming to BAAF, he was head of the social work programmes at Goldsmiths College, University of London. He is a qualified social worker and has substantial experience in child protection, family placement and residential care settings. He has published widely including editing with Gillian Schofield the *Child Placement Handbook* published by BAAF. He is the adoptive father of two children, now adults.

Martin Smith is the Senior Social Work Practitioner of Buckinghamshire Out of Hours Mental Health Team. He has conducted research enquiring into how practitioners are affected by strong emotions in and after crisis situations and how they process their responses. Martin is also interested in ways in which the arts might be helpful to practitioners when reflecting on distressing experiences and he has published previously on these topics.

Robin Solomon was a Consultant Social Worker at the Tavistock Centre working in the Fostering, Adoption and Kinship Care Team. Before joining the Tavistock Centre she worked for 16 years as a senior lecturer at Brunel University where she taught child care social work at both graduate and post-graduate levels. Robin has been involved in research on placement stability, looking at the effectiveness of psycho-educational support groups for foster carers and was the convenor of a multi-disciplinary Masters in Fostering and Adoption Studies at the Tavistock Centre.

Danielle Turney is a Senior Lecturer in Social Work at the University of Bristol, and Head of the Children and Families Research Centre. She worked at Goldsmiths, University of London and The Open University before moving to Bristol where she has had a lead role in developing, managing and delivering post-qualifying social work education for Children and Families practitioners – most recently, the Masters in Advanced Social Work with Children and Families. Danielle's research interests and publications focus on child welfare and protection, with particular reference to child neglect; relationship-based practice; and the role of critical thinking, analysis, and professional judgement in social work assessment and decision making.

Jeremy Walsh is a qualified social worker with extensive experience of work in community-based mental health settings, including crisis and specialist outreach teams. He completed an MA in Health and Social Care at London Metropolitan University where his dissertation examined the response of community mental health services to women who are victims of domestic violence. His doctoral thesis, completed in 2016 at the Tavistock and Portman NHS Foundation Trust and University of East London, focused on the relational experiences of carers and mental health workers from a range of health and social care professional backgrounds. As an NHS manager in the South

West London and St George's Mental Health NHS Trust, Jeremy continues to be responsible for the delivery of mental health services across inpatient and community settings. He has presented his recent doctoral research findings to voluntary and statutory sector groups and is interested in developing practice tools from the findings of his research.

Adrian Ward was a Consultant Social Worker at the Tavistock Centre in London, and formerly worked at the Universities of Reading and East Anglia. He is an experienced practitioner, teacher, writer and consultant in the fields of social work and social care, and in therapeutic child care in particular. His previous books include *Working in Group Care: Social Work and Social Care in Residential and Day Care Settings* (Policy Press, 2006), *What Works in Residential Child Care* (jointly with Roger Clough and Roger Bullock, NCB, 2006) and *Intuition is not Enough: Matching Learning with Practice in Therapeutic Child Care* (jointly with Linnet McMahon, Routledge, 1998). His most recent book is *Leadership in Residential Child Care, A Relationship-Based Approach* (Smokehouse Press, 2014).

Subject Index

Author Index